AQA Physical Education

AS

Learning Exp..........on

Exclusively endorsed by AQA

Paul Bevis
Mike Murray

Nelson Thornes

Published in 2008 by:
Nelson Thornes Ltd
Delta Place
27 Bath Road
CHELTENHAM
GL53 7TH
United Kingdom

09 10 11 12 / 10 9 8 7 6 5 4

A catalogue record for this book is available from the British Library

ISBN 978 1 4085 0015 6

Cover photograph by Photolibrary

Illustrations include artwork drawn by Peters and Zabranskey UK Ltd and Florence
Production Ltd

Page make-up by Florence Production Ltd, Devon

Printed in China by 1010 Printing International Ltd

Acknowledgements
The authors and publisher would like to thank the following for permission to reproduce
photographs and other copyright material:

p2: (a) Getty Images, (b) Emmanuel Faure; p9: David Fischer; p10: Getty Images; p11:
AFP/ Getty Images; p25: Food Standards Agency; p68 (a, c, d) PA Photos/ Empics Sports
Photo Agency, (b) Actionplus/ Neil Tingle, (e) Rex Features/ Heikki Saukkomaa; p71: (a), (b)
JUPITERIMAGES/ Polka Dot/ Alamy; p75: Getty; p79: (a) Epicscotland Ltd/ Alamy, (b) Getty
Images; p82: (a) Getty Images, (b) AFP/ Getty Images; p83: (a) AFP/ Getty Images, (b) AFP/
Getty Images; p84: (a) AFP/ Getty Images, (b) p85: (a) NBAE/ Getty Images, (b) , (c) Getty
Images; p102: (a) Malcolm Fairman/ Alamy, (b) Getty Images p103: Getty Images; p123: (a)
Peter Titmuss/ Alamy, (b) John Powell Photographer/ Alamy; p127: www.cartoonstock.com;
p128: (a) Getty Images, (b) Powered by Light/ Alan Spencer/ Alamy; p129: Tetra Images;
p133: Extreme Sports Photo/ Alamy; p135: AFP/ Getty Images; p137: (a) Actionplus Sports
Images, (b) Getty Images; p138: SHOUT/ Alamy; p148: (a) Colin Underhill/ Alamy, (b) Joe
Tree/ Alamy, p149: Ian Thraves/ Alamy; p151: Anthony Collins/ Alamy; p165: Dundee Art
Gallery; p166: Getty Images; p168 Mary Evans Picture Library; p170: Getty Images; p190:
Alamy/ Nick Turner; p202: Getty Images; p209: Adrian Sherratt/ Alamy; p210: Mike Booth/
Alamy; p211: Kevin Britland/ Alamy; p212: AFP; p260: Radius Images/ Alamy; p261: Index
Stock/ Alamy.

Every effort has been made to trace and contact all copyright holders and we apologise
if any have been overlooked. The publisher will be pleased to make the necessary
arrangements at the first opportunity.

Contents

Contents

AQA introduction

Nelson Thornes has worked in partnership with AQA to ensure this book and the accompanying online resources offer you the best support for your A level course.

All resources have been approved by senior AQA examiners so you can feel assured that they closely match the specification for this subject and provide you with everything you need to prepare successfully for your exams.

These print and online resources together **unlock blended learning**; this means that the links between the activities in the book and the activities online blend together to maximise your understanding of a topic and help you achieve your potential.

These online resources are available on **kerboodle!** which can be accessed via the internet at http://www.kerboodle.com/live, anytime, anywhere. If your school or college subscribes to this service you will be provided with your own personal login details. Once logged in, access your course and locate the required activity.

For more information and help visit http://www.kerboodle.com

Icons in this book indicate where there is material online related to that topic. The following icons are used:

💡 Learning activity

These resources include a variety of interactive and non-interactive activities to support your learning. These include online presentations of concepts from the student book, online case studies and interactive activities.

☑ Progress tracking

These resources include a variety of tests that you can use to check and expand your knowledge on particular topics (Revision quizzes) and a range of resources that enable you to analyse and understand examination questions (On your marks . . .).

How to use this book

This book covers the specification for your course and is arranged in a sequence approved by AQA.

The book content is divided into chapters matched to the sections of the AQA Physical Education specification for Units 1 and 2. Chapters 1–13 cover Unit 1 (Opportunities for and the effects of leading a healthy and active lifestyle) and Chapters 14–16 cover Unit 2 (Optimising performance and evaluating contemporary issues within sport).

The features in this book include:

In this chapter you will:

At the beginning of each chapter you will find a list of Learning objectives that contain targets linked to the requirements of the specification.

Key terms

Terms that you will need to be able to define and understand.

Links

Highlighting any areas where topics relate to one another.

Activity

Suggestions for practical activities that you can carry out.

AQA Examiner's tip

Hints from AQA examiners to help you with your study and to prepare for your exam.

AQA Examination-style questions

Questions in the style that you can expect in your exam.

AQA examination questions are reproduced by permission of the Assessment and Qualifications Alliance.

You should now be able to:

A bulleted list of learning outcomes at the end of each chapter summarising core points of knowledge.

▧ Web links in the book

As Nelson Thornes is not responsible for third party content online, there may be some changes to this material that are beyond our control. In order for us to ensure that the links referred to in the book are as up-to-date and stable as possible, the websites are usually homepages with supporting instructions on how to reach the relevant pages if necessary.

Please let us know at **kerboodle@nelsonthornes.com** if you find a link that doesn't work and we will do our best to redirect the link, or to find an alternative site.

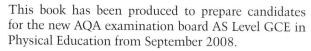

Introduction to this book

This book has been produced to prepare candidates for the new AQA examination board AS Level GCE in Physical Education from September 2008.

The book has been written by two very experienced authors. Both are Heads of PE Departments at their respective centres and have taught AQA AS PE with great success for many years. One is the current AQA Chief Examiner for AS and A2 Physical Education, the other was the previous Chief Examiner.

Physical Education is a popular wide-ranging AS Level subject involving the study of different aspects of many topics including anatomy, physiology, mechanics, psychology, sociology, media studies, history, ethics and politics. The intention of this book is to provide all the material that will satisfy the requirements of the AQA AS Level specification, and aims to make sure that only material relevant to that specification is included. Wherever possible the authors have made this material easy to understand for the student.

This book is clearly set out in sections and chapters which closely follow the AQA specification. The AQA AS Physical Education specification is divided into two units. Unit 1 is concerned with the opportunities for and the effects of leading a healthy and active lifestyle and is examined as section A of the AS examination. To help candidates through this complex range of material, the first part of this book is divided into three sections of anatomy and physiology, skill acquisition and socio-cultural issues. These sections correspond to the sections in the AQA specification. Within each of these sections are a number of separate chapters (Chapters 1–13) covering specific topic areas in suffi-

cient detail to enable the student to gain a full understanding of what is required for the examination.

Unit 2 of the specification is the coursework and involves the analysis and evaluation of physical activity as a performer and/or in an adopted role/s of coach or official. The skills required to demonstrate these abilities and guidance on how to analyse and correct performance are covered in Chapter 14 (Practical coursework). The theoretical aspects of improving practical performance through fitness and skill development which are examined in section B of unit one are covered in Chapters 15 (Practical exercise physiology) and 16 (Practical skill acquisition).

Each chapter begins with a brief introduction to the topic, followed by information that follows the AQA specification at an appropriate depth of knowledge. There are numerous diagrams, graphs and tables to help illustrate the information and clarify understanding for the student. Key terms that need to be understood for the examination are highlighted within the text and defined or explained in the margin. There are learning activities within each chapter for the student to undertake to help them develop their understanding of various topics. Where appropriate, Examiner's tips are included to help the reader appreciate what might be required for the AS examination. At the end of each chapter there are practice examination questions for the student to attempt which mimic the style of the actual AQA examination. Where appropriate, links are shown between the different topic areas so that understanding may be developed.

Applied exercise physiology

Introduction

Physical Education students need to understand how the body and its systems can help lead to a healthy and active lifestyle. In order to perform better, the Physical Education student will need to be fit for their chosen activity and must study and understand the different components of fitness. Developing fitness is part of a healthy lifestyle which will also include regard to the demands of a suitable diet which involves nutrition. In order to improve fitness and perform activities, the body produces controlled movements during physical activity and therefore it is appropriate to study the muscles and bones involved in movement. In a similar way, physical activity involves the delivery of oxygen to muscles and therefore this oxygen transport system is a suitable area of study for AS Level.

Fitness and health and defining the components of fitness are extensions of work already studied at GCSE Level. Similarly, the knowledge gained about food, diet and obesity needs to be developed.

The way we move depends on the action of muscles pulling on bones, which in turn form joints to enable movements. The AQA specification lists the seven movements that need to be understood in detail; these movements are running, jumping, kicking, throwing, forehand racket strokes, press-ups and squats. For each action, the specification requires knowledge of the type of joint involved, the names of the bones forming the joint, the type of joint movement, the types of movements produced, the names of the main muscles causing the action and the plane and axis through which the joint moves.

Oxygen transport involves the interaction of several different body systems including the lungs which take in oxygen from the atmosphere, the blood which carries the oxygen around the body and the heart which pumps the blood.

Your knowledge of this unit will be assessed through two 12-mark questions in the AS examination.

Applied exercise physiology

1 Improving fitness and health

Since the late nineteenth century (1890–1900) physical training and physical education programmes have, as one of their aims, been concerned with improving the fitness and therefore the health of children. After the Boer War (1899–1902) concerns were raised as to whether or not young army recruits had the necessary levels of fitness to perform their duties. As a reaction to that concern drill, physical training and eventually physical education programmes were devised, all of which have had the improvement of fitness and health as one of the core objectives.

In those early days our knowledge of human physiology and the connections between exercise, fitness and health was far less developed than our knowledge today and was often incorrect. We have also learned that an individual's living conditions – diet, housing and work conditions – play a significant part in determining how healthy we are and our ability to become fitter. Despite that improved knowledge and understanding, the development of almost every physical training or physical education programme over the last 100 years has been preceded by concerns for the fitness and health of young people. You can find out more about the development of physical training and physical education programmes in Chapter 12 (page 164), and how to develop fitness as part of sport training and development programme in Chapter 15 (page 222). It is now recognised that individuals are unlikely to embark upon a programme designed to improve their fitness, either designed to help them cope with the demands of everyday living, or designed to make them better able to cope with the specific requirements of a sport, without an underpinning knowledge of what we mean by both health and fitness.

Alongside our improved knowledge of fitness and its positive relationship with general concepts of health, we are more acutely aware of the impact that our lifestyle choices have upon our health and fitness. The impact that our choices about diet, exercise, alcohol and tobacco have upon our health and longevity has been accompanied by the rise of sedentary occupations and the increasing attractions of sedentary leisure activities.

Fig. 1.1 *Aerobics for all*

The fitness industry is now a significant employer and an increasing part of the leisure industry. Most local sport centres offer a range of fitness courses from gentle low impact water aerobics to high level aerobics and 'spinning'. Many people are now joining private fitness and health clubs – although membership cards often lay languishing, unused at the bottom of the wallet or handbag!

To make lifestyle choices that improve our health and fitness and counteract the effect of sedentary occupations we need to understand precisely what is meant by health and fitness and how they are related. Similarly if you are going to advise others and help them plan appropriate health and fitness programmes you will need to understand the basic concepts before embarking upon specific fitness programme design.

Concepts of health and fitness

The general public use the terms 'health' and 'fitness' very loosely and interchangeably, with little understanding of what either term means or how they are related. We should therefore begin with some clear definitions of what we mean by those two terms.

Health

The World Health Organisation (WHO) defines **health** as:

> a state of complete physical, mental and social well-being and not merely the absence of disease or infirmity.

On that basis just because an individual is not obviously suffering from ill health or injury does not mean that we can consider them to be healthy as that would only cover, at best, the 'physical' element of the definition.

Mental wellbeing is defined by the WHO as:

> a state of well-being in which the individual realises his or her own abilities, can cope with the normal stresses of life, can work productively and fruitfully, and is able to make a contribution to his or her community.

As with physical wellbeing, mental wellbeing is not merely the absence of mental illness – not coping with the stress of one's working life may make you unable to 'work fruitfully' but you would probably not be defined as mentally ill. Finally the last element of the WHO definition considers 'social wellbeing'. This is far more difficult to define but involves elements of living within a community, spirituality, fulfilling work, social relationships, etc.

The difficulties of deciding exactly what health is has led some to argue that health cannot be defined as a fixed state at all, but as a process of continuous adjustment to the ever changing demands of an individual's life. It is important that you understand how getting fit and staying fit can contribute to health and better enable us to cope with the changing demands of our life.

Key terms

Health: physical, mental and social wellbeing, not just absence of ill health.

Fitness

Definitions of **fitness** are clearer but more complex and variable. In simple terms fitness may be defined as the 'ability to cope with the demands of everyday life'. The demands made by our lifestyle can vary hugely from the office worker to the elite athlete, from the building worker to the lawyer, from those whose only exercise is reaching for the remote control to the individual who jogs regularly or visits the gym. Even for an individual the demands will vary from day to day. To be fit is to be able to cope with those demands and be able to meet them without undue stress.

Activities

Prepare a 24-hour time plan (divide a page into 24-hour time slots), monitor your activity levels for a 24-hour period. Ask a parent and an older relation to do the same.

1 How did your activity patterns vary?

2 Did vigorous activity or fast walking cause discomfort or distress?

3 How did your activity pattern match up to the recommended levels given by the British Heart Foundation?

4 Using the British Heart Foundation website compare the activity levels of the three people you have researched with the recommendations from the British Heart Foundation.

The term 'fitness' relates to factors that we have some influence over, something that we can change. Fitness therefore fluctuates and our levels of fitness can change, either for the better of for the worse.

How health and fitness are related

It is clear that being fit is one element of being healthy. The health-related components of fitness play an important part in helping us remain healthy. Other important elements would include nutrition, living conditions, our genetic background and the ageing process.

In general it is true to say that the individual who is fit is more likely to be healthy – in both physical and psychological terms. If we engage in activities that help develop or maintain our levels of fitness we are less likely to suffer from certain types of illness, and can delay the effects of the ageing process or reduce the effects of a genetic predisposition to certain medical conditions. But no matter how fit we are we can all be struck down with illness, our genetic traits can still dispose us to suffer from poor physical and mental health and we all age!

To understand more how fitness contributes to a healthier individual or helps us to cope with the demands of our day-to-day life we must understand the range of factors that fall under the umbrella term 'fitness'.

The different components of fitness

Fitness for life, to be able to cope with the demands of work, leisure or our general lifestyle involves a wide range of physical and skill-based competencies. It is sensible therefore to divide the components of fitness into two broad categories – health-related and skill-related fitness.

Health-related fitness refers to physiologically based factors that may also have an effect upon an individual's health. These would include the following:

▥ cardio-respiratory endurance, aerobic capacity, stamina

▥ strength

▥ speed

▥ muscular endurance

▥ flexibility

▥ power.

The work you undertake in this chapter will help you understand the nature of these components and allow you to identify which are necessary for any particular activity.

Skill-related fitness refers to the neuromuscular factors that allow an individual to successfully perform a skill or a technique. These are more likely to be of particular interest to sport performers. The factors concerned with skill-related fitness are:

▥ agility

▥ balance

▥ coordination

▥ reaction time.

Components of health-related fitness

To enable us to manage our day-to-day lives we need to be physically effective and capable. Although we may have a sedentary office job there will be many occasions when physical effectiveness may be required – pushing the car when it won't start in the morning, getting all your belongings into the top floor flat, joining in the impromptu game of football in the park or playing golf with your boss. Our everyday lives are likely to require a level of effectiveness in each of the following health-related fitness components:

▥ cardio-respiratory endurance, aerobic capacity, stamina

▥ strength

▥ speed

▥ muscular endurance

▥ flexibility

▥ power.

Cardio-respiratory fitness and aerobic capacity

Stamina is the component that allows an individual to participate in sustained, whole-body, sub-maximal activities such as swimming, long distance running, cycling and rowing. It is also involved as an underpinning factor in many invasion, racket and strike and field games.

Aerobic capacity is dependent upon:

▥ efficient external respiratory mechanisms involving the lungs – efficient breathing

▥ the efficiency of the blood in taking up the oxygen in the lungs

▥ the efficiency of the cardio-vascular system in transporting the oxygen to the cells throughout the body

---

▦ Key terms

Health-related fitness: an umbrella term for the combination of physiological factors that enable an individual to cope with the demands of their life, and may also have an effect upon their health.

Skill-related fitness: neuromuscular factors that enable an individual to successfully perform skills or techniques.

Stamina: ability to sustain stressful physical exertion for a period of time.

Aerobic capacity: how efficiently the body can take in, transport and use oxygen.

▦ Link

Testing and improving each of the components of health-related fitness will be covered in Chapter 15 – Practical exercise physiology (page 222).

▦ Activity

Draw mind maps showing the components of health-related and skill-related fitness and show how they interact. Reuse the mind maps to show the elements of testing and improvement.

▦ Link

In this chapter you will gain an understanding of the nature of the components of skill-related fitness, but you will study them in greater depth in Chapter 7 – Skills (page 78).

■ the efficiency of the cells in taking up and using the oxygen

■ the efficiency of all the factors above in removing or dealing with unwanted by-products of this process – carbon dioxide, lactic acid.

Heart disease

Recent health reports and newspaper headlines have constantly made the connection between lifestyle choices and heart disease...but are these just scare stories with newspapers taking health statistics out of context?

Research the report published by the British Heart Foundation "2005 Coronary Heart Disease Statistics" and establish the following facts:

Activity

1. Which group of adult men, or men who combine the highest risk factors, are most likely to die from coronary heart disease?

2. Which group of adult women, or women who combine the highest risk factors, are most likely to die from coronary heart disease?

3. Which of those factors is health style related or genetically related?

Key terms

Cardio-vascular system: our blood vessels, arteries, arterioles, capillaries, venules and veins.

Cardio-respiratory system: umbrella term for the heart, lungs and the blood vessels.

💡 *Aerobic capacity and health*

Aerobic capacity is directly related to the efficiency of the lungs and the **cardio-vascular system** in getting oxygen to the cells within the body. The need for good aerobic capacity is not restricted to sports performers. We all have a need for an efficient **cardio-respiratory system** and cardio-vascular system – running for a bus, mowing the lawn, parents playing with their children, decorating, hoovering and pushing the car when it refuses to start!

Deficiencies in the cardio-vascular system account for many health problems suffered today. Heart disease is one of the greatest killers of adults in Britain.

Department of Health

Coronary heart disease (CHD) is a preventable disease that kills more than 110,000 people in England every year. More than 1.4 million people suffer from angina and 275,000 people have a heart attack annually. CHD is the biggest killer in the country

There are clear links between lifestyle factors and heart disease. Poor cardio-vascular efficiency also leads to an inability to participate in many day-to-day activities without feeling breathless, tired or inadequate.

British Heart Foundation recommends that adults should build up to at least 30 minutes of moderate intensity physical activity five or more days a week. Many people aspire to do this by joining gyms, going jogging or cycling, swimming etc. This approach is only partially successful as many people find the time required and the need to get to a gym or pool too much of a disincentive. Current advice suggests that people should try and engage in heart raising activities within their normal lives. Suggestions made are to take the stairs to the office not the lift, walk from the train station to the office, cycle to the local shops.

Concerns over cardio-vascular deficiencies have gone beyond adults and now extend to children. Longitudinal research undertaken by Neil Armstrong at Exeter University has shown that children are now less physically active than in the past. Medical research is now showing high levels of obesity and cardio-respiratory disease in children.

NHS Health Survey for England 2004. Updating of trend tables to include childhood obesity data

Among boys and girls aged 2–15, the proportion who were obese increased between 1995 and 2004, from 11 per cent in 1995 to 19 per cent in 2004 among boys, and from 12 per cent in 1995 to 18 per cent in 2004 among girls.

The same pattern was apparent among boys aged 2–10 between 1995 and 2004, with an increase in the proportion that were obese (10 per cent to 16 per cent). There was a different pattern for girls aged 2–10, with no statistically significant increases in the proportion overweight (14 per cent in 2004) or obese (12 per cent in 2004) in this period.

In boys aged 11–15, as with younger boys, there was an increase in the proportion that were obese between 1995 and 2004 (14 per cent to 24 per cent). There were increases in this period among girls aged 11–15 who were overweight (14 per cent to 19 per cent) and obese (15 per cent to 26 per cent).

It is not a straightforward picture however, as the Earlybird Project in Plymouth concluded. The aim of the Project was to find out more about what lies behind diabetes and obesity. The Project concluded that, over a period of years, there was no basis for a relationship between the physical activity that a child undertakes and obesity.

Strength

When observing physical performance it is clear that **strength** is not a single concept. We see performers applying strength rapidly and powerfully, or in maintaining a position over a period of time, or by repeating an action many times. We can therefore identify three different types of strength – explosive, static and dynamic. All require the brain

---

Activity

Devise a lifestyle-related set of heart raising activities. Use the link to the British Heart Foundation website to help.

Key terms

Strength: the ability to overcome a resistance. This may be explosive, static or dynamic.

Activity

Study the graphs in Figures 1.2 and 1.3.

1. Compare the data from the NHS Health Survey (2004).

2. What is the general trend of obesity over the last 20 years? Has the trend remained constant?

3. Which age group has shown the greatest increase in levels of obesity in the last 20 years?

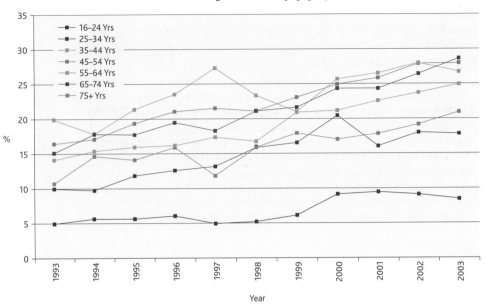

Fig. 1.2 *Graph showing percentage of obese men by age group (1993–2003)*

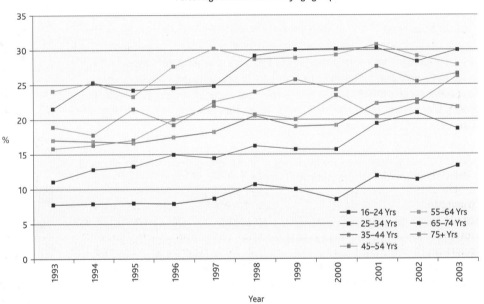

Fig. 1.3 *Graph showing percentage of obese women by age group (1993–2003)*

to control the contraction and relaxation of muscle fibres, thereby generating an infinite range of muscular tension, enabling limbs to be moved or held in a static or held position.

Explosive strength

Explosive strength is the rapid contraction of muscle fibre units to achieve a maximum generation of force. Sporting examples of explosive strength would be when jumping, throwing, sprinting, hitting – any time when maximum force is needed. Explosive strength is also related to power – the rapid application of maximal strength.

Dynamic strength

Dynamic strength is the repeated contraction and relaxation of a single muscle or group of muscles thereby causing a limb to repeat a movement over time. It should not be confused with muscular endurance.

Static strength

Static strength is the holding of a limb or part of the body in a static or immobile position. This is achieved by muscles maintaining a state of contraction or tension, often supported by a paired antagonistic muscle. Examples occur in both sporting and non-sporting situations.

Strength and health

It is not immediately obvious why there should be a connection between strength and health. Indeed most people do not need to engage in serious levels of resistance training to develop any of the forms of strength that have been identified. It is known however that a reasonable level of core body strength (abdominals, back) will do a great deal to avoid back injuries or back pain from degenerative or ageing processes. The use of Pilates or gentle strength conditioning exercises is now known to be a valuable element of maintaining fitness for health.

Speed

The health-related fitness concept of **speed** relates to whole body movement. Speed is achieved through the coordinated application of powerful, often maximal, muscular contractions. Speed is demonstrated by the sprinter, the games player racing down the touchline, the gymnast on the vault run-up in the floor exercise.

Speed and health

The link between speed and health only becomes obvious when you need to sprint up the stairs and muscle pulls and tendon twinges bring you to a halt. If there are times when you need to move quickly and you have not maintained muscular strength and flexibility, then injuries are far more likely. Regular flexibility exercises and gentle muscle conditioning can prevent that happening.

Muscular endurance

Muscular endurance is the repeated contraction and relaxation of a single muscle or group of muscles thereby causing a limb to repeat a movement over time. It should not be confused with endurance, aerobic capacity, stamina, etc. You will often hear sport commentators and others refer to a performer having great endurance and it is not clear if they are referring to the ability to maintain a whole body activity or a repeated limb action. Whilst this may be acceptable in that situation you must be far more precise and use the terms appropriately.

Muscular endurance and health

Again it may not be immediately obvious that the ability to maintain repeated muscular contractions has a direct link to health. Muscular endurance is linked to the body's effectiveness at getting oxygen to the working muscle cells and removing the associated waste products (along with having a high proportion of slow twitch muscle fibres). This is related to both local and whole body aerobic efficiency. A deficiency in this localised muscular endurance may be an indicator of poor aerobic fitness and subsequent health issues.

Flexibility

Flexibility is the ability of a limb or part of the body to show a wide range of movement. It is linked to a range of motion around a joint and reflects the joint structure (type), the length of the related muscles and the limiting effect of the joint ligaments. Flexibility is a contributing factor to

Key terms

Speed: the rate at which the body is moved from one place to another.

Muscular endurance: the ability of a muscle or group of muscles to perform repetitive contractions over a period of time.

Flexibility: the range of movement around a joint.

Fig. 1.4 *Group of adults improving core strength through Pilates*

Activity

Find examples of the use of strength, speed, aerobic fitness, static strength, dynamic strength and muscular endurance in your own sport or activity.

effective skill or technique action, application of muscular contractions for power or speed and when attempting to produce a movement or position that copies a perfect model – for example in gymnastics or diving. High levels of flexibility are also important when avoiding soft tissue injuries such as muscle pulls, ligaments and tendon strains and tears.

Flexibility and health

Flexibility is not just the concern of competitive sport performers; it is something that is important for health, particularly as we get older. Having a high level of flexibility is essential to maintaining a good level of general mobility and avoiding injuries whilst engaging in everyday activities. A flexible joint is one in which the muscles and connective tissues (ligaments and tendons) surrounding it do not restrict the range of movement. Muscles, which are not regularly stretched, are at risk of becoming shorter and less 'elastic'. This reduces the range of movement at the joint and increases the risk of injury from tears and pulls. Regular stretching helps improve general mobility, reduces tension and stiffness and helps to prevent back pain.

Power

Power may be thought of as the application of maximal or large forces from muscular contraction as rapidly as possible. It is very similar to explosive strength and is frequently seen in a wide variety of physical activities – the spike in volleyball, smash in tennis, shot putter, etc. It is dependent upon having a large proportion of fast twitch muscle fibres, and the ability to recruit (stimulate) as many motor units as quickly as possible.

Power and health

Power and health have a very similar connection to speed and health. An individual may be able to undertake their normal everyday activities without requiring rapid, maximal responses. This is unlikely however – a parent may jump off a wall or a tree stump when playing with their children, an individual may swing a sledgehammer when putting up the new fence post, etc. Without appropriate conditioning this kind of irregular and infrequent activity could lead to injury.

Components of skill-related fitness

The components of skill-related fitness are:

- agility
- balance
- coordination
- reaction time.

Agility

Agility is a combination of speed and coordination and can be seen in almost all sports – a side step in rugby, catching and passing on the move in netball, recovering to the middle after a lunge in badminton, etc. Agility requires good body strength, fast reactions, balance and coordination of muscle actions.

Balance

Balance is about maintaining stability or equilibrium. It is formally defined as maintaining your centre of mass over the base of support. Examples of balance would be a handstand in gymnastics, (a static

balance) and a skier weaving in and out of slalom gates (dynamic balance). Many performers require good dynamic balance when dodging and weaving.

Fig. 1.6 *The explosive power of the shot putter*

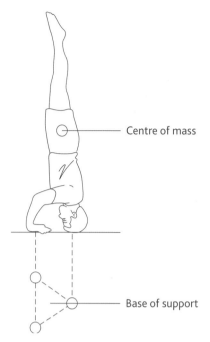

Fig. 1.7 *Gymnast with centre of mass over base*

Coordination

Good **coordination** requires an effective combination of the nervous system and motor systems of the body, in other words the effective inter-relationship of commands from the central nervous system linked to the responses from the muscle motor units required to achieve movement. For example, effectively starting the swing of a cricket bat to ensure that it connects with the ball, or maintaining the contact between stick and ball when dribbling in hockey.

Reaction time

Reaction time is the time taken to begin a response to a stimulus. For example, a swimmer on the starting block starts their dive as soon as they hear the starter's whistle. Reaction time is affected by how quickly an individual can process information and the speed of conduction of the impulse through the motor nerve. It is possible to improve reaction time through practice.

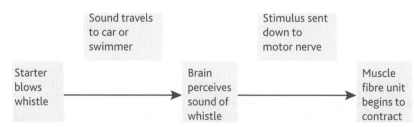

Fig. 1.8 *Reaction time for a swim start*

Activity

Watch a DVD of a live football, basketball, rugby or hockey match and identify the skill-related fitness components.

Key terms

Coordination: a balanced and effective interaction of movements or body actions.

Reaction time: the time taken from the start of the stimulus to the start of the response.

Link

For a more detailed description of reaction time and how it may be improved see Chapter 8 – Information processing (page 87).

💡 How lifestyle choices can affect health and fitness

By 'lifestyle choices' we mean the choices we make about the way we live our lives. We are concerned with those choices that impact upon our health and fitness. These would include our diet, the amounts of physical exercise we take, whether we smoke, drink alcohol or use other recreational drugs and the impact those choices have upon our health and fitness.

Diet

Link

For a more detailed look at nutrition and diet see Chapter 2 – Nutrition (page 16).

A balanced diet is one that contains all the necessary nutrients (carbohydrates, fats, proteins, minerals, vitamins, water and fibre) to enable you to sustain your lifestyle. These will vary depending upon your sex, stage of growth, age, amounts and type of physical activity in your daily life. To have too little or too much of any of the basic nutrients can affect both your health and your fitness. In the developed world the over-consumption of proteins, fats and carbohydrates has led to high amounts of obesity and associated health disorders such as heart disease and high blood pressure. This over-consumption has been accompanied by a decrease in the amount of physical activity that children and adults undertake in their daily lives. This lack of physical activity has also contributed to the problems of obesity and heart disease.

Exercise

Activity

Devise an activity plan that could be used by a 40-year-old non-active adult at the start of an exercise programme.

Exercise is essential for the maintenance of health and fitness. In this chapter we are not concerned with the type of exercise necessary to prepare a performer for a sport competition or sustained high levels of physical activity, but are more concerned with the amount and type of exercise that helps us maintain health and have a level of fitness necessary to undertake our normal lives.

The government, National Health Service and the British Heart Foundation recommend that if we do not exercise regularly we are likely to suffer from:

Diminished aerobic fitness – we will not be able run for the bus, dig the garden, mow the lawn, and walk up the stairs in our office or school building without feeling out of breath. Our heart muscle will become less able to work at an elevated level, the number of capillaries in the lungs and muscles will decrease.

Reduced flexibility – we will become less mobile and have less range of movement around our joints and this is particularly important as we grow older.

Reduced strength – all the different strength components will diminish. Muscles that are not used become wasted and lose tone and strength.

Body composition – our body composition will change. If our energy intake and output is not balanced, i.e. if we consume more energy via food than we expend through physical work, the body stores energy – we store fat. Excess amounts of fat on the body result in raised blood pressure and significantly increased risk of heart disease and diabetes.

If children from an early age do not partake in regular and sustained bouts of exercise, as well as increasing their risk of heart disease and obesity they will also not develop the joint stability, flexibility, muscular strength they will require as they progress to teenagers and adults. There is now significant evidence to suggest that children are not as physically active as they were 30 years ago. And as the earlier learning activities have shown, levels of childhood obesity are rising.

The British Heart Foundation provides advice to parents alongside campaigns in an attempt to get children more active. Sport England with its 'Get Active' campaign and the slogan 'Get Fit, Get Healthy, Get the Sporting Habit' is sending the same message. The National Curriculum for England has a specific element in the schemes of work relating to fitness and health.

Department of Health

For Key Stage 4 (14–16 yr olds)

Knowledge and understanding of fitness and health

Students should be taught:

How preparation, training and fitness relate to and affect performance

How to design and carry out activity and training programmes that have specific purposes

The importance of exercise and activity to personal, social and mental health and well-being

How to monitor and develop their own training, exercise and activity programmes in and out of school.

The Qualifications and Curriculum Authority through its PE and School Sport initiative (PESS) and the Healthy Schools Initiative are also encouraging schools to encourage their pupils to engage in regular physical activity and to be aware of a healthy diet.

Other lifestyle choices such as consumption of alcohol, smoking and the taking of recreational drugs can have a direct and highly damaging impact on your health and of course your fitness.

▓ Activity

Draw a mind map to show the ways in which children could gain more physical activity apart from taking part in sport and PE.

Alcohol

The Department for Health advice on the drinking of alcohol is that men should not regularly drink more than 3–4 units of alcohol per day, and women should not regularly drink more than 2–3 units of alcohol per day. Research evidence indicates that young people (aged 11–18 years) are drinking more and drinking earlier. The effects of sustained over-consumption of alcohol are given below:

▓ liver damage – fatty liver, alcoholic hepatitis and cirrhosis

▓ cancer – of the mouth, larynx, pharynx and oesophagus, liver, stomach, colon and rectum and possibly breast

▓ heart disease and high blood pressure – alcohol raises blood pressure

▓ problems with the digestive system – inflammation of the stomach lining, irritating ulcers, damage to the pancreas

▓ Psychiatric disorders – heavy drinking is closely linked with mental health problems, including clinical depression and with an estimated 65% of suicides. Up to one-third of young suicides have drunk alcohol at the time of death.

Fig. 1.9 *Health and fitness advertising*

Link

There is more detail on the role of Physical Education in school in Chapter 12 – National Curriculum PE and school sport (page 164). You will undertake a more detailed examination of how the Government and other providers offer opportunities for participation in physical activity in Chapter 11 – Leisure provision (page 146).

 You should now be able to:

■ know the difference between fitness and health and be able to use those terms in a precise way when discussing how individuals can improve the quality of their lives

■ observe or engage in a physical activity and know which element of health- or skill-related fitness is being used or required

■ explain to others how becoming fitter can help them cope with the demands that life makes upon them

■ analyse the health- and skill-related fitness demands of the activity you are offering for practical assessment

■ make an informed decision about your own lifestyle choices.

■ Reproductive problems – in men, temporary impotence and longer-term loss of potency, shrinking testes and penis and reduced sperm count. In women the menstrual cycle can be disrupted, it may increase the risk of miscarriage, can result in low birthweight babies, birth defects and foetal alcohol syndrome.

■ Alcohol dependence – 7% of adults in the UK are mildly dependent on alcohol and 0.1% are moderately to severely dependent. It can happen to anyone.

Source: Wired for Health

Smoking

In the UK one person dies from a smoking-related disease every four minutes. Smoking causes:

■ lung cancer (smoking causes over 80 per cent of all lung cancer deaths)

■ heart disease

■ bronchitis

■ strokes

■ stomach ulcers

■ leukaemia

■ gangrene

■ other cancers, e.g. mouth and throat cancer.

It can also worsen colds, chest problems and allergies such as hay fever, bronchitis and emphysema, as well as have unpleasant side-effects such as wrinkles and bad breath. Smoking can also make you cough, sneeze or feel short of breath when you exercise.

The effects of smoking or the over-consumption of alcohol cannot be undone by improved diet or regular exercise. It should be clear that as well as an effect on health, lifestyle choices involving poor diet, smoking and sustained over-consumption of alcohol will have a significantly detrimental effect on fitness and sport performance.

Lifestyle choices, fitness and health

As quickly as medical knowledge and technology enable us to combat illness and disease our relative wealth allows us to damage our health through over-consumption or poor lifestyle choices. Medical research is giving us a much clearer picture of the effects of these choices and what we can do to improve our health chances. Our health is a complex interaction of our genetic endowment, environmental factors and the personal choices we make. Physical education's contribution is to help young people understand the relationship between fitness and health and encourage them to engage in an active lifestyle throughout their lives by introducing them to enjoyable and challenging physical activities. The government's role is to ensure that resources are allocated so that all sections of the community have access to physical activity opportunities. As individuals we make our own choices based upon information, advice and a clear understanding that we are (partly) what we eat, drink and do.

AQA Examination-style questions

1   Many people participate in a physical activity to maintain their health and to improve their fitness.

   (a)   Give an appropriate definition for each of these terms. *(2 marks)*

   (b)   Give two reasons why it is possible that a person may be considered to be fit but not healthy. *(4 marks)*

2   Power may be considered to be a major fitness component required by gymnasts.

   (a)   What do you understand by the term 'power'? *(2 marks)*

   (b)   Name and describe two other fitness components that you consider to be important for gymnastics. *(4 marks)*

3   A defender in a team game has to sprint for the ball, stop and then change direction to mark an attacker. The attacker moves towards goal and the defender has to stretch to win the ball.

   (a)   Define three components of skill-related fitness components that have been used in this period of play and state when they were used. *(6 marks)*

4   The choices we make about our lifestyle can have negative effects upon our health and fitness.

   (a)   State three lifestyle choices that can have an effect upon our health and fitness. *(3 marks)*

   (b)   Choose one of the answers given in part (a) and discuss how you could help somebody else change their lifestyle. *(3 marks)*

2 Nutrition

Activity

Look at the back of the packaging from several different foods. Write down the main constituents and the amount of energy (kilojoules/kjs) they provide you with.

Key terms

Basal metabolic rate (BMR): how fast energy is being used. This depends on gender, age and physique.

Percentage body fat: the proportion of body fat to lean body tissue.

The topic of nutrition follows on from what you may have previously learned at GCSE Level. We need food in order to provide ourselves with energy. We need energy to maintain body functions such as breathing and keeping the body alive; for muscle contraction; for growth and repair.

Energy comes from the sun (solar energy). Living plants can convert solar energy to chemical energy by a process called photosynthesis. Plants then use this chemical energy to make other substances such as carbohydrate, fat and protein, all of which provide energy. We cannot use solar energy directly, but can use the chemical energy contained in food. Humans can oxidise food to produce energy, carbon dioxide and water.

▓ Energy

The actual amount of energy needed will vary from person to person and depends on their basal metabolic rate (BMR) and their level of activity.

Basal metabolic rate

The **basal metabolic rate** can be thought of as the rate at which a person uses energy to maintain the basic functions of the body. BMR varies from person to person. Infants and young children have a high BMR for their size due to their rapid growth and development. Men usually have a higher BMR than women since they tend to have more muscle. The BMR accounts on average for about three-quarters of an individual's energy needs.

The total amount of energy required by individuals depends on their level of activity and on their body weight. In particular, the more active they are, the more energy they can consume without gaining weight.

Percentage body fat

How much energy/food you need may be calculated by multiplying the BMR by a factor that takes account of the physical activity level. The more active you are the higher your BMR becomes. There is a need to balance your energy intake through food with the amount of energy you use. People vary, but for adults, change in body weight is a good guide to this energy balance.

Ideally, people should be encouraged to find the energy intake that enables them to maintain their weight within the desirable range for their height. Any excess energy taken in as food that is not used during daily energy expenditure is stored by the body as fat. A person who is very fat will have a body weight 20 per cent or more above the desirable range. Your body mass is made up of two components, your lean body mass (muscles, bones and organs) and your body fat. On average men have 10–20 per cent body fat, while women have 15–25 per cent.

Sport scientists can estimate your **percentage body fat** in different ways. The skinfold method involves measuring the thickness of your skin at specific locations around the body. The total of these various readings is then looked up in norm tables to give a guide to percentage body fat.

Table 2.1 *Calories used per minute for various activities*

ACTIVITY	cal/lb/min*	BODY WEIGHT (lb)				
		110	125	150	175	200
		CALORIES PER MINUTE				
Aerobic dance (vigorous)	0.062	6.8	7.6	9.3	10.9	12.4
Basketball (vigorous, full court)	0.097	10.7	12.1	14.6	17.0	19.4
Bicycling						
13 miles per hour	0.045	5.0	5.6	6.8	7.9	9.0
15 miles per hour	0.049	5.4	6.1	7.4	8.6	9.8
17 miles per hour	0.037	6.3	7.1	8.6	10.0	11.1
19 miles per hour	0.076	8.4	9.3	11.4	13.3	15.2
21 miles per hour	0.090	9.9	11.3	13.5	15.8	18.0
23 miles per hour	0.109	12.0	13.6	16.4	19.0	21.8
25 miles per hour	0.139	15.3	17.4	20.9	24.3	27.8
Canoeing (flat water, moderate pace)	0.043	5.0	5.6	6.8	7.9	9.0
Cross-country skiing (8 miles per hour)	0.104	11.4	13.0	15.6	18.2	20.8
Golf (carrying clubs)	0.045	5.0	5.6	6.8	7.9	9.0
Handball	0.078	8.6	9.8	11.7	13.7	15.0
Horseback riding (trot)	0.032	5.7	6.5	7.8	9.1	10.4
Rowing (vigorous)	0.097	10.7	12.1	14.6	17.0	19.4
Running						
5 miles per hour	0.061	6.7	7.6	9.2	10.7	12.2
6 miles per hour	0.074	8.1	9.2	11.1	13.0	14.8
7.5 miles per hour	0.094	10.3	11.8	14.1	16.4	18.8
9 miles per hour	0.103	11.3	12.9	15.5	18.0	20.6
10 miles per hour	0.114	12.3	14.3	17.1	20.0	22.9
11 miles per hour	0.131	14.4	16.4	19.7	11.9	26.2
Studying	0.011	1.2	1.4	1.7	1.9	2.2
Soccer (vigorous)	0.097	10.7	12.1	14.0	17.0	19.4
Swimming						
20 yards per minute	0.032	3.5	4.0	4.8	5.6	6.4
45 yards per minute	0.058	6.4	7.3	8.7	10.2	11.6
50 yards per minute	0.070	7.7	8.8	10.5	12.3	14.0
Table tennis (skilled)	0.045	5.0	5.0	6.8	7.9	9.0
Tennis (beginner)	0.032	3.5	4.0	4.8	5.6	6.4
Walking (brisk pace)						
3.5 miles per hour	0.035	3.9	4.4	5.2	6.1	7.0
4.5 miles per hour	0.048	3.3	6.0	7.2	8.4	9.6

*To calculate calories spent per minute of activity for your own body weight, multiply cal/lb/min by your exact weight and then multiply this number by the number of minutes spent in the activity. For example, if you weigh 142 pounds and you want to know how many calories you spent doing 30 minutes of vigorous aerobic dance, 062 x 142 = 6.8 calories per minute. 8.8 x 30 (minutes) = 264 total calories spent.

Source: Adapted in part with permission from the Consumers Union of the United States, Physical Fitness for Practically Everybody: The Consumers Union Report on Exercise (Mr. Vernon, N. Y.: Consumers Union, 1983), and from G.P. Town and K. B. Wheeler, Nutritional concerns for the endurance athlete (1986) 7–12.

Table 2.2 *Less strenuous activities*

Activity	Rate for men (kcal/min)	Rate for women (kcal/min)
Sleeping and lying	1.1	1.0
Sitting	1.5	1.1
Standing	2.5	1.5
Strolling	4.5	3.0

Note that this method depends on the accuracy of the person taking the skinfold measure. A second method uses the body's natural resistance to electricity to make an estimate. This bioelectrical impedance method simply involves entering your gender, age, height and weight measures into a device that is then held while a tiny electric current is sent from one electrode to another and a percentage body fat estimate is generated. The most accurate way of measuring body fat is through total submersion in water and measuring the amount of water displaced.

▉ Activity

Prepare a diary of what activities you have undertaken in the last three days and use the chart to decide how much additional energy (above BMR) you have used in the different types of activities you have been involved in.

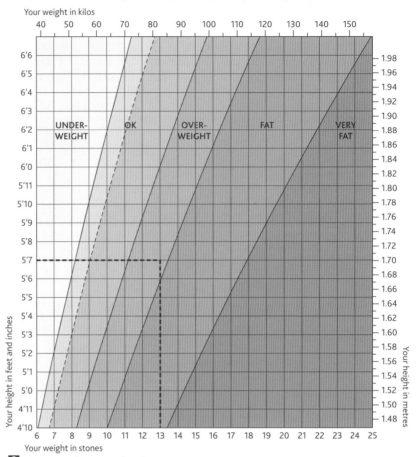

Fig. 2.1 *Body mass index chart*

Obesity

Obesity is a condition in which excessive fat accumulation in adipose tissue impairs health. It is defined in adults as a **body mass index** (BMI) above 30. Another definition regards 40% body fat as obese. Because obesity is a symptom rather than a measurable quantity, it is a difficult term to define. Body weight is influenced by energy intake and energy expenditure. If a person regularly consumes more energy than they use up, they will start to gain weight and eventually become overweight or obese. If a person regularly consumes less energy than they use up they will lose weight.

A useful way to judge whether a person is the appropriate weight for their height is to work out their BMI. This can be assessed by dividing a person's weight (kg) by height (m)², or by using a body mass index (BMI) chart.

In general, BMIs are classified as follows:

- Less than 20 – Underweight
- 20–25 – Desirable or healthy range
- 25–30 – Overweight
- 30–35 – Obese (Class I)
- 35–40 – Obese (Class II)
- Over 40 – Morbidly or severely obese (Class III).

A strong relationship exists between BMI and risk of associated diseases whereby individuals with a BMI above 40 have a very severe disease risk. Obesity is second only to smoking as a cause of cancer. People who are overweight or obese are more likely to suffer from coronary heart disease, diabetes, osteoarthritis (knees) and high blood pressure.

In many countries, there are cultural pressures for people to be slim. Many people try to lose weight even though they are in the normal weight range for their height or only slightly 'plump'. Unnecessary slimming is not recommended, as this may lead to a person becoming underweight, and in severe cases may be a factor in the development of eating disorders, such as anorexia nervosa.

In the UK many people have very inactive lifestyles through watching television, playing computer games and using a car rather than walking for short journeys. Very few people have physically active jobs or do significant amounts of exercise in their free time. Lack of activity is an important factor in the increasing prevalence of obesity. Walking or cycling instead of using a car, going to exercise classes and taking part in sporting activities can all help a person maintain a healthy body weight by increasing energy expenditure.

People who are very overweight find it more difficult to be physically active and this may add to their health problems. People who are already overweight are usually encouraged to become more active as well as reducing the amount of energy in food provided by their diet. Preventing obesity is important, as 'dieting' can be difficult, especially if dietary changes cannot easily be maintained as part of someone's lifestyle in the long term. Diets often 'fail', but this is usually because people revert to their old eating habits and/or levels of activity, rather than making changes for life.

The Department of Health recommends that in order to benefit health, individuals should participate in at least 30 minutes of at least moderate intensity activity on five or more days a week. Moderate intensity activity is defined as a level of activity that will:

- lead to an increase in breathing rate
- lead to an increase in heart rate (the pulse can be felt during this level of activity)
- lead to a feeling of increased warmth, possibly accompanied by sweating.

AQA Examiner's tip

You may need to know why the Government is keen to increase levels of participation in physical activity among the general population. Your answer to this type of question should include the idea of improving health and decreasing costs to the National Health Service as well as the wider sociological issues that are discussed in Chapter 12 – National Curriculum PE and school sport (page 164).

Activity

Conduct a survey to see the level of participation of different groups from the population such as students taking AS PE, a similar sized group of students not taking AS PE, a similar sized group of adults (you could use parents of the PE students), a similar sized group of year 7 children. You could hand out a questionnaire to find out how many hours per week that people are involved in physical activity of varying levels such as low level, moderate and intense.

1 From your results, what are the average levels of participation for each group?

2 Which group is the most and least active?

3 How do your results compare to those national findings described above?

Physical activity levels in Britain are low and a cause for concern across virtually all sections of the adult population and amongst some groups of children, notably teenage girls. Only 37 per cent of men and 25 per cent of women achieve at least 30 minutes of moderate intensity physical activity on five or more days of the week. Over the last 20 to 30 years, despite a small increase in the proportion of people participating in physical activity during leisure time, physical activity levels have fallen as a result of physical activity becoming a smaller part of the daily routine.

There are also concerns about activity levels of children in Britain; although more active than adults, many may not be taking part in enough exercise for good health. Seventy per cent of boys aged 2–15 years achieve at least 60 minutes of physical activity every day whereas only 61 per cent of girls aged 2–15 years achieved this level of physical activity. This level of activity tends to be maintained up to 15 years of age in boys, but falls in girls as they reach 15 years old. Seventeen per cent of boys and 22 per cent of girls are inactive, and only achieve less than 30 minutes of activity per day. This is one possible reason for the increase in prevalence of obesity in children.

💡 The seven classes of food

Carbohydrates

Carbohydrate has several important functions, but most importantly, it provides energy. The body's cells and tissues require a constant supply of **glucose**, which is used as a fuel. The main source of glucose is dietary carbohydrate. Most foods contain some carbohydrate.

The carbohydrate in food is digested and converted into glucose and enters the blood. The level of glucose in the blood is carefully monitored and kept within narrow limits by the action of the hormone insulin. Excess glucose may be stored as glycogen in the liver and in muscle, but such stores are limited. Any extra glucose is not wasted, but converted into **glycogen** or fat and stored.

Carbohydrate is the body's preferred source of energy at all levels of activity from rest to intense exercise. Hence, carbohydrate is a very important constituent of food from the athlete's point of view. The more exercise that is undertaken, the more carbohydrate that is required. If exercise uses up the available glucose, then stored glycogen may be used for energy. To replace the used glucose and glycogen, fat is converted into glucose.

Carbohydrates are compounds of carbon, hydrogen and oxygen. Carbo-hydrates can be classified in different ways. One common way is according to their structure. They can be divided into three main groups, according to the size of the molecule:

▦ *Monosaccharides* are the simplest carbohydrate molecules. The most commonly occurring monosaccharides in food are glucose and fructose.

▦ *Disaccharides* are sugars formed when two monosaccharide molecules join together with the removal of one molecule of water. Examples of disaccharides are sucrose, lactose and maltose.

▦ *Polysaccharides* are made up of many monosaccharide molecules (usually glucose) joined together. Examples of polysaccharides are starch, glycogen and cellulose.

For dietary purposes, carbohydrates can be described as sugars or complex carbohydrates. Some sugars are found in whole fruits, milk, honey, fruit juices and vegetables, others are found in table sugar and confectionery. Starch is a complex carbohydrate found in potatoes, bread, rice and pasta. Fibre is a mixture of mainly complex carbohydrates which cannot be digested in the small intestine by humans.

Key terms

Seven classes of food: carbohydrates, fats, proteins, vitamins, minerals, fibre and water.

Carbohydrate: group of foods containing carbon and hydrogen and oxygen in the same proportion as found in water (hydrate). Used as principal source of energy by the body.

Glucose: carbohydrate found in blood.

Glycogen: carbohydrate found in liver and muscles.

Fat

Fat is composed of carbon, hydrogen and oxygen. The building blocks of fat are fatty acids and glycerol. If the fatty acid has all the hydrogen atoms it can hold it is said to be saturated. If some of the hydrogen atoms are missing and have been replaced by a double bond between the carbon atoms, then the fatty acid is said to be unsaturated. If there is one double bond, the fatty acid is known as a monounsaturated fatty acid. If there is more than one double bond, then the fatty acid is known as a polyunsaturated fatty acid.

Three fatty acids combine with one molecule of glycerol to form a **triglyceride**, or simple fat. The body can make all the fatty acids it needs except for two so-called essential fatty acids which must be supplied in the diet.

The nature of the fat depends on the types of fatty acids which make up the triglycerides. All fats contain both saturated and unsaturated fatty acids but are sometimes described as 'saturated' or 'unsaturated' according to the proportions of fatty acids present. As a rough guide, saturated fats are solid at room temperature and tend to be derived from animal sources. Most unsaturated fats are liquid at room temperature and are usually vegetable fats. Just to confuse the issue, most unsaturated fats are called oils!

Fat is a concentrated source of energy. Fat provides more than double the energy provided by carbohydrate. It is also a carrier for fat-soluble vitamins A, D, E and K. Fat is only used as an energy source at rest and during low intensity exercise. This is because fat requires much more oxygen to break it down than the equivalent amount of carbohydrate. Hence, when exercising at a high intensity, when oxygen supply to muscles is limited, fat cannot be efficiently broken down and so carbohydrate is used as the energy source. A high fat intake, and in particular a high intake of saturated fat, has been associated with a raised blood cholesterol level, which is one of the risk factors for coronary heart disease.

Protein

Foods vary in the amount of **protein** they provide but the main sources include meat, fish, eggs, milk, cheese, cereals and cereal products (e.g. bread), nuts and pulses (beans and lentils).

The building blocks of protein are amino acids. Amino acids are compounds containing carbon, hydrogen, oxygen, nitrogen and in some cases sulphur. There are about twenty different amino acids commonly found in plant and animal proteins. After a protein is eaten it is broken down by digestion into amino acids, which are then absorbed and used to make other proteins in the body. The human body is able to make some amino acids for itself. These are known as non-essential amino acids. However, it is not possible to do this for every amino acid, so a certain number must be supplied by the diet. They are known as the essential amino acids.

Protein is necessary for the growth and repair of body tissues. It is also a relatively minor source of energy. Athletes who are training in strength/power-type activities will be repairing and developing muscle tissue, and will therefore require sufficient protein in their diet.

Key terms

Fat: group of foods containing carbon, hydrogen and oxygen; used as an energy source during rest and low intensity exercise.

Triglycerides: simple fat found in adipose (fat) tissue and muscle.

Protein: complex group of amino-acid containing foods. Used for growth and repair and as a minor energy source.

Activity

Look at the back of the packaging from several different foods. Write down their proportions of carbohydrates, fats and proteins and fibre they provide you with. Compare your findings to those that are recommended by doctors.

Fibre

Dietary fibre comprises the edible parts of plants that are not broken down and absorbed in the small intestine. Most people do not eat enough dietary fibre. The major sources of dietary fibre in the British diet are whole-grain and high-fibre breakfast cereals and bread (because they are rich in fibre and are eaten frequently). Dietary fibre can act as a bulking agent and help prevent constipation. Some forms of fibre eaten in large amounts can help reduce blood cholesterol levels. They can also help people with diabetes to control their blood glucose levels.

Minerals

Minerals are inorganic substances required by the body for a variety of functions including the formation of bones and teeth; as essential constituents of body fluids and tissues; components of enzyme systems; nerve function.

Calcium

Calcium is the main mineral in bones and teeth. Calcium is also necessary for nerve and muscle function. Foods that are particularly rich in calcium are milk, cheese and other dairy products. White and brown flour, but not wholemeal is fortified with calcium by law so bread and other products made from this are important sources of calcium in the UK diet.

Magnesium

Magnesium is present in all tissues including bone. It is required for normal energy metabolism and electrolyte balance. It is also needed for muscle function and for bone and tooth structure. It is present in all foods but it is abundant in dark green leafy vegetables. Grains and nuts are also rich in magnesium.

Phosphorus

Phosphorus is present in all plant and animal cells, and 80 per cent of the phosphorus in the body is present as calcium salts in the skeleton. It is essential for bone and tooth structure, for the structure of cell membranes and for energy metabolism. It is found in many foods.

Sodium

Sodium helps regulate body water content and electrolyte balance, and is involved in energy use and nerve function. Too much salt in the diet is associated with an increased risk of raised blood pressure, which is a risk factor for heart disease and stroke. Excess sweating may cause some sodium depletion and sodium intake may need to increase temporarily to replenish the loss in sweat. Most raw foods contain very small amounts of sodium chloride (salt). But salt is often added during the processing, preparation, preservation and serving of foods.

Potassium

Potassium is found in body fluids and is essential for water and electrolyte balance and for the proper functioning of nerve cells. It is present in almost all foods but fruit (e.g. dried fruits, bananas and berries), vegetables and milk are rich sources.

Iron

Iron is required for the formation of haemoglobin in red blood cells, which transport oxygen around the body. Iron is also required for normal

> ### Key terms
>
> **Minerals:** inorganic chemicals required for body functions such as bone growth, energy metabolism and nerve function.

energy metabolism, and for metabolism of drugs and foreign substances that need to be removed from the body. The immune system also requires iron for normal function. A lack of iron leads to anaemia.

Iodine

Iodine is used to make thyroid hormones. The thyroid hormones control many metabolic processes and if there is insufficient iodine in the diet, the result is lethargy and swelling of the thyroid gland in the neck to form a goitre. Iodine is also required for normal neurological development and for energy metabolism.

Vitamins

Vitamins are complex organic substances that are needed in very small amounts for many of the essential processes carried out in the body. Most vitamins cannot be made by the body, so have to be provided by the diet. Vitamins are usually grouped into two categories: the fat soluble vitamins, and the water soluble vitamins. Originally, vitamins were given letters (A, B, C, etc.) but now some are referred to by their chemical names, e.g. folic acid.

The fat soluble vitamins

Vitamin A

Vitamin A is essential to the normal structure and function of the skin and mucous membranes (e.g. lining the digestive system and lungs). It is also required for cell differentiation and therefore for normal growth and development, for normal vision and for the immune system. Vitamin A is found in liver, whole milk, cheese, butter, carrots and green leafy vegetables.

Vitamin D

Vitamin D is made by the action of ultraviolet rays on the skin and this is the most important source for the majority of people as few foods contain significant amounts of vitamin D. It works as a hormone in controlling the amount of calcium absorbed by the intestine. It is also essential for the absorption of phosphorus and for normal bone mineralisation and structure. Vitamin D is also involved in the process of cell division. Vitamin D occurs naturally in some animal products, including oily fish, eggs, butter and meat.

Vitamin K

Vitamin K is found in foods from both plant and animal sources and is also made by bacteria in the gut. Vitamin K is essential for the clotting of blood and is required for normal bone structure.

The water soluble vitamins

Vitamin C (Ascorbic acid)

Vitamin C is involved in the production of collagen – the protein in connective tissue (skin, cartilage and bone). It is also involved in the normal structure and function of blood vessels and neurological function. Vitamin C is found almost exclusively in foods from plant sources, although fresh milk and liver contain small amounts.

Vitamin B1 (Thiamine)

Thiamine is needed to release energy from carbohydrate. It is involved in the normal function of the nervous system and the heart. Thiamine is

Key terms

Vitamins: complex compounds with variety of functions including energy metabolism and formation of various tissues.

found in whole grains, nuts and meat, especially pork. In the UK, white and brown flour and many breakfast cereals are fortified with thiamine.

Vitamin B2 (Riboflavin)

Riboflavin is required to release energy from protein, carbohydrate and fat. It is also involved in the transport and metabolism of iron in the body and is needed for the normal structure and function of mucous membranes and skin. Major dietary sources of riboflavin are milk, eggs, fortified breakfast cereals, liver and green vegetables.

Niacin

Niacin is found in most foods, although meat is the major source in the UK diet. It is required for the release of energy from food, for the normal structure of the skin and mucous membranes and for normal functioning of the nervous system.

Vitamin B6

Vitamin B6 is essential in the metabolism of protein. It is also involved in iron metabolism and transport. Together with folic acid and vitamin B12, vitamin B6 is required for maintenance of normal blood homocysteine levels – raised blood homocysteine is a risk factor for cardiovascular disease. Vitamin B6 is found in a variety of foods: beef, fish and poultry are rich sources. It also occurs in eggs, whole grains and some vegetables.

Vitamin B12

Vitamin B12 is required for normal cell division and normal blood formation and function. It is also needed for the normal structure and function of nerves. Dietary intake is exclusively from animal sources, e.g. milk, meat and eggs.

Folic acid

Folic acid is essential for normal cell division and in the formation of blood cells. It is also needed for the normal structure of the nervous system. Folic acid is found in liver, yeast extract, orange juice and green, leafy vegetables.

Water

Over half the human body consists of water and it is essential for the correct functioning of virtually all living cells. Water is essential for our bodies to work properly. Water has many functions in the body:

▓ It provides the medium in which most reactions in the body occur.

▓ It acts as a lubricant for joints and eyes.

▓ It helps to regulate body temperature.

The amount of water that we need to drink each day varies from person to person, depending on age, time of year, climatic conditions, diet and the amount of physical activity we do. Water requirements are particularly increased in hot climates and following exercise.

Dehydration is common amongst athletes, particularly those exercising in hot climates and/or at altitude, and can be very serious. As little as a 2 per cent loss of body weight (which can be a consequence of dehydration) can result in impaired physiological responses and performance. Symptoms of mild dehydration include headache and fatigue.

Activity

Look at the back of the packaging from several different foods. Write down the proportions of different vitamins and minerals they provide you with. Compare your findings to those that are recommended by doctors.

Water replacement is essential before, during and after exercise. Tap water is suitable for replacing any lost fluid following mild or moderate exercise, but research has demonstrated that water alone is not the best solution for fluid replacement during or after vigorous or prolonged exercise. **Isotonic** drinks are more suitable and will replenish water and carbohydrate stores (e.g. glycogen stores in muscle). These do not necessarily have to be bought from shops as they are easily made from diluted squash, some additional sugar and tiny amounts of salt.

Balanced diet

No single food contains all the essential nutrients the body needs to be healthy and function efficiently. A **balanced diet** is an intake of food containing sufficient amounts of the nutrients required by the individual. This varies between different people, but in general consideration should be given to increasing fruit and vegetable intake.

The Balance of Good Health is a pictorial food guide showing the proportion and types of foods that are needed to make up a healthy balanced diet. The guide is divided into five food groups: bread, other cereals and potatoes; fruit and vegetables; milk and dairy foods; meat, fish and alternatives; foods containing fat and foods containing sugar. Foods from the largest groups should be eaten most often and foods from the smallest group should be eaten least often. The guide is shaped like a dinner plate which has been designed to make 'healthy' simpler to understand and interpret.

Key terms

Isotonic: in the same concentrations as body fluids. Proprietary isotonic drinks are popular with some performers as they are said to affect metabolism quicker. Similar drinks that have similar effects are easily made from simple (cheap!) ingredients.

Balanced diet: is one that is likely to include a large number or variety of foods, so adequate intakes of all the nutrients are achieved.

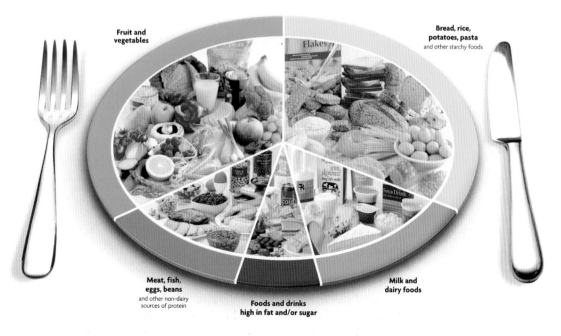

The eatwell plate

Use the eatwell plate to help you get the balance right. It shows how much of what you eat should come from each food group.

FOOD STANDARDS AGENCY
food.gov.uk

Fruit and vegetables

Bread, rice, potatoes, pasta
and other starchy foods

Meat, fish, eggs, beans
and other non-dairy sources of protein

Foods and drinks high in fat and/or sugar

Milk and dairy foods

💡 **Fig. 2.2** *Balance of good health*

In order to achieve the recommendations many people would need to make significant changes to their pattern of eating. For most people, achieving a balanced diet will mean:

■ eating more starchy foods such as bread, potatoes, rice and pasta

■ eating more fruit and vegetables

■ choosing leaner cuts of meat and lower fat versions of dairy products will help to reduce the amount of fat, particularly saturated fatty acids in the diet.

There is strong scientific evidence to suggest that physical activity benefits wellbeing and is necessary for good health. It has beneficial effects on a wide number of diseases, but also plays a role in disease prevention. Participating in physical activity has been shown to reduce the risk of a number of chronic diseases including cardiovascular disease and diabetes as well as the risk of premature death.

Children benefit from physical activity because it improves disease risk factors, strengthens the skeleton, improves mental wellbeing and helps to maintain a healthy body weight. Adults will benefit from increasing physical activity levels through protection against a number of diseases and through achievement and maintenance of a healthy body weight. In addition, individuals will benefit from improved mental health, wellbeing and muscle and bone health. In older people, activities that promote strength, coordination and balance are particularly valuable for maintaining capability for everyday activities.

Physical inactivity and low fitness are major risk factors for coronary heart disease; those who are inactive and unfit have almost double the risk of dying from coronary heart disease. Physical activity also has a beneficial effect on preventing strokes and modifying cardiovascular risk factors such as high blood pressure and blood lipids (e.g. cholesterol). Physical inactivity is a major risk factor for diabetes.

Physical activity is associated with a reduced risk of certain cancers, particularly colon cancer and breast cancer. Physical activity can also have an indirect effect on reducing cancer risk through its effects on body fatness, as a number of cancers are associated with obesity.

Activities that produce physical stresses on bones (e.g. running, dancing, skipping) are necessary throughout life to provide protection against degeneration (osteoporosis). In adolescents this type of physical activity strengthens the skeleton by increasing bone mass. After adolescence, physical activity reduces the rate of bone loss which takes place naturally with ageing.

Incorporating more physical activity into daily life, for example walking or cycling instead of catching the bus and taking up more active hobbies, would be the easiest way to increase physical activity. Overall, the benefits associated with participating in the recommended levels of physical activity are great.

Activity

Research on the internet to find tables that list the energy and nutritional value of common foods and use this to suggest a suitable daily diet for a marathon runner and a power athlete.

💡 Different diets for different athletes

In general, any person involved in physical activity will need a greater food intake than those that are not provided their basal metabolic rate (BMR) is similar. The greater the degree of involvement the greater will be the need to take in sufficient food. But simply eating more is not good enough for the elite performer. Care must be taken that a balanced diet is maintained rather than simply eating lots of burgers and fries to get the quantity of food needed.

The diet of an endurance-based performer such as a marathon runner needs special consideration. Endurance training makes the performer better at metabolising fats; therefore fat intake needs to be increased. Using fat will save carbohydrate use for later in an exercise or performances (glycogen sparing). Similarly there needs to be a larger intake of carbohydrates to satisfy the energy demands of the elite performer. Marathon runners would therefore need to have a diet that has a larger proportion of carbohydrates and fats than the 'average' diet. Any elite performers , including marathon runners, because of their training load have a much higher metabolism than the average person, and therefore require more vitamins and minerals. Hence the need for more fruit, vegetables, dairy products and cereals than most other people.

The power/strength performer will also need to adjust their carbohydrate intake because of the energy demands, but they will also need to increase their protein intake because of the increase in muscle repair and growth that will accompany their training.

 You should now be able to:

- describe the concept of BMI and body composition
- suggest what is meant by obesity and why it is difficult to define
- list the six classes of food and give a general description of their roles in the body
- explain and describe what is meant by a balanced diet
- suggest the different forms of food intake that might suit a marathon runner as compared to a weightlifter.

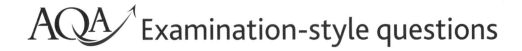

1   (a)   Name the six classes of food. *(3 marks)*

     (b)   How should the diet required by a marathon runner differ from an inactive person? *(3 marks)*

2   (a)   What are the benefits of having sufficient fibre in a performer's diet? *(2 marks)*

     (b)   Why do people engaged in physical activity need to make sure that they eat foods containing sufficient iron and calcium? *(4 marks)*

3   (a)   Fat is an important component of an athlete's diet. Describe two beneficial functions of dietary fat. *(2 marks)*

     (b)   Why is excess fat considered to be a disadvantage to an endurance athlete? *(4 marks)*

4   (a)   What is basal metabolic rate? *(2 marks)*

     (b)   How could you measure the amount of fat in the body of an athlete? *(2 marks)*

     (c)   What are the main health risks of being obese? *(2 marks)*

3 Lung function

To maintain life humans must supply the body with oxygen and remove the waste product of carbon dioxide. Oxygen is required to release energy from food, this energy then being used to sustain all the different cells within the body. A by-product of this release of energy from the breakdown of digested and stored food is carbon dioxide. The process of getting oxygen to the cells also involves the cardiovascular system. Our focus will be on muscle cells but remember that this information applies to all of the cells in the body. The combination of breathing, respiration and transporting the gases to and from the cells is undertaken by the cardio-respiratory system.

During this chapter you will learn how the mechanical process of breathing ensures that we get air into and out of the lungs. You will also learn how gases may be exchanged between air and blood in the lungs and how similar processes occur between the blood and the muscle cells. To understand how this can occur you also need an understanding of the physical process of diffusion and how this depends upon a concept known as partial pressure. Although carbon dioxide is a waste product of these respiratory processes it plays a vital role in controlling our breathing and also our heart function.

The process of exchanging gases in the lungs is known as external respiration, and when this occurs between the muscle cell and the blood it is known as internal respiration.

The energy that is released from stored food is used in a process known as ATP reformation or re-synthesis. This is a topic of study in the A2 element of the specification but it is useful to have a general idea of the process as it explains why the oxygen provided from respiration is so important. ATP is a chemical that is found in all cells. The breakdown of ATP releases energy that is used to sustain all cells. We have a limited amount of ATP in the body and for us to get through a day, run a marathon or play a game of badminton we have to reform or re-synthesise large amounts of ATP. The re-synthesis of ATP requires energy. The energy is supplied from the breakdown of food which requires oxygen – hence the need for breathing and respiration.

It should already be clear to you that an efficient set of lungs and structures associated with respiration is essential for the maintenance of life and to be healthy. It should also be clear that sport performers, who require and use more energy than the average person, will also require an above average pulmonary efficiency – pulmonary means to do with the lungs and respiratory systems. When you train, particularly endurance train, you force the body to adapt so that it supplies the muscle cells with the required amounts of oxygen – these adaptations or changes occur in the lungs and in the muscle tissue and are vital in ensuring that we can perform at a high level. The individual who engages in little or no physical activity, or in physical activity only at a very low level of intensity (sitting on the sofa or walking to the fridge or drink cooler!) will not develop a respiratory system that allows them to cope even with the normal stresses and strains of everyday life – walking up flights of stairs, mowing the grass in the back garden or dancing at the local nightclub.

Links

- The heart, blood vessels, and the role of carbon dioxide in breathing and heart function will be studied in more depth in Chapter 4 – Blood transport system (page 41).

- To find out more about the role of ATP, see Chapters 1 and 2 in *AQA Physical Education for A2 Level*.

- Efficient processes of breathing and respiration play a vital part in being healthy and fit, as you will have seen in Chapter 1 – Improving fitness and health (page 2).

Activity

Whilst sitting and reading this book, count (or get a partner to count) the number of breaths you take in a minute. Note how deep your breathing seems to be (look at the rise and fall of your chest) and listen to other body functions such as the sound of your breathing and beating of your heart. Note down your observations.

Now take a brisk walk around the room for 60 seconds. Repeat the observations. Do a similar activity the next time you are engaged in more intense physical work.

The mechanics of breathing

To understand how we breathe we need some understanding of the structure of the lungs and the respiratory airways (the tubes that take air to and from the lungs).

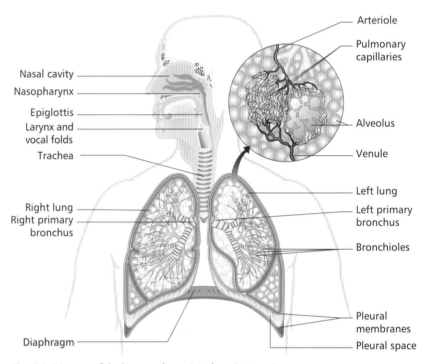

AQA Examiner's tip

You will not be examined on the structure of the lungs or the respiratory airways.

Fig. 3.1 *Diagram of the lungs and associated respiratory airways*

Activity

Draw a flow chart to show the passage of air from the mouth into the alveoli. Make up a mnemonic to remember the route, e.g. 'No Little Time Before Breakfast Again' – Nasal cavity, Larynx, Trachea, Bronchus, Bronchioles, Alveoli/Air Sacs.

Air is a mixture of gases – oxygen, nitrogen, carbon dioxide, inert gases and often some water vapour. We are only interested in oxygen and carbon dioxide. Air enters the mouth and travels through the nasal cavity, through the larynx, down the trachea, into the right or left bronchus, then into the bronchioles and finally into the alveoli or air sacs.

If you were studying human biology you would need to learn much more about the structure of the lungs and respiratory passages than is required here. We are only concerned with the overall structure of the lungs, the pleural membrane, diaphragm, alveoli and the small blood vessels surrounding the alveoli known as capillaries.

Lungs

The lungs are two sac-like organs, spongy in appearance that lie in our chest or thoracic cavity. The spongy appearance is due to the millions of small air sacs or **alveoli**. The lungs are surrounded by a membrane called the pleural membrane and bordered on the bottom by a sheet of muscle known as the diaphragm. See Figure 3.1.

Air moves from areas of higher pressure to areas of lower pressure. To breathe in (inspire) it is necessary for the air pressure in our lungs to be lower than the pressure of the air in the atmosphere. Atmospheric air pressure is 100 **kPa** and when we inspire we lower the air pressure in the alveoli to 99.74 kPa. This allows air to flow into the lungs from the outside air.

Inspiration (breathing in)

During **inspiration**, we lower the air pressure in our lungs and therefore alveoli by increasing the volume of the lungs. During quiet breathing (when at rest) this increase in volume is achieved by the diaphragm muscle contracting and therefore flattening. This increases the volume inside the chest cavity or thorax. At the same time the intercostal muscles between the ribs contract and lift the ribcage up and out also increasing the volume inside the chest cavity. The lungs are connected to the pleural membrane, and therefore to the ribs, so the lungs are pulled outwards. Because the intercostal muscles and diaphragm are actively working this is known as an active process.

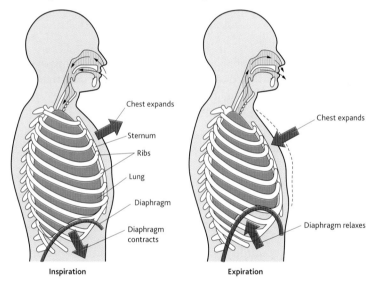

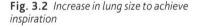

Fig. 3.2 *Increase in lung size to achieve inspiration*

During exercise the rate and depth of breathing increase (look at the notes you made after the learning activity at the beginning of the chapter). The depth of breathing is increased by a greater expansion of the thoracic cavity. This is caused by the action of three other muscles – the strernocleidomastoid raises the sternum (breast bone) and scalene and pectoralis minor lift the ribs further. The greater expansion of the ribcage stretches the lungs further and allows for a larger inspiration of air.

The amount of air we can inspire in one breath, known as the tidal volume, can vary from 0.5 lt at rest to 3.5 lt when exercising. Our rate of breathing can also increase from 11–14 breaths per minute up to approximately 45. This allows for a significant amount of air breathed during exercise as we shall see in the next section.

Key terms

Alveoli: tiny thin-walled air sacs found in large numbers in the lungs.

kPa: kilo Pascal (measure of pressure).

Inspiration: the act of breathing in.

Activity

After quiet breathing for about ten seconds, breathe in and out as hard as you can. Note the muscles you have used, chest and abdominal action.

Expiration (breathing out)

To breathe out during quiet breathing the external intercostal muscles relax as does the diaphragm, the volume of the thoracic cavity decreases, lungs return to their resting size and the air pressure inside the lungs increases and air is forced out of the respiratory passages. During rest this process is passive, with the diaphragm and the external intercostals relaxing.

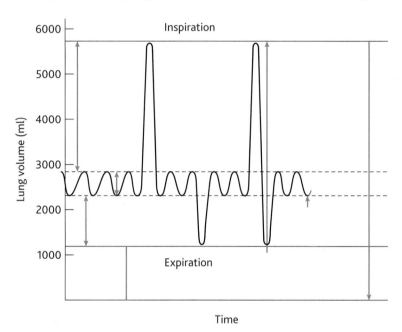

Fig. 3.3 *Spirometer trace of an adult male during quiet breathing and when exercising.*

Activity

Draw a flow diagram to show the step by step process of quiet breathing and breathing during exercise.

During exercise **expiration** is more active, with the internal intercostal muscles contracting to pull the ribcage inwards and downwards, the abdominals also contract which helps to push the diaphragm up with a much more rapid reduction in the volume of the thoracic cavity.

It should be obvious that the volume of air breathed in and out changes greatly between quiet breathing and forced breathing. These changes in lung volume are considered in the next section.

💡 Lung volumes and capacities

We can see we are able to vary the depth (and volume) of our breathing enormously. It is also the case that no matter how hard we try we are never able to totally empty our lungs of air. This is a good thing because if we could our lung tissue would collapse and stick together. This is due to the surface tension created by the film of moisture on the inner side of the alveoli tissue. You may have tried to pull apart a balloon before inflating – it is quite difficult.

We therefore have a great deal in reserve when engaged in quiet breathing. This leads to an identification of different parts of our total lung volume. The different types of lung volumes are defined below.

This can best be seen by examining the chart in Figure 3.3 which shows the changes in lung volumes and how they are identified.

As we exercise our depth of breathing increases. This means that the tidal volume increases because we are increasingly using our inspiratory reserve volume and expiratory reserve volume. Our vital capacity (the maximum amount of air that can be exhaled after a maximum inspiration) does not change as can be seen from the following equation:

Vital Capacity = Tidal Volume + Inspiratory Reserve Volume +
Expiratory Reserve Volume

VC   = TV + IRV + ERV

Table 3.1 *Lung volumes (average male) – descriptions, values and changes during exercise*

Volume name	Description	Value at rest (ml). Average male	Change during exercise
Tidal Volume (TV)	Amount of air breathed in or out per breath	500	Increases
Inspiratory Reserve Volume (IRV)	Maximal amount of air forcibly inspired in addition to tidal volume	3100	Decreases
Expiratory Reserve Volume (ERV)	Maximal amount of air forcibly expired in addition to tidal volume	1200	Decreases
Vital capacity (VC)	Maximal amount of air exhaled after a maximal inspiration (TV+IRV+ERV)	4800	Slight
Residual Volume (RV)	Amount of air left in the lungs after a maximal expiration	1200	None
Total Lung Capacity (TV)	Vital capacity plus residual volume (TV+IRV+ERV+RV)	6000	None

Minute ventilation

Moving air in and out of our lungs is known as ventilation, or more specifically **minute ventilation**. Minute ventilation (V_E) is the amount of air that is moved in and out of the lungs in one minute.

It is a function of our depth of breathing (tidal volume, TV) and the frequency or rate of breathing (breaths per minute). Remember that our rate of breathing can vary from 12–15 to up to 60 breaths per minute. Our tidal volume can also vary during exercise – from 0.5 litres during quiet breathing up to 3 litres.

$$V_E = \text{Frequency of breathing} \times \text{Tidal volume (ml)}$$

Activity

Study the values shown in Table 3.1. Using the values shown in the table, copy Fig. 3.3 and add in the lung volumes (ml) at points A, B and C on the x-axis.

Questions:

1. What happens to the tidal volume from A to C?
2. What happens to the IRV and the ERV?
3. Why does this happen?
4. What happens to the RV during that period?

At rest:

$$V_E = 12 \times 500 \text{ ml}$$

$$V_E = 6000 \text{ ml. min}^{-1} \text{ (or 6 Lmin}^{-1}\text{)}$$

Key terms

Minute ventilation: the amount of air moved in and out of the lungs in one minute. Measured in millilitres per minute (ml. min^{-1}).

AQA Examiner's tip

Always use correct units when discussing or describing terms such as minute ventilation.

Activity

Using a hand held spirometer measure your vital capacity. Then take your resting breathing rate and calculate your minute ventilation.

Following a warm up take your breathing rate again, and undertake the multi-stage fitness test (bleep test). As soon as you have completed the test take your breathing rate again.

Calculate the V_E for both the warm up and post test, plot the values on a graph (V_E, breathing rate, tidal volume (estimated)).

Link

The transportation mechanism of the body is our blood and the cardiovascular system – heart and blood vessels. For more information see Chapters 4 – Blood transport system (page 41) and 5 – Heart function (page 51).

During exercise both the depth of breathing (tidal volume) and the rate of breathing can increase to such a level that minute ventilation can approach $180 - 200 \, \text{Lm}^{-1}$ for male endurance athletes. A ventilation rate of $208 \, \text{Lm}^{-1}$ was recorded for an American football player. Such increases in V_E are achieved by increasing the rate of breathing up to approximately 60 breaths per minute and increasing tidal volume to 3000 ml – 3300 ml.

$$V_E = 60 \times 3000 \text{ ml}$$

$$V_E = 180,000 \text{ ml. min}^{-1} \text{ (or 180 L. min}^{-1}\text{)}$$

Gas exchange

The whole point of breathing is to get the oxygen in air into the lungs so that it can be transported to the cells of the body. In this section we are concerned with how oxygen gets into the blood and into the cells, and how the reverse process happens for carbon dioxide which you will recall from the introduction is a waste by-product of the breakdown of glucose.

Air is a mixture of gases but we are only concerned with two – oxygen and carbon dioxide. All gases tend to distribute themselves evenly. Therefore if a gas on one side of a semi-permeable membrane is at a higher concentration than the same gas on the other side there will be a movement from the higher concentration to the lower until they are equal. This process is

A
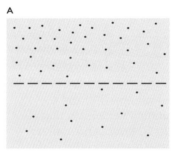

The difference between the two concentrations of the gas either side of the semi-permeable membrane creates a concentration gradient or diffusion gradient

B
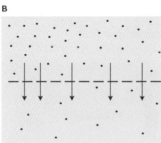

Gas molecules distribute themselves evenly by moving from area of high concentration to a lowconcentration until equal

Gas will diffuse from the area of higher concentration to the area of lower concentration. The bigger the difference in concentrations, the steeper the diffusion gradient and the faster the gas diffuses

C
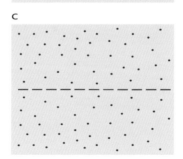

With the same concentration either side of the semi-permeable membrane there is no diffusion or concentration gradient – therefore no movement

Fig. 3.4 *The process of diffusion*

known as **diffusion** (see Figure 3.4). Diffusion, or the movement of a gas from an area of high pressure to an area of lower pressure, will only occur if there is this difference in pressure – the diffusion gradient. The movement of the gas distributes the molecules more evenly until they are all evenly distributed and there is no pressure difference. No pressure difference means no diffusion gradient means no diffusion. Diffusion is dependent upon there being a diffusion or pressure gradient.

Diffusion in the lungs

The wall of the alveoli is semi-permeable which means that it has holes in it large enough to allow the passage of oxygen and carbon dioxide molecules. The concentration of a gas is known as its **partial pressure**. Partial pressure is the pressure exerted by a single gas in a mixture of gases and is measured in mmHg (**millimetres of mercury**).

In the alveoli the partial pressure of oxygen (PO_2) is 100 mmHg and in the blood from the heart, now in the pulmonary capillaries it is 40 mmHg. The difference in partial pressure sets up a diffusion gradient and oxygen molecules flow across the semi-permeable membranes of the alveoli walls and the walls of the capillary – oxygen diffuses from the air in the alveoli into the blood. The oxygen combines with haemoglobin in the red blood cells to form oxyhaemoglobin. The blood, now known as oxygenated blood, leaves the lungs via the pulmonary vein and returns to the heart.

The partial pressure of carbon dioxide (PCO_2) in the alveoli is 40 mmHg and in the blood 46 mmHg. This creates a diffusion gradient in the opposite direction and carbon dioxide diffuses from the blood into the air in the alveoli, crossing the semi-permeable membranes of the capillary and alveoli walls. Carbon dioxide diffuses more easily and rapidly through the semi-permeable membranes than oxygen (20 times as fast in fact).

The partial pressures of oxygen and carbon dioxide in the pulmonary capillaries do not vary greatly, even during times of heavy exercise. This is not the case for the diffusion gradients that occur at the muscle site.

Key terms

Diffusion: The movement of gas molecules from an area of high concentration or partial pressure to an area of low concentration or partial pressure.

Partial pressure: the pressure a gas exerts in a mixture of gases.

Millimetres of mercury (mmHg): a unit for measuring atmospheric pressure.

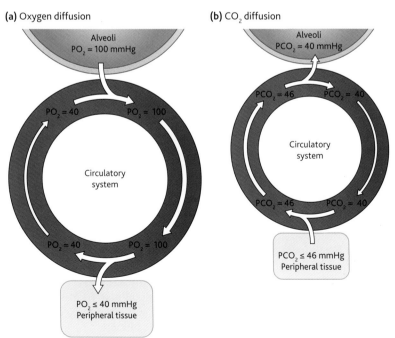

(a) Oxygen diffusion

(b) CO_2 diffusion

Fig. 3.5 *Diffusion of oxygen and carbon dioxide between the alveoli and a pulmonary capillary*

In summary there are a number of factors which make the diffusion of oxygen from the lungs into the blood very efficient:

- permeability of the alveoli and capillary cell walls
- short distance from alveoli to capillary
- readiness of haemoglobin to combine with oxygen to form oxyhaemoglobin
- diffusion gradient caused by different partial pressures of the gases involved
- large surface area of alveoli
- slow movement of blood through thin narrow capillaries
- moisture layer enhancing the uptake of oxygen.

Link

For a more detailed explanation see Chapter 4 – Blood transport system, page 41.

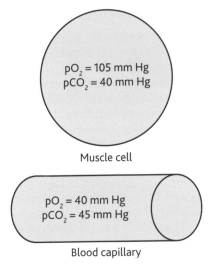

Muscle cell

Blood capillary

Fig. 3.6 *Diffusion of oxygen and carbon dioxide at the muscle cell*

Activity

Draw a diagram to show the blood route:

- from the alveoli
- to the heart
- to a muscle cell
- back to the heart then
- back to the lungs.

At the alveoli and muscle cell sites, add the partial pressures of oxygen and carbon dioxide and show the diffusion directions.

Oxygenated blood leaves the lungs, returns to the heart and is then pumped to all parts of the body via arteries, arterioles and finally capillaries. As the oxygenated blood flows slowly past the muscle cell, oxygen diffuses from the blood through the semi-permeable capillary and muscle cell walls, into the cell. Inside the cell, oxygen combines with myoglobin to form oxymyoglobin and is then transferred to a structure inside the cell known as the mitochondria.

During a period of exercise two factors change the steepness of the diffusion gradients. During periods of sustained or intense levels of exercise the breakdown of glucose to provide energy for the reformation of ATP is increased (see chapter introduction to remind yourself of this), using more oxygen in the process. This lowers the partial pressure of oxygen (PO_2) in the muscle cell (it in can go as low as 0 mmHg) and this results in a steeper pressure gradient and therefore a faster rate of oxygen diffusion.

The greater breakdown of glucose in the muscle cell to fuel the reformation of ATP results in more carbon dioxide being produced. The partial pressure of carbon dioxide (PCO_2) in the muscle cell can increase from 45 mmHg to 90 mmHg. In the capillary blood it is 40 mmHg and once again we have a steeper diffusion gradient and an increased rate of diffusion of carbon dioxide from the cell into the blood.

The blood returning to the heart now has a PO_2 of 40 mmHg (reduced from 100 mmHg) and a PCO_2 of 46 mmHg (increased from 40 mmHg).

The control of breathing and the role of carbon dioxide

Respiration is controlled (the rate and depth of breathing) by the **respiratory centre** in a part of the brain know as the medulla oblongata. The medulla oblongata is located in the brain stem, found between the spinal cord and the upper brain. The respiratory centre controls both the rate and depth of breathing and uses both neural control and chemical control.

Quiet breathing when at rest

There is both an inspiratory and expiratory centre. During normal, quiet breathing the inspiratory centre sends nerve impulses to the diaphragm and the external intercostal muscles causing them to contract, and we breathe in. After approximately 2 seconds the inspiratory centre ceases sending impulses and the intercostals and the diaphragm relax and the elastic recoil of the lungs means we expire or breathe out.

Breathing during exercise

As an earlier learning activity demonstrated during exercise we breathe more rapidly and deeply. This is due partly to the expiratory centre stimulating the internal intercostal muscles which causes us to breathe more deeply. But other factors have a significant effect upon the respiratory centre in the medulla oblongata. During exercise both chemical changes and neural influences are responsible for the significant changes in depth and rate of breathing (ventilation) that can occur. The chemical changes that are responsible for this change in respiration are caused by:

- an increase in carbon dioxide dissolved in the blood thereby making it more acidic (lower pH)
- an increase in lactic acid production during intense exercise which also lowers the pH level of the blood.

Carbon dioxide, formed as a by-product of the breakdown of glucose, can only escape from the cell by diffusing into the bloodstream and then leaving via expiration from the lungs. Carbon dioxide is transported in the blood in three ways.

- Approximately 5% is dissolved in the blood plasma (the fluid part of the blood). The carbon dioxide that is dissolved in the plasma determines the partial pressure (PCO_2) of carbon dioxide in the blood.
- Some 20% is combined with haemoglobin.
- Finally 60–80% combines with water to form bicarbonate in the plasma.

The body never tries to rid itself of all the carbon dioxide. The blood is never completely free of carbon dioxide, even after it has been through the lungs and carbon dioxide has been diffused into the alveoli and expired. The PCO_2 in oxygenated blood is 40 mmHg, which means that each litre of blood is carrying about 50 ml of carbon dioxide. This background level of carbon dioxide provides a chemical stimulation to control breathing.

An increase in the amount of carbon dioxide causes an increase in blood acidity. This change in blood acidity stimulates structures in the carotid artery known as **chemoreceptors**. Chemoreceptors are tiny structures, found in the carotid artery and in the aortic arch, that are sensitive to changes in blood acidity and when blood acidity rises they stimulate the respiratory centre to increase ventilation until the blood acidity has returned to normal.

Key terms

Respiratory centre: an area in the brain stem that is responsible for the control of breathing rate and depth.

Chemoreceptor: tiny structure in the carotid artery and aortic arch that is stimulated by an increase in blood acidity.

During exercise the arterial partial pressure of oxygen is not reduced sufficiently to stimulate a change in ventilation levels (rate and depth of breathing). It is the change in carbon dioxide level that causes this effect. It is the case that in conditions where arterial PO_2 is significantly lowered (at altitude, as a result of asthma, or by lung damage caused by smoking) the chemoreceptors are stimulated and ventilation is increased.

The neural influences that have an effect during exercise are connected to three factors:

- activity from the brain caused by the anticipation of exercise and increased stimulation from the motor centres of the brain (those parts of the brain that control muscle contractions)
- increased stimulation from proprioceptors in the joints and muscles as a result of increased rate of muscle contraction and joint movements
- increases in body temperature.

The control of our rate and depth of breathing is through the monitoring of the chemical state of the blood, our anticipation and control of movement, the feedback from movement and the temperature of the body. It is a highly dynamic system, which constantly manages and fine tunes our ventilation rates with no conscious input from ourselves.

a

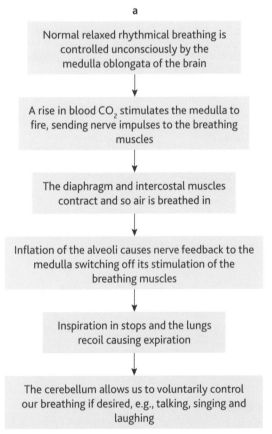

b

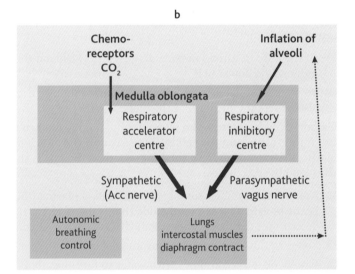

Fig. 3.7 **a** *Schematic diagram of the control of breathing;* **b** *Control of breathing by the nervous system*

✓ *You should now be able to:*

- explain how the process of inspiration and expiration works, enabling us to breathe in and out and also increase the depth of breathing
- name, analyse and explain the varying lung volumes that are shown on a chart of spirometer readings
- explain the term 'minute ventilation' and explain how it is calculated
- explain how oxygen is transferred from the lungs into the muscle cells
- explain how carbon dioxide is removed from the muscle cell and transported to the alveoli ready for expiration
- describe the chemical, physical and neural change that cause a change in our breathing rates and depth of breathing.

1 Figure 1 shows the spirometer trace of a games player.

    (a)   What lung volumes are represented by A, B and C? *(3 marks)*

    (b)   What would be the effect of a period of continuous running on the spirometer trace for lung volume A? *(3 marks)*

2 Describe the process of breathing from the point just before the start of inspiration until the end of expiration. *(6 marks)*

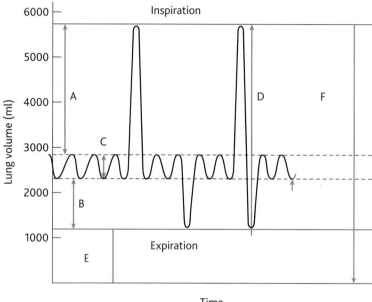

Fig. 1

3 Table 1 gives some data relating to the percentage concentrations of gases in air at various points of the breathing cycle.

    (a)   Use the information in the table to explain the functions of the lungs at rest and during exercise. *(3 marks)*

    (b)   Describe those characteristics of the structure of lungs that make them an efficient respiratory surface. *(3 marks)*

Table 1

	Inspired (%)	Expired (%) At rest	Expired (%) During exercise
Oxygen	20	16	14
Carbon dioxide	0.04	4	6
Nitrogen	79	79	79
Water vapour	variable	saturated	saturated

4 The diffusion of oxygen and carbon dioxide at the muscle site is an essential process for muscle activity.

Describe how the process of diffusion works at the muscle site with reference to concepts of partial pressure and diffusion gradients. *(6 marks)*

Blood transport system

Key terms

Artery: thick-walled blood vessel carrying blood away from the heart.

Vein: thin-walled blood vessel carrying blood towards the heart.

Arterioles: small arteries.

Venules: small veins.

Capillaries: tiny blood vessels supplying nutrients to cells and removing waste materials.

AQA Examiner's tip

- Arteries <u>a</u>lways take blood <u>a</u>way from the heart.

- <u>V</u>eins have <u>v</u>alves and carry blood to the heart.

Introduction

In order for our muscles to contract during exercise, they need a supply of oxygen. As we saw in the previous chapter, the supply of oxygen to the body is a function of the lungs. The lungs deliver oxygen to the blood, and the blood transports this oxygen around the body. Blood is moved through the body in a series of tubes, the blood vessels. The blood vessels and the blood itself form the blood transport system.

The role of the blood transport system is to move blood to all parts of the body. Our interest is in transporting the oxygen supplied by the lungs to muscles so that they can produce the energy they require for contraction. A waste product of the energy production process is carbon dioxide. This is transported by the blood from the muscles to the lungs where it is breathed out into the atmosphere. Blood has several other functions apart from transporting oxygen and carbon dioxide. It transports other important substances such as glucose, amino acids and nutrients. It also transports hormones which allow cells to communicate with each other. Blood being a fluid responds to changes in temperature and by redistributing our blood we are able to control our body temperature. Blood is also involved in protecting the body from infection through its role in clotting to prevent loss of blood.

Circulation

Each and every part of the body, including the muscles, has a major **artery** supplying it with blood from the heart, and a major **vein**, which carries blood back to the heart.

Blood flows away from the heart within arteries and as the blood gets further from the heart then various branches of the artery take the blood to the various parts of the body such as the arms, legs and organs. These branches are called **arterioles**. In much the same way, small veins called **venules** collect blood that has passed through the different parts of the body, including the muscles, and these unite to form the large veins that take the blood back to the heart.

When the arterioles take blood to the muscles, smaller and smaller divisions of the blood vessels occur. Eventually these smallest arterioles supply blood to small units of muscle through a network of the smallest of blood vessels called **capillaries**. This network of tiny blood vessels is called a capillary bed. Capillaries are tiny blood vessels that are so small they cannot be seen without a microscope. It is from the capillaries that cells and tissues such as muscle can gain the oxygen and glucose they require, whilst at the same time allowing their waste products such as carbon dioxide to be removed.

Having passed alongside the muscle cells, the capillaries then reunite to form tiny venules, which in turn combine to former larger venules and veins.

There are two transport systems in a human, so that blood follows a roughly figure-of-eight route around the body.

Pulmonary circulation: blood from the heart to the lungs and back to the heart picking up oxygen.

Systemic circulation: oxygenated blood carried from the heart to the body tissues and back to the heart.

The main job of the blood transport system is to get oxygen to the muscles. The oxygen comes into the body through the lungs. In order to pick up this oxygen, the blood flows from the heart to the lungs, picks up the oxygen and then travels back to the heart. This part of the transport system, from the heart to the lungs and back to the heart, is known as the **pulmonary circulation**.

The oxygen is then carried by the blood from the heart to the rest of the body tissues, including the muscles, where the oxygen is taken up by the tissues, and then the blood flows back to the heart again. This part of the transport system from the heart to the body tissues and back to the heart is called the **systemic circulation**.

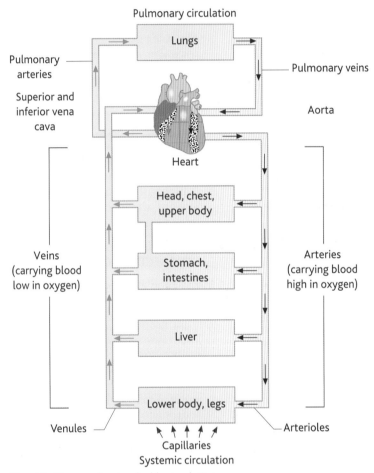

Fig. 4.1 *Diagram showing double circulation*

Arteries and veins

The walls of both arteries and veins consist of three layers:

- an inner endothelium
- a middle layer of smooth muscle and elastic fibres
- an outer fibrous layer.

The endothelium is the smooth inner layer that allows the blood to flow relatively free of friction through the blood vessels. In arteries, the middle layer of smooth muscle and elastic tissue is much thicker than that of veins. This allows the arteries to withstand the high pressure of blood caused by the contractions of the heart. The other big difference is that

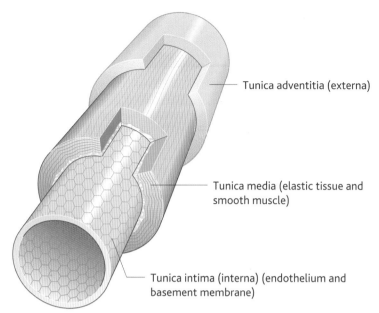

Tunica adventitia (externa)

Tunica media (elastic tissue and smooth muscle)

Tunica intima (interna) (endothelium and basement membrane)

Fig. 4.2 *Diagram showing structure of blood vessels*

veins have valves that prevent blood from flowing back the way it came. Arteries and capillaries do not have valves. The diameter of arteries gets smaller as they are found further away from the heart. The diameter of veins tends to increase as they approach the heart.

Redistribution of blood during exercise

There is a limited amount of blood within the body, roughly between 4 and 5 litres. There are however, miles of capillaries in the body that could be filled with blood. There is more space for blood than the amount of blood we have so not all the capillaries can be supplied with blood at the same time. There is therefore competition for blood between different regions of the body, especially during exercise, when blood must be moved or shunted to where it is needed at the working muscles, and consequently withdrawn from other regions.

The shunting of blood between competing tissues is achieved by the opening (dilation) and closing (constriction) of the arterioles that supply the blood that is entering the capillary beds.

In these arterioles there are rings of circular muscle that act as sphincters. When this ring of muscle contracts the size of the opening to the arteriole is reduced and blood supply to that particular capillary bed is similarly reduced. When these sphincters relax, blood flow returns to normal into the capillary beds.

Control of this blood shunting is regulated automatically through the sympathetic nervous system. Stimulation by impulses from these nerves causes the smooth muscle in arterioles and the pre-capillary sphincters to contract and **vasoconstriction** occurs. Vasoconstriction reduces the diameter of the blood vessels which in turn reduces the flow of blood through these vessels to the following capillaries.

In cardiac muscle and skeletal muscle however, these same sympathetic nerves act as vasodilators, increasing the diameter of the blood vessels supplying these tissues. This **vasodilation** means that more blood flows through these blood vessels and into the capillary network.

Activity

Draw a table to summarise the differences between arteries and veins.

AQA Examiner's tip

You may be required in an examination to outline the structure of different types of blood vessels and link those to their functions.

Activity

Make a list of parts of the body that would need more oxygen if you were running a 1500-metre race. Are there any parts of the body that will not need as much oxygen, and that can have a reduced blood flow?

Key terms

Vasoconstriction: reducing flow of blood into capillaries by action of sympathetic nerves.

Vasodilation: increasing flow of blood into capillaries.

Table 4.1 *Estimated blood flow in cm³ per minute*

Organ	At rest (cm³ per min)	Percentage of total blood flow	Maximum effort (cm³ per min)	Percentage of total blood flow
Skeletal muscles	1000	20	26000	88
Coronary vessels	250	5	1200	4
Skin	500	10	750	2.5
Kidneys	1000	20	300	1
Liver/gut	1250	25	375	1.25
Brain	750	15	750	2.5
Other	250	5	625	0.75
Whole body	5000	100	30000	100

AQA Examiner's tip

You may be asked questions about how vasoconstriction or vasodilation happens. In this case you will need to talk about changes in blood acidity because of the increase in carbon dioxide content; automatic control through the sympathetic nervous system and the opening and closing of pre-capillary sphincters to affect blood flow.

▓ Activity

Compare the table shown above to the list you made in the previous learning activity.

▓ Can you explain why blood flow to the skin and coronary blood vessels increases during exercise?

▓ Why does blood flow to the brain remain constant during rest and exercise?

There are also local factors which have a direct effect and cause vasodilation in working muscles. These include a drop in oxygen and a rise in carbon dioxide levels; an increase in acidity; and several others, including movement in the joints and tendons, which will give an instantaneous vasodilation because these are the result of muscle activity.

During exercise there is an increase in blood flowing to the skeletal muscles that are being used. This is in order to supply these exercising muscles with the oxygen and nutrients that they require for energy production, and also to remove the waste carbon dioxide produced. Blood supply to the heart muscle through the coronary arteries also increases as the heart has to pump harder and faster to supply this extra oxygen. Blood supply to the skin also increases. This is because exercise generates heat in the working muscles, but we need to keep our body temperature constant. Therefore there is a need to lose this heat. This heat loss is a function of the skin which can lose heat mainly through radiation and evaporation. Radiation is a process where heat is lost through a body being warmer than the surrounding environment. Vasodilation of skin capillaries near the skin's surface will result in the skin warming because of the warm blood flowing, and therefore heat can be lost by radiation. Evaporation is concerned with sweating. When we are hot we sweat, and sweat forms a layer of water on the skin's surface. When this water evaporates from the skin it loses heat and so the skin gets cooled. So to lose the heat produced through exercise we sweat and our skin reddens because of the increase in blood flowing close to the skin's surface.

It should come as no surprise that blood flow to the brain remains constant. The brain doesn't switch off during exercise; it carries on working, just as hard. It therefore still requires oxygen and nutrients so it can keep functioning.

This blood has to come from somewhere. When we exercise the extra blood flow to the active parts of the body is maintained by reducing the flow of blood in those arterioles supplying some abdominal organs such as the liver, kidneys and digestive organs. This involves vasoconstriction. Note that flow of blood is not stopped, merely reduced as digestion still takes place, but this is not as immediately important as the need for blood to reach the exercising muscles.

This redistribution of blood during exercise explains why performers should not eat immediately before exercise. After eating there will be a demand for blood to pass through the gut to digest the food. If exercise begins there will also be a demand for blood to flow to the exercising muscles. There is not enough blood in the body to deal with both digestion and exercise efficiently at the same time. There will be a less than maximal redistribution of blood flow to the exercising muscles, which will in turn limit the supply of oxygen and so performance suffers. Similarly there will be insufficient blood available for digestion, which slows down. There will also be the possibility that exercising with a full stomach adds additional weight to the body, which might affect performance. Excess food in the gut may also lead to feelings of nausea.

It should also be noted that Table 4.1 applies to the trained individual. The effects are less obvious on the untrained person, with the effects on the kidneys and heart minimised, and the only major shunt being that to the working muscles.

Blood pressure and velocity

As the heart pumps blood through the blood vessels, the vessels offer resistance, much like friction, to the flow of blood, and this creates a pressure, the blood pressure. This pressure varies depending on whether the flow of blood has been forced through the vessels, or this forced flow of blood is reduced. In other words the blood pressure varies according to whether the heart is contracting or relaxing.

Hence there is a **systolic pressure** when the heart is contracting and a **diastolic pressure** when the heart is relaxing.

As the blood leaves the heart and flows through the main arteries, it has a high systolic pressure from the contraction of the heart. This blood pressure reduces as blood moves further and further away from the heart. This is because the resistance to flow of the blood depends in part on the cross-sectional area of the blood vessels, and this increases as blood moves away from the heart. Similarly, because smaller arterioles have a larger total surface area than the larger arteries, blood pressure also falls as blood vessels get smaller. The friction of blood against the blood vessel walls also reduces the pressure of the blood. The longer the blood vessel is, the longer the blood is in contact with the blood vessels walls and the greater the effects of friction are. These effects of increasing cross-sectional area and resistance to flow are even greater in the capillaries, where blood pressure is so low that there is no pulsing flow of blood corresponding to the systolic and diastolic pressures, but rather a continuous smooth flow. As a result of this low capillary blood pressure, the pressure in veins is very low, and the friction of blood against the walls of the veins adds to this reduction even further. Thus, blood pressure diminishes as we move from arteries to arterioles to capillaries to venules to veins.

The velocity of the blood also reduces as we move away from the heart, with blood in the capillaries flowing very slowly. Again this is because of the increasing cross-sectional area of the blood vessels concerned. However, the blood speeds up as it enters the venules and veins because the total cross-sectional area decreases in these vessels.

These changes in total cross-sectional area and the corresponding changes in blood pressure and velocity are shown in Figure 4.3 overleaf.

Key terms

Systolic pressure: pressure of heart contracting.

Diastolic pressure: pressure of the relaxed heart.

Activity

Use a hosepipe or a piece of rubber tubing attached to a tap. Turn on the flow of water. Now try to adjust the flow of water – the pressure – by adjusting the opening (cross-sectional area) of the hose using your thumb.

What do you do to increase the pressure and to decrease the pressure? This simulates how the opening of the cross-sectional area affects the flow of blood and blood pressure.

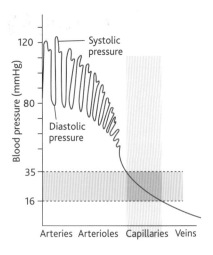

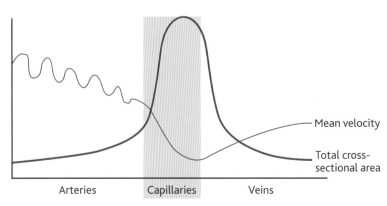

Fig. 4.3 *Relationship between blood pressure and blood velocity and the cross-sectional area of blood vessels*

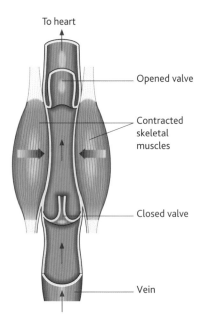

Fig. 4.4 *Diagram of skeletal muscle pump*

■ **Key terms**

Venous return: mechanisms involved to assist the return of blood to the heart.

Skeletal muscle pump: muscle action squeezes veins and forces blood towards the heart.

Respiratory pump: breathing movements force blood to flow towards the heart.

So blood does not flow at a constant speed around the body. It moves fastest in the large arteries, slower in the small arterioles and the veins, and slowest in the capillaries. The reasons for these differences are that the speed (velocity) of the blood is related to the cross-sectional area of the blood vessels. Blood flows most rapidly where the cross-sectional area is least, in the arteries.

🔆 Venous return

The pressure of the blood in the large veins is so low that it is insufficient to return the blood to the heart. This is because we tend to be upright most of the day, and therefore flow of blood in the veins has to move against the effects of gravity. We therefore need some mechanism to aid this **venous return**.

The most important mechanism for venous return is valves found in veins. These pocket valves allow blood to flow towards the heart, but open to prevent the blood from flowing in the wrong direction. There is also a **skeletal muscle pump**. The majority of our major veins lie either in-between muscles, or between muscles and bones. When we contract these muscles, the veins, being thin-walled, are squeezed and get compressed. This action pushes the blood back towards the heart, because the valves in the veins prevent flow in the other direction.

Exercise increases this effect. However if you suddenly stop exercising, the skeletal muscle pump slows, even though the heart is still working hard whilst you recover. This results in blood 'pooling' in the muscles, which means that less blood is reaching the heart, and therefore less is being pumped out.

The first organ to suffer from a lack of blood is the brain, and athletes can get dizzy or even faint from this mechanism, because of a lack of oxygen supply to the brain. This emphasises the need for a 'cool down' after exercise to prevent this venous pooling.

The second mechanism to aid venous return is the **respiratory pump**. When we breathe in and out, there are pressure changes within the chest cavity. Breathing out increases the pressure within the chest, and this compresses the veins within the chest, forcing blood to flow towards the heart (remember the one-way valves!). When we breathe in, the diaphragm flattens; this squeezes the abdominal organs against the veins, and again blood is forced to flow back to the heart.

💡 Transport of respiratory gases

Oxygen transport

Oxygen is slightly soluble in plasma, and a small proportion (about 3 per cent) of the oxygen entering our blood is carried in this way. However, the vast majority of the oxygen we need and use is carried in chemical combination with the red pigment **haemoglobin** that is found in red blood cells. Each haemoglobin molecule is able to carry a maximum of four molecules of oxygen:

Hence: $Hb + O_2 <==> HbO_2$ (**oxyhaemoglobin**)

This reaction is easily reversible, and the amount of oxygen combining with haemoglobin depends on the partial pressure of oxygen (PO_2). The partial pressure of a gas is equivalent to its concentration, and is sometimes referred to as the oxygen tension. Both of the terms 'oxygen tension' and 'partial pressure of oxygen' are comparable to the concentration of oxygen. When all the haemoglobin is combined with oxygen and formed into oxyhaemoglobin, then the haemoglobin is said to be fully (100 per cent) saturated with oxygen. This occurs where the oxygen concentration in the surrounding tissues is high, for example, when the blood is flowing through the lungs.

At lower oxygen concentrations the percentage saturation of haemoglobin is lower, as for example when the blood is flowing through actively respiring tissues (muscles). Hence at tissues such as the muscles, the nearly 100 per cent saturated haemoglobin that has arrived from the lungs gives up its oxygen to the surrounding cells, as it reduces its percentage saturation down to below 75 per cent. On returning to the lungs, where the oxygen tension is much higher, the haemoglobin once again picks up more oxygen to become highly saturated.

This idea is shown in the oxyhaemoglobin dissociation curve (Figure 4.5).

Typically, the partial pressure of oxygen in arterial blood is 90–100 mmHg and therefore blood leaving the lungs is about 97–98 per cent saturated with haemoglobin. When this blood reaches the tissues, the partial pressure of oxygen falls to about 40 mmHg, a point where haemoglobin is only about 75 per cent saturated, and a large proportion of the oxygen being carried by the blood is released into the tissues. This release of oxygen occurs in even greater amounts in exercising muscles, where the partial pressure of oxygen may drop well below 40 mmHg, so that nearly all the oxygen is released from the haemoglobin.

The amount of oxygen released from haemoglobin is affected by several other factors apart from the partial pressure of oxygen. In acidic conditions, oxygen splits more readily from haemoglobin. This effect is seen as a shift of the dissociation curve to the right, a phenomenon known as the **Bohr shift**. Higher acidity in the blood can occur from the presence of more carbon dioxide and more lactic acid as a result of exercise.

■ Key terms

Haemoglobin: red pigment that transports oxygen in the blood.

Oxyhaemoglobin: chemical combination of haemoglobin with oxygen.

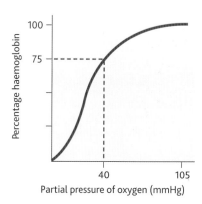

Fig. 4.5 *Oxyhaemoglobin dissociation curve*

■ Key terms

Bohr shift: change in shape - movement to the right of oxyhaemoglobin dissociation curve which results in the release of more oxygen in exercising muscles.

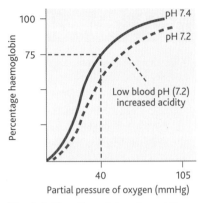

Fig. 4.6 *The effect of changing acidity on the oxyhaemoglobin dissociation curve – the Bohr shift*

Key terms

Hydrogen carbonate: main means by which carbon dioxide is transported by the blood.

Arterio-venous oxygen difference: amount of oxygen removed from the blood by muscles.

Increases in temperature decreases haemoglobin's affinity for oxygen and thus causes more oxygen to be released from oxyhaemoglobin at the tissues. This effect will also occur as a result of exercise-generating heat in the muscles.

Haemoglobin is thus a very efficient respiratory pigment. Males normally have a higher level of haemoglobin than females, as well as a greater blood volume. This means that males generally have better adaptations to endurance training.

In order to make sure that sufficient oxygen is available to working muscles, another respiratory pigment, myoglobin, is involved. Myoglobin is found only in muscles. Myoglobin has a higher affinity for oxygen than haemoglobin, and therefore it picks up all the oxygen released from haemoglobin, and transports it through the muscles. Myoglobin acts like a reservoir for oxygen should the muscle begin to contract.

Carbon dioxide transport

The carbon dioxide that enters the body via the alveoli diffuses into the blood and is transported in three different ways:

- 7% dissolves into the plasma.
- 23% combines with proteins in the plasma, including haemoglobin in red blood cells.
- 70% is transported as bicarbonate ion (hydrogen carbonate ion).

As the carbon dioxide diffuses into blood, it enters red blood cells and combines with water to form carbonic acid, which readily splits into **hydrogen carbonate** and hydrogen ions:

$$CO_2 + H_2O <=> H_2CO_3 <=> H^+ + HCO_3^-$$

The excess H^+ is buffered by the haemoglobin, thus preventing the blood from becoming too acidic. This also helps dissociate oxyhaemoglobin. The deoxygenated blood returning to the lungs contains carbon dioxide dissolved in the plasma. Carbon dioxide combined with plasma proteins and carbon dioxide incorporate into bicarbonate ions. In the lungs the carbon dioxide diffuses out of the blood and into the alveoli.

💡 Gaseous exchange at tissues

Gaseous exchange at the tissues (muscles) is mainly dependent on the partial pressure gradient between the blood and tissues for the gases concerned. When muscles are exercising, the partial pressure of oxygen within the muscles becomes quite low and this increases the diffusion gradient between the muscles and the blood. This releases oxygen from the red blood cells, which diffuses into the muscle.

Other factors that occur with exercise, such as increased temperature and a decrease in pH, also encourage oxygen to diffuse into the muscles from the blood. The muscles (tissues) thus take up oxygen from the blood. This means that there is a difference in the amount of oxygen in arterial blood arriving at the muscles, from that in venous blood that is leaving the muscles. This **arterio-venous difference** or a-vO_2 diff per 100 cm³ blood depends on the level of oxygen extracted by the muscles. At rest, the a-vO_2 diff is low, but during exercise muscles extract large amounts of oxygen from the blood, and hence the a-vO_2 diff is high. This increase in a-vO_2 diff affects gaseous exchange at the alveoli, because venous blood returning to the lungs during exercise has correspondingly more carbon dioxide and less oxygen, thus increasing the diffusion gradients for these gases. Training increases the a-vO$_2$ diff, as trained individuals can extract more oxygen from blood.

✓ *You should now be able to:*

- describe the double circulation of the blood
- describe the differences between different types of blood vessels
- explain the redistribution of blood that occurs as a result of exercise
- explain the transport of oxygen and carbon dioxide at rest and during exercise
- explain the venous return mechanism
- explain what is meant by the a-vO$_2$ difference.

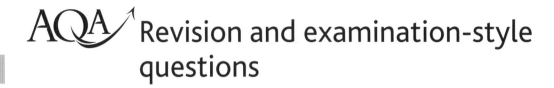

1   Figure 1 below shows the oxyhaemoglobin dissociation curve.

   (a)   Use the figure to explain how oxygen is released by the blood and supplied
         to muscles.   *(2 marks)*

   (b)   Explain how exercise affects the shape of the curve and the effect this has
         on oxygen delivery to the muscles.   *(4 marks)*

2   (a)   State three ways in which carbon dioxide is transported in the blood.   *(3 marks)*

   (b)   Explain how oxygen is taken up by haemoglobin from the lungs and released
         at the muscle site.   *(3 marks)*

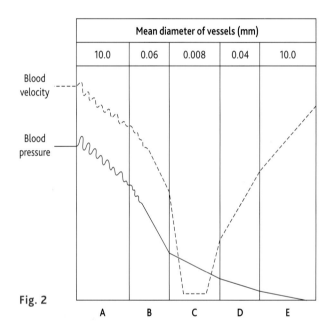

Fig. 1

Fig. 2

3   When involved in physical activity, a performer's blood velocity and pressure is
   similar to the graph shown in Figure 2.

   (a)   Using the graph identify blood vessels represented by A, B, C, D and E.   *(3 marks)*

   (b)   Explain the variation in blood pressure and blood velocity occurring
         from A to E.   *(3 marks)*

4   When competing at maximum effort, a performer will experience changes in the
   way that blood is distributed around the body, as shown in Table 4.1 on page 44,
   compared to rest.

   (a)   Explain why the blood flow to the brain remains the same at rest and
         during the game.   *(2 marks)*

   (b)   Explain why there is a need for blood flow to increase to the skeletal
         muscles during the game and how this is achieved.   *(4 marks)*

5 Heart function

AQA Examiner's tip

Although the structure of the heart is not examined, it needs to be known in order to understand how it functions.

There are two systems of blood flow in the body: the **pulmonary circulation** to the lungs and back to the heart, and the **systemic circulation** which takes blood around the rest of the body and back to the heart.

▓ Key terms

Pulmonary circulation: blood circulates from the heart to the lungs and returns to the heart.

Systemic circulation: blood circulates from the heart to the body tissues and returns to the heart.

One of the more obvious effects of exercise is that your heart beats faster. This is because during any form of exercise, muscles will be contracting. These contractions require energy to make them happen. In order to produce the energy for contractions, the muscles will use oxygen. There is therefore a need for oxygen in order to supply the energy required for muscle contraction. This oxygen is found all around as a component of air. When we breathe in, air enters our lungs and some of the oxygen enters our body. This oxygen is transported from the lungs to the muscles by the blood. In order to force the oxygen-rich blood around the body we need a pump. The heart is the pumping mechanism for the blood and must keep pace with the demand for oxygen made by the muscles.

The heart is a complex organ both in terms of its structure and how it works (function). You will have studied the structure of the heart earlier in your school career as part of general science. The structure of the heart is not examined in AQA Physical Education, but you cannot understand how the heart functions without a clear understanding of its structure. In the examination you could easily be asked questions about how the heart functions in terms of the sequence of events that make it contract and push blood around the body. You could also be asked questions about the various amounts of blood that are released from the heart and how exercise and/or training affects the heart by making it beat faster and grow bigger.

The heart is a two-sided pump. The right side of the heart is separated from the left side by a wall of muscle called the septum. The right side of the heart receives deoxygenated blood from the body via the inferior and superior vena cava and blood from these blood vessels enters the heart into the right atrium. The right atrium is the upper collecting chamber of the right side of the heart. As the right atrium fills, some of this blood passes through the tricuspid valve and enters the lower chamber, the right ventricle. When full the right ventricle pumps this deoxygenated blood to the lungs via the pulmonary artery, which forms part of the **pulmonary circulation**.

The left side of the heart receives oxygenated blood from the lungs via the pulmonary veins. The blood enters into the left atrium and passes through the bicuspid valve, before moving into the left ventricle. When the left ventricle contracts, that blood is sent around the rest of the body, including the muscles, via the aorta, eventually returning through the inferior and superior vena cava, part of the **systemic circulation**.

Because the ventricles are the main pumping components of the heart, they are more muscular than the atria. Similarly, because the left ventricle has to force blood around the whole body while the right ventricle has to pump blood the short distance to the lungs, the left ventricle has thicker muscle layers in its wall, to generate greater forces during contraction.

The blood is kept flowing in the correct direction through the heart through the action of four heart valves. On the right side of the heart, there is a tricuspid valve between the atrium and the ventricle and a semi-lunar valve between the right ventricle and the pulmonary artery. On the left side of the heart there is a bicuspid valve between the atrium

SAN or sino-atrial node: small mass of cardiac muscle, found in the wall of the right atrium that generates the heartbeat.

Intrinsic: the name given to the idea that the heart generates its own contraction from within itself.

Myogenic: impulses generated without nervous stimulation.

■ Activity

Draw a large square on a piece of paper. Divide this square in half with both a vertical line and a horizontal line so that you finish up with four smaller squares inside the large square. This is your diagram of the heart. Now label the four heart chambers. Draw on and label the main blood vessels connected to each heart chamber. Draw on and label the four sets of heart valves. Compare your diagram to Figure 5.1.

and the ventricle and another semi-lunar valve between the ventricle and the aorta.

The opening and closing of these valves is brought about by changes in pressure within the heart chambers themselves. Increasing pressure is caused by the presence of blood initially and further pressure rises are due to the force of the heart muscle contracting and squeezing on the chamber contents. Increasing pressure in the atria will force open the tricuspid and bicuspid valves and blood will surge into the ventricles. Increasing pressure in the ventricles will force the tricuspid and bicuspid valves to close and the semi-lunar valves to open.

■ How the heart contracts

The heart is mainly composed of cardiac muscle which has the unique ability to not only contract like skeletal muscle, but also to generate and conduct its own electrical signal for contraction without the need for nervous stimulation. The impulse for contraction is generated by a small mass of specialised cardiac muscle called the **sino-atrial node (SAN)** found in the wall of the right atrium. The SAN sets the heart's rhythm and is sometimes called the heart's 'pacemaker'. The heartbeat is said to be **intrinsic** because it comes from within the heart itself, and **myogenic** because it occurs without nervous stimulation. The electrical impulse generated by the SAN spreads as a wave of depolarisation through the atria and causes the muscle in the atria to contract.

Physiologists call the period of time that the heart is contacting systole (the period of relaxation is called diastole). Therefore the start of a heartbeat is contraction of the atria or atrial systole. The stimulation to contract that is generated by the SAN cannot spread down to the ventricles because the valves of the heart act as a physical barrier to the conduction of the impulses. The wave eventually reaches another mass

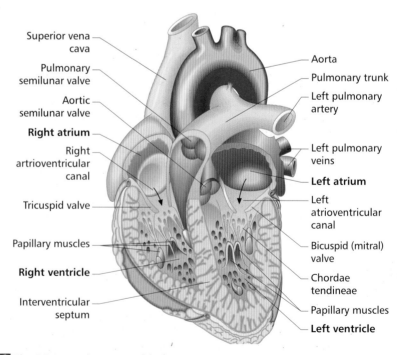

Superior vena cava
Pulmonary semilunar valve
Aortic semilunar valve
Right atrium
Right artrioventricular canal
Tricuspid valve
Papillary muscles
Right ventricle
Interventricular septum

Aorta
Pulmonary trunk
Left pulmonary artery
Left pulmonary veins
Left atrium
Left atrioventricular canal
Bicuspid (mitral) valve
Chordae tendineae
Papillary muscles
Left ventricle

💡 **Fig. 5.1** *Internal structure of the heart*

of tissue called the **atrio-ventricular node** (AVN), which conducts the impulse from the atria to the ventricles. There is a delay as the impulse passes through the AVN. This delay is very important to the efficient functioning of the heart. It gives the atria time to fully contract and fill the ventricles before the ventricles themselves contract.

The impulse from the AVN passes down the septum in a bundle of conducting tissue (**bundle of His**) to the tip of the ventricle where it branches out into many smaller sub-branches that spread throughout the wall of the ventricles. These terminal parts of the bundle of His are called **Purkinje fibres**, and it is these that carry the impulse to the ventricular wall to cause contraction.

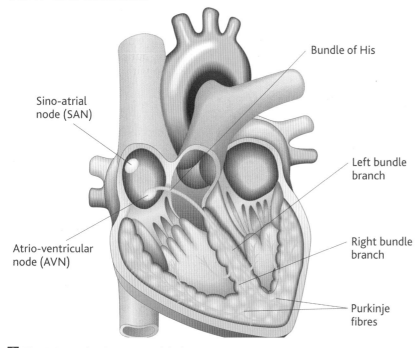

🔗 **Fig. 5.2** *Conduction system of the heart*

The intrinsic impulses of the SAN set the rhythm of the heartbeat, but the timings can be altered through the sub-conscious autonomic nervous system (think automatic!) and the action of hormones. The autonomic nervous system has two branches. The parasympathetic branch has its effect on SAN via the vagus nerve. Impulses from this nerve cause heart rate to slow by affecting the intrinsic rhythm of the SAN. This vagal tone also decreases the force or strength of contraction of the heart.

The other branch of the autonomic nervous system, the sympathetic branch, has the opposite effect in that it speeds up heart rate. The maximum heart rate that an individual can achieve varies, but can reach over 200 beats per minute. Sympathetic stimulation of the SAN also increases the strength of contraction of the heart.

💡 An analogy for understanding the regulation of heart rate

Think of a cyclist going downhill. They can control their speed by means of their brakes and their pedals. The speed of the bike is similar to the speed of the heartbeat. The brakes on the bike are like the vagus nerve, and the pedals are like the sympathetic nerve.

Key terms

Atrio-ventricular node: bundle of tissue found in atrio-ventricular septum that forms part of the heart's conduction system.

Bundle of His: specialised bundles of nerve tissue, found in the interventricular septum that forms part of the conduction system.

Purkinje fibres: specialised nerve fibres found in the ventricles.

AQA Examiner's tip

Questions about the cardiac cycle are invariably 4 or 5 mark questions and therefore you should learn just sufficient key points to gain full marks; such as:

- SAN is heart's pacemaker – intrinsic rhythm
- impulses spread through atria causing contraction of atria
- picked up by AVN
- spread through the septum in the bundle of His
- then through ventricles in Purkinje fibres causing contraction.

■ Key terms

Stroke volume: volume of blood leaving the left ventricle per beat.

Ejection fraction: proportion of blood in left ventricle pumped out each beat.

Cardiac output: volume of blood leaving the left ventricle per minute or stroke volume × heart rate.

AQA **Examiner's tip**

Key points for answering questions about the regulation of heart rate:

■ SAN rate is altered by autonomic nervous system

■ parasympathetic vagus nerve slows heart rate

■ sympathetic nerve speeds up heart rate

■ release of adrenaline increases heart rate prior to exercise.

Typical questions:

■ the relationship between heart rate, stroke volume and cardiac output needs to be learned: Cardiac output = stroke volume × heart rate.

■ Questions on this topic can include calculations as well as definitions and explanations.

When travelling downhill you would adjust the speed of the bike through adjusting the amount of braking used – just like the vagus nerve. To go faster, reduce the amount of braking, to slow down, increase the braking. If you need to cycle really fast downhill, then take off the brakes completely – vagus nerve, and pedal faster – sympathetic nerve.

The hormone adrenaline is released from the adrenal glands in times of stress and this affects the SAN, mimicking the action of the sympathetic system in that it speeds up heart rate and strength of contraction. When you are getting ready to exercise or preparing to compete you invariably think about what is going to happen, and this can increase your level of arousal which in turn leads to a release of adrenaline in anticipation of exercise. This causes an anticipatory rise in heart rate.

The time taken for the heart's chambers to go through a complete cycle of contraction (systole) followed by a period of relaxation (diastole) is called the cardiac cycle. During rest and with a normal heart rate of 75 beats per minute, the cardiac cycle lasts 0.8 seconds (60 seconds ÷ 75 beats). Most of this time is taken up with the heart filling during diastole (0.5 s) and a much smaller time period (about 0.3 s) is for systole.

During systole, a certain amount of blood is forced out from each ventricle. This is the **stroke volume**. When contracting, the ventricles do not completely empty. The proportion of blood that was in a ventricle that eventually leaves the ventricle is called the **ejection fraction**. The **cardiac output** is the total volume of blood pumped out by a ventricle per minute, or simply stroke volume × heart rate. This averages at about five litres per minute for a resting adult male.

Your resting heart rate will be something in the region of 60–90 beats per minute. During exercise your heart rate increases. This increase is in direct proportion to the intensity of the work you are undertaking, until nearing exhaustion, when your heart rate starts to level off, giving you a maximum heart rate. An estimate of maximum heart rate may be made by subtracting your age from 220.

■ Activity

Plot a graph of the following experimental results of changes to heart rate when using an exercise bike at different workloads:

Workload (Watts)	50	100	150	200	250	300
Heart rate (Bts/min)	84	102	114	132	144	160

1 How does heart rate vary with workload?

2 What would happen if the workload was increased to 350 Watts?

3 What about 500 Watts?

When workloads are kept constant at sub-maximal levels, the heart rate increases rapidly but does eventually level off, reaching a plateau. This is the steady state heart rate and indicates the optimal heart rate for the amount of exercise being undertaken. Increase or decrease the workload and a new steady state heart rate will develop within a minute or two.

Your stroke volume will also change during exercise. As the workload gets higher, so does your stroke volume, peaking at about 50 per cent of maximum effort and then levelling out as workload approaches maximum. It must be noted that changes in stroke volume are a

Activity

Plot a graph of the following experimental results of changes to heart rate when using an exercise bike at a constant workload of 100 Watts:

Time (Seconds)	30	60	90	120	150	180
Heart rate (Bts/min)	85	100	116	130	133	131

1 What do you think the heart rate would be after 4 minutes (240 seconds)?

2 What do we call this phenomenon?

much-debated area, with many conflicting studies. The increase in stroke volume that occurs when exercising is due to two mechanisms.

Firstly it is known that if more blood enters the ventricle during diastole, then the walls of the ventricle will correspondingly stretch and contract more forcefully. This is **Starling's Law of the Heart**. The increase in blood flow into the heart is a result of increased **venous return** which occurs as a result of blood flowing faster around the body. Secondly, at higher workload intensities, it appears that the cardiac muscle contracts with greater force. This occurs to combat the shortened duration of diastole, meaning there is less time for the heart to fill with blood. Because the heart does not have enough time to fill while it is relaxed, there is a stronger, more forceful contraction to make sure more of the contents of each ventricle is expelled form the heart.

The effects of an increased exercising heart rate and stroke volume on the cardiac output are quite dramatic. Remember that cardiac output = heart rate × stroke volume. Exercising heart rate may reach 200 beats per minute and exercising stroke volumes of 180 mls are not unknown, giving us an exercising cardiac output of 36 litres per minute (200 × 180 ÷ 1000). Remember that the main reason for this increase in cardiac output is to supply the working muscles with extra oxygen.

Key terms

Starling's Law of the Heart: the greater the venous return, the greater the strength of contraction.

Venous return: the mechanisms that return blood to the heart.

Activity

Calculate the cardiac output of the following individuals:

- Subject A – heart rate = 80 bts per min; stroke volume = 90 mls
- Subject B – heart rate = 110 bts per min; stroke volume = 100 mls
- Subject C – heart rate = 160 bts per min; stroke volume = 120 mls.

AQA Examiner's tip

The effects of exercise on the heart is a 4 or 5 mark question. Learn the following bullet points in order to gain maximum marks:

- heart rate increases
- stroke volume increases
- because of Starling's Law
- cardiac output increases
- because cardiac output = stroke volume × heart rate.

Regulation of heart rate

The increase in heart rate that accompanies exercise is due to the action of the sympathetic nerves on the SAN. But what causes these nerves to increase their firing? It should be noted that there are many different stimuli that affect heart rate, including increased brain activity, increased blood pressure, detection of movement and decreased levels of oxygen in the blood, but it is thought that changes to blood carbon dioxide levels is the most important. Exercise increases the levels of carbon dioxide in the blood, which in turn increases the acidity of the blood. These changes in blood chemistry are detected by **chemoreceptors** found mainly in the carotid arteries. These receptors send nerve impulses to the cardiac centre

Key terms

Chemoreceptors: group of cells sensitive to changes in blood acidity.

■ **Key terms**

Hypertrophy or athlete's heart: the increase in size of the heart that accompanies training.

■ **Key terms**

Bradycardia: the reduction in resting heart rate that accompanies training.

in the medulla of the brain which in turn adjusts the nerve stimulation to the SAN with decreased vagal and increased sympathetic impulses to increase the heart rate.

Reduction in heart rate is most likely due to the resulting increase in blood pressure which would be detected by baroreceptors found again in the carotid arteries, which via the medulla, increase vagal tone and decrease sympathetic stimulation.

💡 Effects of training

The effects of training on the heart are to change the parameters involved so that exercising becomes easier. Thus training, especially endurance training over months/years causes the heart to increase in size, especially in terms of the thickness of the cardiac muscle in the left ventricle. Cardiac muscle, like skeletal muscle gets bigger the more it is overloaded. It undergoes **hypertrophy**. This is the so-called 'athlete's heart'. This enlargement is caused by both an increased thickness of the cardiac muscle in the ventricular wall, and an increase in the size of the ventricular chamber. A less dramatic increase is found in power-trained athletes.

These two changes mean that the hypertrophied heart is capable of increased filling during the diastolic (resting) phase and increased strength of contractions as a result of thicker cardiac muscle.

■ **Activity**

■ Use a bottle of water to mimic the stroke volume/ejection fraction idea and effects of training. Outside, or over a bath, gently squeeze a bottle full of water. Water flows out of the top of the bottle. The amount of water coming out of the bottle is equivalent to the stroke volume. The proportion of water coming out is the ejection fraction.

■ Refill the bottle; now because of training the heart muscle is stronger and the contraction more powerful – squeeze the bottle harder. More water comes out of the bottle – an increased stroke volume and ejection fraction.

Stroke volume also increases as a result of training. There is a greater blood volume available in the body as a result of training and hence venous return during exercise becomes greater and Starling's Law tells us that this will result in increased force of contraction, meaning more blood is ejected from the heart with each beat. Add this to a stronger heart and it is easy to see that resting and exercising stroke volume increases with training.

Training reduces resting heart rate. When initially started, training has been shown to reduce resting heart rate by as much as one beat per week of training. Highly conditioned athletes have been known to have resting heart rates of less that 30 beats per minute. Clinically, a resting heart rate of below 60 beats per minute is known as **bradycardia**. It is usually suggested that the reduction in resting heart rate is due to training increasing resting stroke volume. Remember that cardiac output = stroke volume × heart rate. Training increases stroke volume, but has little effect on resting cardiac output. Thus heart rate must decrease to balance the increase in stroke volume. Extensive endurance-type training will also decrease the maximum heart rate because the high cardiac output demanded by the body during maximum exertion can be maintained with a lower heart rate due to the increase in stroke volume.

So, how do these changes to the heart benefit the performer? Perhaps surprisingly, it is mainly as a result of less demand for oxygen by the heart. The heart functions as a working muscle. The harder it works the more oxygen it requires to generate energy. With training, the heart rate decreases and therefore less energy and consequently less oxygen is required by the heart muscle, leaving more oxygen available to the other working muscles.

The trained individual's exercising heart rate is also lower than the untrained person for any given workload. Increasing the workload means that there is a need for an increased cardiac output. In untrained individuals this is mainly achieved by increasing heart rate, but in trained individuals it is achieved by an increased ejection fraction.

As the exercise continues the stoke volume begins to get smaller while the heart rate increases. There is also an increase in cardiac output during sustained exercise. These changes to cardiac function are known as **cardiovascular drift** and is thought to be caused by a reduction in fluid in the blood (due to sweating and loss of fluids because of the heat generated by muscle contraction), which in turn decreases the venous return and thus the stroke volume (remember Starling's Law of the heart). The increase in cardiac output that occurs during prolonged exercise is also due to sweating and the increased oxygen need for energy to assist the skin in cooling the body.

Activity

Explain in your own words how training benefits the performer in terms of cardiac function.

Key terms

Cardiovascular drift: an increase in heart rate that occurs during prolonged exercise that compensates for a decrease in stroke volume in an attempt to maintain cardiac output.

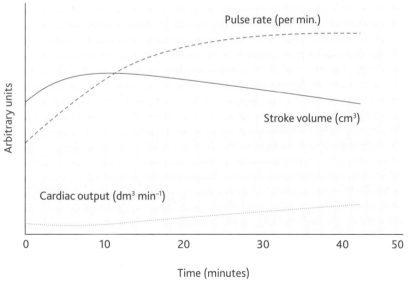

Fig. 5.3 *Graph showing effects of cardiovascular drift*

✔ *You should now be able to:*

- describe how the heartbeat is generated
- define the terms 'cardiac output' and 'stroke volume' and the relationship between them
- explain how heart rate is regulated
- define and explain the effects of exercise and training on the heart.

1   The graph in Figure 1 shows the stroke volume, pulse rate and cardiac output
     of a performer completing a 30-minute run at sub-maximal pace on a treadmill.

     (a)   Using Figure 1, explain why the performer's cardiac output increases
            during a run of constant pace and workload.   *(4 marks)*

     (b)   Explain how it is possible for a trained and an untrained individual to
            have the same cardiac output for a given workload.   *(2 marks)*

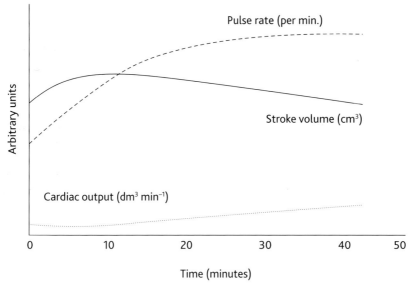

Fig. 1 *Graph showing effects of cardiovascular drift*

2   When a person is participating in a sporting activity, the physical demands of
     exercise are met by increasing blood flow to some areas of the body.

     (a)   Explain the terms cardiac output and stroke volume and the relationship
            between them.   *(3 marks)*

     (b)   What are the effects of training on resting cardiac output, heart rate and
            stroke volume?   *(3 marks)*

3   Describe how the sinoatrial node (SAN) and the atrioventricular node (AVN)
     control the increase in heart rate during exercise.   *(6 marks)*

4   Both heart rate and stroke volume increase during exercise.

     (a)   What causes the increase in stroke volume?   *(2 marks)*

     (b)   Explain how structures within the heart control the rate of the heartbeat. *(4 marks)*

6 Analysis of movements

Key terms

Articulations: another name for a joint.

Agonist (or Prime Mover): muscle or muscle group whose action is mainly responsible for producing a given motion.

Most GCSE PE courses involve the naming of specific muscles and bones of the body. Even if you haven't studied GCSE PE you are quite likely to know the names of several bones and muscles because of your interest in sport. AS Level study takes these ideas a stage further by looking at how these muscles and bones work together to produce certain common sporting movements. It is therefore important that you are able to understand the actions that are involved in each of the movements required. Quite often images will be provided in the examination papers that you may use as a reference, but you are never going to be provided with a moving image. You must be able to visualise the movement involved so that you may answer any questions accurately.

Activity

▦ Work with a partner/friend. Write the names of any muscles or bones that you know onto sticky labels and after discussion with your partner, place them on yourself in the correct location.

▦ Compare your labels to those of the rest of the class and label those muscles and bones that you have missed out. Ask your teacher to identify any muscles or bones you are not sure of.

💡 How we move

The bones and the joints of the body provide leverage for movement and form the framework of the body; they are not capable of providing movement by themselves. Movement is brought about by the contraction and relaxation of muscles.

Muscles produce movements by exerting force on tendons, which in turn pull on bones. Most muscles cross at least one joint, and are attached to the bones that form that joint. Joints consist of two or more bones that make contact and can move against each other. The moving bones in a joint are called articulating bones, and the joints themselves are called **articulations**.

When a muscle contracts it pulls one articulating bone towards the other. The two bones that form a joint do not move equally in response to the muscle contraction. One bone is generally held in its original position by the action of other muscles. Usually the attachment of a muscle tendon to the stationary bone is called the origin. The attachment to the moving bone is called the insertion.

Most muscles that move joints lie alongside bones and do not lie on top of the joint. It's usually the tendon at the insertion end of a muscle that lies over the joint.

Most movements are produced from several muscles working together rather than as isolated muscles, and most skeletal muscles are arranged in pairs that oppose each other at joints, that is flexors-extensors, abductors-adductors, etc.

A muscle that produces the desired action is called the prime mover (**agonist**). For example, in flexion of the forearm at the elbow, the biceps muscle is the prime mover. At the same time, another muscle, the triceps, called the **antagonist**, is relaxing.

The antagonist has the opposite effect to the prime mover. The roles of these two muscles are reversed when the action is changed to that of extension. As well as prime movers and antagonists, most movements involve muscles called **synergists**. The role of these muscles is to steady a movement and thus prevent unwanted movements whilst helping the prime mover function more efficiently.

Some synergists also act as fixators during movements, helping to stabilise the origin of the prime mover so that it can act more efficiently. For example, the scapula must be held in place by fixators so that the deltoid muscle can abduct the upper arm.

All muscle contractions are either **isometric** or **isotonic**. An isometric contraction happens when the muscle develops tension (force), but no movement occurs. These are sometimes called static contractions, and are often used in sport to hold the body in a fixed position, such as during gymnastic balances, or when a sprinter remains still in the 'set' position.

Isotonic contractions occur when there is tension produced within a muscle whilst it shortens or lengthens. They are sometimes called dynamic contractions, because movement occurs.

Concentric contractions occur when the muscle shortens during contraction. This happens when the muscle develops enough force to overcome a resistance as for example in the biceps during the flexion phase of a biceps curl.

Eccentric contractions involve the muscle lengthening under tension. These contractions occur when the muscle gradually lessens its tension to control movement that is happening because of gravity. This is what takes place in the biceps during the extension phase of the biceps curl.

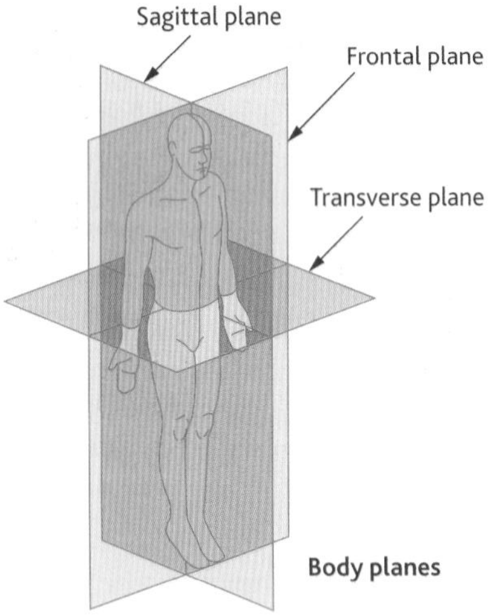

Planes of motion

There are three planes of motion, which make the description of various joint movements easier to understand. As movements occur, the direction or line through which the part of the body moves is called a plane. At the same time, the joint moves or rotates around an axis that is at right angles to that plane. For simplicity, all movements are described as if the performer was standing upright with their arms by their sides and their palms facing forward, see Figure 6.1.

Sagittal plane

The **sagittal plane** splits the body into left and right halves. Movements in the sagittal plane could be described as forward and backward movements, and take place around a **transverse axis** that passes through the body from side to side. Generally, flexion and extension movements, such as biceps curls, sit-ups and knee extensions occur in the sagittal plane and around a transverse axis.

Frontal plane

The **frontal plane** splits the body into front and back halves. Movements in the frontal plane could be described as side to side movements, and take place around a **frontal axis** that passes through the body from front to back. Abduction and adduction movements such as raising and lowering of a limb to the side, which occur at the hip and the shoulder, take place in the frontal plane and around the frontal axis.

Sagittal plane

Frontal plane

Transverse plane

Body planes

Fig. 6.1 *Planes and axes*

Transverse plane

The **transverse plane** divides the body into top and bottom halves. Movements in the transverse plane could be described as turning movements, and take place around a **longitudinal axis** that passes through the body from top to bottom. Rotational movements such as pronation and supination occur in the transverse plane around a longitudinal axis, as does horizontal flexion and extension.

💡 Analysis of specific movements

Running

The leg action in running is one that takes place in a sagittal plane about a transverse axis. The actions are concerned with three joints: the hip, knee and ankle.

The hip joint is a large **ball and socket joint** that permits a large range of movement in many directions. The joint is formed between the ball, the spherical head of the femur (thigh bone), and the socket, a deep depression in the side of the pelvis. The ball and socket fit together to give a strong, stable joint with a good range of movements.

Activities

Locate and feel the hip joint at the side of the top of your thigh. The hip joint is three or four inches lower than the crest of your pelvis, and many people confuse the two. You'll find it easier to locate the hip if you move the leg. What you are actually feeling is the femur.

1 Move your leg forwards and backwards. Through which plane and what axis is this movement taking place in?

2 Move your leg out to the side. Through which plane and what axis is this movement taking place in?

3 Now keeping your leg locked straight, turn your foot outwards and inwards. Through which plane and what axis is this movement taking place in?

Various ligaments and cartilages are involved with providing the knee with stability and these tend to make the knee the most complex and discussed joint in the body. But in simple terms the joint is relatively straightforward.

AQA **Examiner's tip**

One plane is only ever paired with one particular axis. The vast majority of movements that you need to know take place in a sagittal plane around a transverse axis; a few take place in a transverse plane around a longitudinal axis.

Key terms

Transverse plane and longitudinal axis: directions for turning/rotational movements.

Ball and socket joint: formed at the hip between pelvis and femur.

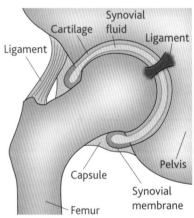

Fig. 6.2 *Diagram of hip joint*

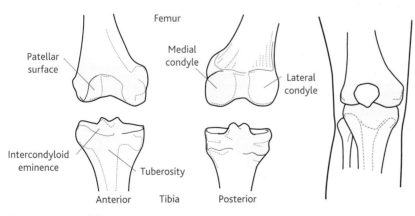

Fig. 6.3 *Bones of the knee joint*

■ **Key terms**

Hinge joint: formed at the knee between femur and tibia.

Drive phase: period when foot is pushing against the ground to produce forward movement.

The knee joint is a junction of two bones. The femur and the tibia (shin bone) meet to form a **hinge joint**. In front of them is the patella (kneecap). The patella sits over the other bones and slides when the leg moves, but doesn't form part of the joint.

■ Activity

■ Locate and feel the knee joint. At the sides of the knee you will feel the projections of the sides of the tibia and femur. At the front of the knee joint you will feel the patella, which acts as a protective covering.

■ Bend and straighten your knee. These are the only movements permitted by the joint. Through which plane and what axis is this movement taking place in?

The ankle joint also acts like a hinge joint being formed by the connection of three bones. The ankle bone itself is really part of the foot and is more properly called the talus. The top of the talus fits inside a socket that is formed by the lower end of the tibia and the fibula (the small bone of the outer lower leg).

■ Activity

■ Locate and feel the ankle joint. The bones at the side of the joint are the tibia on the big-toe side of the foot and the fibula on the little -toe side of the foot.

■ Bend and flex your foot. Bending is called dorsi-flexion and straightening is called plantar flexion. These movements take place in a sagittal plane around a transverse axis.

Fig. 6.4 *Diagram showing structure of the ankle joint*

Fibula

Tibia

Talus

Sustentaculum tali

Calcaneus

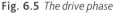

Fig. 6.5 *The drive phase*

Although it can be quite hard to visualise what is happening, when we run, there are two distinct periods of time involved. There is the time when the foot is in contact with the ground. This is the **drive phase**, when the muscles of the leg are contracting in order to push us forward. These ideas are best seen in slow-motion video footage, or even better a series of still images showing the movements involved.

Activity

- Find a movie or picture sequence of somebody running from side on. Play the movie through slowly, if necessary freeze-framing the image every few frames.
- Watch how the legs move when we run. Notice especially the short period of time when the foot is in contact with the ground. Produce a stick drawing of how one leg changes shape during a complete running cycle.

During each phase the joints in the leg go through actions that both increase and decrease the angle between the bones forming the joint. Actions which decrease the angle between the bones in a joint are called **flexion**. When the angle between the bones increases it is called **extension**.

During the drive phase, the angle between the pelvis and the femur increases, hence there is extension. In fact the angle increases so much that it goes beyond 180 degrees and this is specifically called **hyperextension**.

Remember that muscles can only pull to cause movement; they cannot push. Therefore the muscles causing the upper leg to be pulled backwards (the agonists) are the muscles on the back of the hip joint – the **gluteal** muscles. Note that the **hamstring** muscles on the back of the thigh are also involved in this movement.

The knee joint is also involved during the drive phase. It moves from being slightly bent to fully straight. In other words, the angle between the bones forming the knee increases. This is extension. The main agonist that extends or straightens the knee is the group of muscles at the front of the thigh, the **quadriceps**.

At the ankle joint, the action looks like extension as the angle between the lower leg (tibia) and the foot itself increases. But anatomically this particular movement is called **plantar flexion**. This action is brought about through contraction of the **gastrocnemius** muscle found in the calf.

Key terms

Flexion: decreasing the angle between the bones of a joint.

Extension: increasing the angle between the bones of a joint.

Hyperextension: increasing the angle between the bones of a joint beyond 180°.

Gluteals: group of muscles at back of hip that causes extension and hyperextension of the hip joint.

Hamstrings: group of muscles at the back of the thigh that causes flexion of the knee joint.

Quadriceps: group of muscles that cause knee extension.

Plantar flexion: action of pointing toes; increasing angle between tibia and foot.

Gastrocnemius: muscle in calf that causes plantar flexion.

Recovery phase: period when leg bends to return to the front of the body ready for the drive phase.

Activity

Complete the summary of the joint and muscle actions of the drive phase of running:

Joint	Plane and axis	Type of joint	Bones forming joint	Joint action	Main agonist
Hip					
Knee					
Ankle					

During a single stride, when the foot leaves the ground, we enter the recovery phase which is designed to get the leg back into position for the next drive phase.

During the **recovery phase** we are again concerned with the three joints, the hip, knee and ankle. The movements still occur in the sagittal plane and around a transverse axis. The same bones make up the joints as did during the drive phase. But now the actions are essentially reversed. The muscles that were the agonists during the drive phase now become the antagonists for the recovery phase.

Key terms

Hip flexors: group of muscles at the front of the hip that causes hip flexion.

Dorsiflexion: decreasing angle between foot and tibia; action of pulling toes up to the shin, caused by tibialis anterior.

Tibialis anterior: muscle in front of lower leg that causes dorsi flexion.

AQA Examiner's tip

■ Sometimes simplifying the movement makes it easier to understand and therefore name the agonist. For example if you lock your leg straight, it's easy to feel that it is the quadriceps that is contracting. Hence it's the quadriceps that causes the knee to extend.

■ Movements at the ankle can prove difficult. Try to remember **P** for plantar flexion and **P** for pointed toes.

Fig. 6.6 *The recovery phase*

At the hip, the angle between the pelvis and the femur decreases. This is flexion. The main agonists are a group of muscles commonly known as the **hip flexors**.

The action at the knee is a bending of the leg; the angle between the femur and tibia decreases. This is flexion. The main muscles causing flexion are those found at the back of the thigh – the hamstrings.

Once again, the ankle joint is slightly more complex. The angle between the tibia and the foot actually decreases, but once again we use a special name for this joint action. It's called **dorsiflexion**. The main muscle causing this movement lies alongside the tibia and is called the **tibialis anterior**.

Activity

Complete the summary of the joint and muscles actions of the recovery phase of running:

Joint	Bones forming joint	Joint action	Main agonist	Main antagonist
Hip				
Knee				
Ankle				

Jumping

Jumping is a somewhat similar action to the drive phase of running in that the hip, knee and ankle are again involved, with actions taking place in the sagittal plane about a transverse axis.

As a prelude to take off, the athlete lowers him- or herself slightly at the hip, knee and ankle. The main action at take off is at all three joints in the leg. At the hip is extension, brought about mainly by the gluteal muscles, although there is some assistance from the hamstrings groups.

Activity

- Find a movie or picture sequence of somebody taking off for a jump. Play the movie through slowly, if necessary freeze-framing the image every few frames.
- Watch how the take off leg moves when we jump. Produce a stick drawing of how the take off leg changes shape during the take off for a jump.

At the knee, there are powerful contractions of the agonist, the quadriceps group which produce extension.

At the ankle, there is plantar flexion, brought about by the gastrocnemius.

Activity

Complete the summary of the joint and muscle actions in jumping:

Joint	Plane and axis	Joint action	Main agonist
Hip			
Knee			
Ankle			

Kicking

Activity

- Find a movie or picture sequence that shows a side-on view of somebody kicking a ball. A rugby player taking a penalty kick might be an easy movie to find.
- Play the movie through slowly, if necessary freeze-framing the image every few frames. Watch how the kicking leg moves when we kick a ball. Produce a stick drawing of how the kicking leg changes shape during a kick.

There are two phases to kicking; the **preparatory phase** when one leg is drawn back in readiness to kick a ball, and the actual **kicking phase**, both of which take place in a sagittal plane and around a transverse axis.

During the preparatory phase, the upper leg is moved backwards. This involves hyperextension at the hip, which as in running, occurs as a result of contraction of the gluteal muscles, and to a lesser extent the hamstrings group.

At the knee, there is flexion as the angle between the tibia and femur is reduced. This flexion is brought about by the action of the hamstrings group of muscles acting as the agonist.

At the ankle, plantar flexion occurs, caused by contraction of the agonistic gastrocnemius.

During the kicking phase, there is flexion at the hips, due to the action of the hip flexors, and to a lesser extent, the quadriceps. While at the knee, there is a powerful extension, due to the contraction of the quadriceps.

Key terms

Preparatory phase: taking leg back prior to kicking.

Kicking phase: action of bringing leg forward to kick a ball.

■ **Activity**

Complete the summary of the main joint and muscle actions involved in kicking:

Joint	Preparatory phase		Kicking phase	
	Joint action	Main agonist	Joint action	Main agonist
Hip				
Knee				
Ankle				

When you consider the ankle, the expected dorsiflexion does not normally happen, instead the toes tend to remain pointed in plantar flexion, again due to the action of the gastrocnemius.

Overarm throwing

■ **Activity**

▪ Find a movie or picture sequence that shows a side-on view of somebody throwing a javelin. Play the movie through slowly, if necessary freeze-framing the image every few frames.

▪ Watch how the throwing arm moves when we throw. Produce a stick drawing of how the throwing arm changes shape during the throwing sequence.

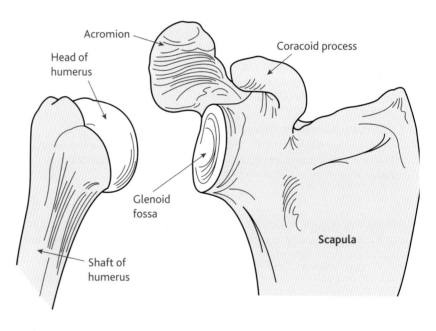

Acromion

Head of humerus

Coracoid process

Glenoid fossa

Shaft of humerus

Scapula

Fig. 6.7 *The structure of the shoulder joint*

■ **Key terms**

Withdrawal phase: period of time when arm is extended backwards.

Throwing phase: period of time when actual throw occurs.

There are various types of overarm throws; we shall concentrate on the javelin throw. Throwing is a more complex action than running, and in the exam you will probably be provided with images that show sequences of action. It will be your job to identify the movements involved and the muscles causing the joint actions.

In javelin throwing there are two phases to the movement, the **withdrawal phase** and the **throwing phase**, both mainly involving actions at the shoulder and the elbow.

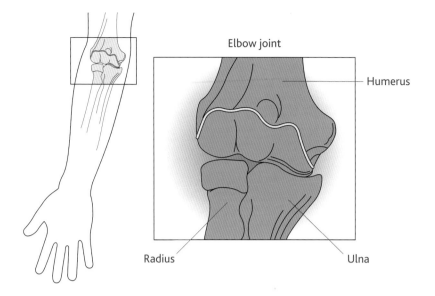

Fig. 6.8 *The elbow joint*

The shoulder is a ball and socket joint formed from the shoulder blade, more properly called the **scapula,** and the **humerus** of the upper arm.

The elbow joint is a hinge joint formed from the meeting of the humerus bone of the upper arm, and the **radius** and **ulna** of the lower arm.

The start of a javelin throw involves the carry when the javelin is held up, parallel to the ground with the elbow flexed and the hand close to the ear.

Taking the arm back from the carry position in preparation is called the withdrawal and involves extension at the elbow. This action is produced by contraction of the **triceps** muscle. At the shoulder the upper arm moves back. This is called hyperextension. But the upper arm is approximately parallel to the ground and therefore it is more properly called **horizontal hyperextension**. Horizontal hyperextension of the shoulder is caused by the action of the **posterior deltoid** muscle of the shoulder, assisted by the **latissimus dorsi** of the back. This horizontal hyperextension takes place in a transverse plane and around a longitudinal axis.

The throwing phase up to the starting position is shown in the following images of a throw by Steve Backley.

The first stage involves flexion of the elbow due to the action of the biceps as the agonist. The upper arm also travels forwards; this is flexion, or more properly, horizontal flexion at the shoulder, caused by the action of the pectoral muscles of the chest and the anterior deltoid muscle of the shoulder. This movement also takes place in a transverse plane around a longitudinal axis.

The throwing phase continues beyond the position shown in Figure 6.12 overleaf.

There is now extension at the elbow, caused by the action of the triceps, and continued horizontal flexion at the shoulder caused by the pectorals and anterior deltoids working as agonists. Extension at the elbow, like flexion at the elbow, takes place along a sagittal plane and around a transverse axis.

Key terms

Scapula: shoulder blade; flat, triangular bone that lies at the back of the shoulder.

Humerus: bone of the upper arm.

Radius: bone of the forearm; runs from elbow to thumb side of wrist.

Ulna: bone of the forearm; runs from elbow to little finger side of wrist.

Triceps: muscle on the back of the upper arm causing extension at the elbow.

Horizontal hyperextension: action of taking arm back behind the shoulder, but keeping arm parallel to the ground.

Posterior deltoid: small part at the back of the muscle that 'caps' the shoulder.

Latissimus dorsi: large muscle in the back that pulls the arms backwards.

Activity

Complete the summary of the structures involved in throwing:

Joint	Bones forming joint
Elbow	
Shoulder	

Fig. 6.9 *The carry position in javelin throwing*

Fig. 6.10 *The withdrawal*

Fig. 6.11 *The first stage of a javelin throw*

Fig. 6.12 *The latter stages*

Activity

Complete the summary of main actions involved in throwing:

	Withdrawal phase		Throwing phase	
Joint	Joint action	Main agonist	Joint action	Main agonist
Elbow	Extension	Triceps	Flexion then extension	Biceps then triceps
Shoulder	Horizontal hyperextension	Posterior deltoids	Horizontal flexion	Anterior deltoids and pectorals

Racket strokes

The preparatory phase is essentially the same to that of overarm throwing. The shoulder joint goes through horizontal hyperextension to take the arm back. This action is caused by the contractions of the posterior deltoids and the latissimus dorsi, and takes place in a transverse plane around a longitudinal axis. The elbow joint is extended due to the action of the triceps muscle. Extension takes place in a sagittal plane around a transverse axis.

The striking phase is based on movements that occur at the elbow and shoulder.

Fig. 6.13 *Tennis action*

At the elbow there is initially extension (images a–c), caused by the action of the triceps as the agonist, but in the last part of the action, the elbow bends (image c–d). This is flexion, caused by the agonistic action of the biceps.

At the shoulder there is horizontal flexion, caused by the pectorals and the anterior deltoids.

Squats

Remember that muscles can only pull and that muscle contractions either involve movement (isotonic) or no movement (isometric). We also previously talked about there being two types of isotonic contractions: concentric contractions occur when a muscle shortens and eccentric contractions occur when a muscle lengths.

In reality, most muscle contractions are concentric, but when a movement takes place in the same direction as the force of gravity, where the demand is that the body moves downwards in a controlled manner, then such contractions will be eccentric.

We need to study two examples of these types of situations, the first of which is a squat.

Many sporting situations involve squats. For example the volleyball player often squats to get into position to perform a 'dig'; the basketball player when on the free-throw line will use their legs in a squat-type action; and of course the weight-lifter does a squat as an exercise.

In the following sequence of images (Figure 6.14), the performer is moving from a deep squat up into a standing position. Movement

Fig. 6.14 *Squats*

Activity

- Find a movie or picture sequence that shows a side-on view of somebody playing a forehand stroke at tennis. Play the movie through slowly, if necessary freeze-framing the image every few frames.
- Watch how the racket arm moves when we hit a ball. Produce a stick drawing of how the racket arm changes shape during the throwing sequence.

Activity

- Find a movie or picture sequence of somebody performing a weight-lifting squat. Play the movie through slowly, if necessary freeze-framing the image every few frames.
- Watch how the legs move when the squat is performed. Produce a stick drawing of how the legs change shape on the way down and when standing up.

Work with a partner. One of the pair performs a squat while the other feels the front and back of the subject's legs, trying to identify which of the quadriceps or hamstrings is the agonist during the upward and downward movements.

occurs at the hip, knee and ankle. You should recognise the joint actions involved and the muscles causing the movement.

At the hip there is extension, caused by the action of the gluteal muscles. At the knee there is extension. Extension is caused by the action of the quadriceps as the agonist. At the ankle there is plantar flexion, caused by the action of the gastrocnemius. The muscle contractions will be concentric contractions, and all take place in a sagittal plane around a transverse axis.

The return movement from standing upright and lowering yourself down will need to be controlled against the force of gravity. The joint actions are hip – flexion, knee – flexion, ankle – dorsiflexion. The controlling muscles are the same ones that were involved in standing up; the agonists remain the same, but now they are working eccentrically.

So there is hip flexion where the gluteals are the agonists, knee flexion controlled by the quadriceps and dorsiflexion where the agonist is the gastrocnemius.

Activity

Complete the summary of the main actions involved in a squat:

| Joint | Upward phase | | | Downward phase | | |
	Joint action	Main agonist	Type of contraction	Joint action	Main agonist	Type of contraction
Hip						
Knee						
Ankle						

Press-ups

When looking at press-ups we are again concerned with the elbow and shoulder joints. The elbow is a hinge joint that is capable of flexion and extension, and therefore the movements are in a sagittal plane around a transverse axis. The bones that form the elbow joint have already been discussed but you should remember that they are the humerus, radius and ulna.

The shoulder is a ball and socket joint formed by the scapula and humerus.

In Figure. 6.15 opposite, the upward movement, involves extension at the elbow due to the action of the triceps muscle as the agonist. This involves a concentric contraction. At the shoulder the action is horizontal flexion caused by the contractions of the pectorals.

The return downward movement shown in Figure 6.16 involves flexion at the elbow, but because the movement has to be controlled against the effects of gravity, the muscle contraction is eccentric and involves the triceps again acting as the agonist. At the shoulder there is horizontal extension controlled by an eccentric contraction of the pectorals.

AQA Examiner's tip

Muscle actions at the shoulder during a press-up depend on the position of the hands in relation to the shoulder joint. The wider the arms are apart, the more obvious the horizontal flexion and extension becomes.

Fig. 6.15 *Pressing up*

Fig. 6.16 *Lowering down*

Levers

In order for your arm, leg or any body part to move, the appropriate muscles and bones must work together as a series of levers. A lever has three components:

- fulcrum or pivot – the point about which the lever rotates
- resistance or load – the force applied by the lever system
- effort – the force applied by the user of the lever system.

In your body, the fulcrum is the joint involved in the movement, and the effort is the muscle acting as the agonist. So in a biceps curl, the elbow joint is the fulcrum and the biceps act as the effort, causing the movement.

The resistance is the load that is being moved and is often simply a question of moving part of the body against the force of gravity, in other words weight.

The way in which a lever will operate is dependent on the type of lever.

Classification of levers

First class – the fulcrum lies between the effort and the resistance.

Second class – the fulcrum is at one end, the effort at the other end and the resistance lies between the effort and the fulcrum.

Third class – the fulcrum is at one end, the resistance at the other end and the effort lies between the load and the fulcrum .

First class lever

There are only two examples of this lever system in the human body. One is the way the head moves forwards and back on top of the neck, but more relevant to the movements described previously in this chapter, this type of lever is found at the elbow.

During extension when the triceps is the agonist, the triceps muscle provides the effort; the elbow joint itself is the fulcrum, and the weight of the arm is the resistance. This arrangement is shown in the following diagram.

Activity

- Work with a partner. One of the pair performs a press-up while the other feels the front and back of the subject's arms, trying to identify which of the triceps or biceps is the agonist during the upward and downward movements.
- Try other up and down movements – dips, sit-ups, pull-ups and biceps curls. Work out which muscles are working.

AQA Examiner's tip

An easy way to remember the order of the components in a particular class of levers is the mnemonic '1, 2, 3, – FRE'. Where 1, 2, 3 refers to the class of lever and F, R, E refers to the middle component. Hence a first class lever has a fulcrum as the middle component.

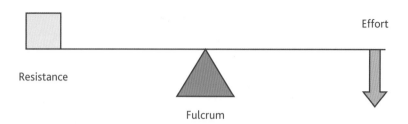

Fig. 6.17 *First class lever*

So in throwing, racket strokes and press-ups, when the triceps causes extension at the elbow, it acts on the elbow as a first class lever system.

Second class lever

In second class lever systems the resistance is in the middle. There is only one example of this type of lever system operating in the body, and that is found in the foot. The bones of the foot act as the lever, with the joint at the ball of foot acting as a fulcrum, the gastrocnemius muscle providing the effort, and weight of body providing the resistance. When plantar and dorsiflexing in running, kicking, jumping and performing squats, the gastrocnemius acts on the foot as a second class lever system, as the following diagram shows.

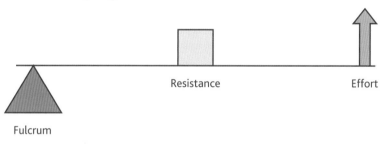

Fig. 6.18 *Second class lever*

Third class lever

In third class lever systems, the effort is between fulcrum and resistance. This type of lever system accounts for all other joints in the body. So in hip and knee flexion and extension that occurs in running, jumping and kicking, the hip flexors, gluteals, quadriceps and hamstrings all act on their respective joints as third class lever systems.

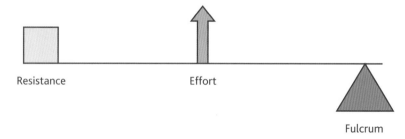

Fig. 6.19 *Third class lever*

There are two other parts of a lever system that we need to consider. The **force arm** is the shortest perpendicular distance between fulcrum and effort; and the **resistance arm** is the shortest perpendicular distance between fulcrum and resistance. As shown on the following diagram:

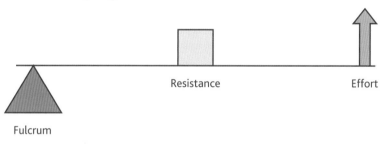

■ Key terms

Force arm: distance of force from fulcrum.

Resistance arm: distance of resistance from fulcrum.

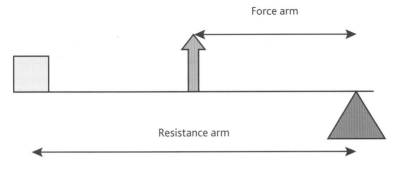

Fig. 6.20 *Force and resistance arms*

All lever systems have both a mechanical advantage and a mechanical disadvantage, the degree of which depends on the relative lengths of the effort and resistance arms. In the third class lever systems that are found at most joints, the force arm is very short and the resistance arm is quite long.

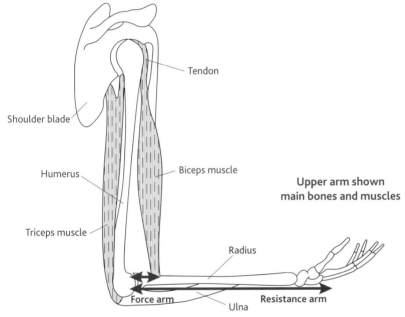

Fig. 6.21 *Force and resistance arms in third class lever*

This means that there is quite a mechanical disadvantage in terms of what the lever system can achieve when working. The force arm is very short and the muscles involved will be unable to apply very much force to move objects. However there is a mechanical advantage as well in that the long resistance arm means that such systems may have a very large range of movement, and because the force is applied so close to the fulcrum, the resistance can be moved quite quickly. For example, the biceps acting on the elbow joint is a third class lever and cannot move large resistances, but the range of movement from extension to full flexion of the lower arm is almost 180 degrees. Because of the very short force arm and relatively long resistance arm of this system, small movements of the biceps muscle produce large movements of the resistance arm and thus the hand moves very rapidly.

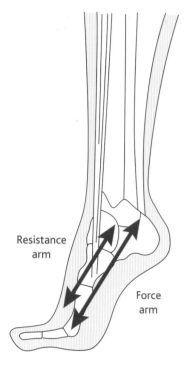

Resistance arm

Force arm

Fig. 6.22 *Force and resistance arms in second class lever*

Second class lever systems have a greater mechanical advantage. They have a force arm that is longer than the resistance arm, and they can therefore generate much larger forces, but they have the mechanical disadvantage of only having a limited range of movement, and the movements tend to be quite slow.

Activities

1 Compare potential forces being applied to muscles of comparable size – biceps in biceps curls and gastrocnemius in calf raises. Try doing a biceps curl with a 10 kg bar. It is probably quite hard work, but look at the range of motion achieved; you can move your arm from being straight at the elbow to bring your hand up so it almost touches your shoulder. Biceps curls involve a third class lever system.

2 Now use a second class lever system. Raise yourself up onto your toes and back down again. You are moving a lot more than 10kg! But look at the limited range of movement at the ankle. Most people cannot point their toes sufficiently to get the angle anywhere near straight, and none can get their toes to touch their shin!

3 The third class lever system gives an advantage by allowing a great range of movement but gives the disadvantage of limiting the amount of force that can be applied. The second class lever system gives the advantage of allowing much greater forces to be applied, but has the disadvantage of having a very limited range of movement.

✔ *You should now be able to:*

■ identify the different stages and the main articulating bones, joint types, joint actions, muscle actions and muscle contractions involved in running, kicking, jumping, throwing, racket strokes, squatting and completing press-ups

■ name, draw and label an identified lever system

■ explain what is meant by mechanical advantage and disadvantage.

1   The leg action in running has a drive phase and a recovery phase as shown below.
For the hip joint, identify:
(a)   the plane and axis.   *(1 mark)*
(b)   the agonist, action and type of contraction in the drive phase.   *(3 marks)*
(c)   the agonist, action and type of contraction in the recovery phase.   *(3 marks)*

Fig. 1

2   Figure 2 shows a weightlifter performing a squat.
(a)   With reference to the figure copy and complete the following table and identify the joint action, main agonist and the type of muscle contraction at the hip and ankle joint in the upward phase of the squat.   *(6 marks)*

	Hip	Ankle
Joint action		
Main agonist		
Muscle contraction		

Fig. 2

3   The tennis player in Figure 3 is executing a forehand stroke.

   (a)   Copy and complete the diagram, identifying the type of joint, the joint
          action and the main agonist of the shoulder from a–c and of the elbow
          from c–d used in the execution of the forehand stroke.   *(6 marks)*

a   b   c   d   Fig. 3

4   Skilled performance is made possible through the effective use of lever systems.

   (a)   Sketch and label a third class lever system.   *(3 marks)*
   (b)   In your diagram, draw and label the effort arm and the resistance arm.   *(1 mark)*
   (c)   What are the advantages and disadvantages of third class levers over the
          other types of lever systems?   *(2 marks)*

	Type of joint	Joint action	Agonist
Shoulder			
Elbow			

UNIT 1.2 Skill acquisition

Introduction

This section of the specification is concerned with how we can receive and process information as an important part of being able to acquire, develop and use skills. As such we are as much concerned with what happens in our brains and nervous system as we are with the physical movements of limbs and bodies.

To be able to acquire, develop and perform complex movements in what are physically demanding and constantly changing tactical situations requires a combination of seeing, perceiving, recognising, deciding, moving and evaluating – in short a combination of perceptual, cognitive and psychomotor skills and their underlying abilities. It is not always possible to place those factors in watertight compartments – differentiating between perception (receiving and recognising information) and cognition (decision making), or between cognition and controlling a movement is almost impossible.

Ideas about skill, information processing and the acquisition of skill and skill development are based upon psychological research. Therefore it is theoretical and theories are subject to further development and change. Many of our ideas about skill and how we acquire it, use it and develop it are derived from general learning research in fields unrelated to sport. As we undertake sport science related research our understanding of skill acquisition will probably change. This development of skill is covered in more depth in Chapter 9.

It must be understood therefore that our knowledge is less precise and specific when it comes to understanding what the brain does in comparison to our knowledge of the body's anatomy and physiology. If you decide to read more widely you will come across alternative and indeed contradictory definitions and theories. What you read in this section of the book is the knowledge and understanding that is required to be successful in AQA AS Level PE examinations.

The acquisition, development and use of skill is a fascinating but less precise part of the specification. You will be required to gain an understanding of psychological processes and apply them to real-world, human performance situations. You will also be asked to use these theories to evaluate movement and to suggest how it may be improved.

7 Skills

In this chapter you will:

- recognise a skill by its characteristics, define it and be able to tell the difference between skill and ability

- know the difference between motor and perceptual skills and how they underpin all skills

- recognise different types of skill – cognitive, perceptual and psychomotor and how these are also underpinned by motor and perceptual abilities

- classify by using a range of continua (open-closed, discrete-serial-continuous, gross-fine, self paced-externally paced).

Key terms

Skill: learned behaviour to bring about pre-determined results with maximum certainty often with the minimum outlay of time, energy or both as a result of evaluating information and decision making.

The A Level specification requires students to have a full understanding of the nature and characteristics of a skilled performance. Skill lies at the heart of performance and it is therefore essential that you know how to recognise it and to be sure that you are talking about a skill rather than ability. It should also be clear from your own observations that skills vary from repetitive movements made in unchanging situations to movements that are being adapted and modified to deal with a constantly changing environment. Before you can improve skill or help others to acquire and develop skill you must understand the very nature of skill.

We first need to be able to recognise skill and to understand the characteristics of a skilled movement.

Characteristics of skill – how do you recognise it?

Physical performance uses combinations of three different types of **skill** – cognitive, perceptual and psycho-motor. The balance between those skills is determined by the objectives of the movement and situation within which they are performed.

First of all we need to understand and define what we mean by a skilled performance. There are many definitions of skilled performance but they all share the following characteristics:

- Skill actions have an objective – they are goal directed and pre-determined.
- Skill is learned – it is not innate, nor is it the result purely of maturation – the process of growing up.

Activities

Either by observing another class, a sports fixture or practice, or by watching a sporting activity on television, answer the following questions:

1. Note down examples of what you consider to be a skill or a skill action.

2. Give a reason as to why each of the actions you have noted above was carried out.

3. It is likely that different performers will have tried to use the same movement or skill. Identify any differences in the quality of the movement as shown by the different performers.

4. On the basis of the notes you have made in answering questions 1–3, with a partner write a definition of skilled performance.

- Skilled movements are economic and efficient – they do not waste energy.
- Skilled movements are flowing and aesthetically pleasing – they look good.
- Skilled action may be described as the use of a technique at the right time and place.

- Skilled actions are consistently successful – they regularly achieve the objective or copy the technical model.
- Skilled actions are often the result of receiving and evaluating information (perception) and then making the correct decision (cognition).

Difference between skill and ability

When talking about human performance, commentators (and some PE students!) frequently talk about a performer 'having a high level of ability' when what they actually mean is that the performer has a high level of skill. From a sport science perspective there is a clear difference between skill and **ability**.

Fig. 7.1 *A netball pass on the run*

Ability is an innate quality that we have – it is something we are born with, and the relative magnitude of that quality is determined by our genetic inheritance. As such abilities are unchanging or stable, except as a result of growing up or maturing. Examples of abilities would be reaction time, agility, coordination and balance. The use and combination of abilities underpins the development of skilled actions.

Types of abilities – perceptual and motor

From the perspective of physical movement we are concerned with two different types of ability – motor ability and perceptual ability.

Motor ability is a series of underlying characteristics that contribute to moving a limb or limbs successfully. Motor abilities are innate inherited traits that determine an individual's coordination, balance ability and speed of reactions. Fleishmann (1964) produced a list of 14 different motor abilities that he believed underpinned and were the determinants of an individual's potential to develop skill. His theory argued that every skill would require the combination of two or more of these abilities in varying proportions and that it is possible through a process of factor analysis to identify which motor abilities are required as a means of determining potential skill development for an individual.

Fig. 7.2 *Skill or ability?*

Activity

Produce a mind map to show the characteristics and examples of abilities and skill.

Key terms

Ability: inherited, innate, stable traits that determine a person's potential to acquire skills, e.g. coordination, balance, agility, speed of reaction.

Motor ability: a series of genetically inherited traits that determine an individual's coordination, balance and speed of reactions.

AQA Examiner's tip

It is not necessary to quote a definition of skilled performance; it is important that you understand the characteristics and criteria of a skilled action.

Link

The ability to observe a movement and analyse its skilfulness will be useful skill in the practical performance you undertake for coursework. For more information, see Chapter 14 – Practical coursework (page 209).

Key terms

Perceptual ability: to be able to take in information, recognise it and make sense of it.

Cognitive skill: the use of the brain to reason and problem solve as a result of learning and experience.

Activities

View a live performance of a team game or activity and observe a defender versus attacker(s) situation.

1 What information is the defender being presented with?

2 Is all the information useful or necessary?

3 Which information is most necessary?

4 What questions might the defenders ask themselves before deciding upon a course of action?

Link

An understanding of the abilities required as the basis for skilled performance will be useful when learning how to improve skill. For more information, see Chapter 16 – Practical skill acquisition (page 250).

This theory has been criticised on the basis that Fleishman's research was carried out for very specific skills (not sport-based) and in stable conditions. Sport skills are rarely as simple or undertaken in an unchanging environment, which takes no account of perceptual and cognitive factors.

Perceptual ability is related to the process of receiving, recognising, selecting and organising information that we receive from our senses – sight, sound, touch and our internal senses or kinaesthesis.

It should be clear that the defender has a great deal of information to take in as the two attackers move towards him. This information is known as the display or field of vision, and having taken it in he must then decide between what is useful or irrelevant. Then the defender must organise that information into something meaningful so that a course of action can be decided upon (cognition) – all in a split second!

The perceptual abilities that allow us to process the information in the display (field of vision) are:

- speed of perception – how fast you can compare the various elements within the display
- being able to divide your attention between more than one part of the display (more than one attacker perhaps)
- analysing movement (other performer or object such as a ball) within the display and predicting future movement/position
- selection – to filter out unwanted, unnecessary or irrelevant pieces of information from the display.

Researchers are less confident in stating whether these attributes are clearly abilities (innate, enduring and unchanging) or skills (can be developed through practice and experience).

💡 Type of skill

For us to act in a skilled way we must receive information from our environment, select relevant from irrelevant information and then understand the information we have received and attended to. We then select and use the correct physical response. This uses a combination of cognitive, perceptual and psycho-motor skills. For example a tennis player who is about to receive a return from their opponent is firstly watching their opponent – their foot position, body shape, arm action, etc. (perceptual). They also have some prior knowledge about the player – their strengths, weaknesses, the shots they prefer to play, etc. (cognitive). You then begin to make a prediction about where the ball is going to go (cognitive), and as they play the shot you begin to move to play your own return (**psycho-motor**). As you do this you are deciding which shot to play (**cognitive**), to get your feet and body in the correct position, and then you play your stunning forehand top spin (**psycho-motor**) to win the point!

Cognitive skill – selecting what to do, choosing which action to use and when, decision making, reasoning. Our cognitive skill develops as we learn from an ever wider range of experiences. As an example a tennis player makes better decisions about how to play an opponent if they have played them before and evaluated their opponent's strengths and weaknesses. A performer is able to give attention to the more tactical and decision making elements within a performance if a technique has become grooved, habitual or can be performed with less attention to the required muscle contractions.

Activities

Stop! Write down all the things that you have heard, seen, smelt, tasted or felt over the last 60 seconds!

Having done that, spend 60 seconds trying to accumulate as much information about your surroundings as you can – try and remember all the things that you hear, feel and smell as well as see. Try to do this whilst a partner is talking to you.

After the 60 seconds are up write down as much as you can remember.

1. How many things could you remember? Compare with others in the group.
2. Were some things more memorable than others?
3. What would be the effect if you did this all the time?
4. Were things from different senses more difficult to remember?
5. Did you find it more difficult to recall things that you think you were expected to – your partner's words for example?

Perceptual skill – how well we select, organise and recognise information gained from our senses. This will be built on our perceptual abilities and is developed as a consequence of maturation (getting older) and practice. We learn how to select the essential or relevant information from all the information that bombards our senses. For example the tennis player attends to the call of a teammate despite all the background noise and clamour. This is known as selective attention and you will learn more about this in Chapter 8 – Information processing (page 87).

Psycho-motor skill – our physical movements, controlled by the brain towards a pre-determined goal or objective. For example being able to combine and coordinate the muscle contractions and relaxations to control movement such as a badminton overhead clear.

Key terms

Perceptual skill: selecting, interpreting and making sense of the information from our senses.

Pyscho-motor skill: movement decided upon and controlled by the brain.

Classifying skills

To understand the nature of a skilled performance and to provide a basis on which to plan training and practice it is helpful to classify skills into different types or groups. Classifying may be defined as 'categorising' or 'placing in a class or a group'. The performance of skills may vary greatly as they are performed in varying and changing situations. For example, executing a pass in rugby will change depending on what my team-mates or opponents do, or what the tactical situation demands. This makes classification difficult and to simplify the process we analyse and classify skills on the basis of a range of continua.

A continuum is a link between two extremes that blend from one to the other gradually and seamlessly – it is impossible to say where one becomes the next.

Most skill analysis and classification is concerned with four factors:

- How much the performance of the skill is affected by factors outside of the performer – the environment. This is known as the Open-Closed continuum.
- How much control the performer has over the rate and the timing of the action. This is known as the Self Paced-Externally Paced continuum.
- The level or precision or fine control that the performer uses when performing the skill. This is known as the Gross-Fine continuum.
- Whether it is possible to determine the movement has a definite beginning or end. This is known as the Discrete-Serial-Continuous continuum.

Open-Closed continuum

Deciding where on the Open-Closed continuum a skill may be placed involves a consideration of the following factors:

▓ How stable is the environment, how much it is changing prior to and during the performance of the skill?

▓ Does what is happening outside of the performer (in the environment) have an impact upon the skill – when it is performed or how it is performed?

▓ How cognitive or perceptual is the skill?

Fig. 7.3 *Where would you place these on the Open-Closed continuum and why?*

▓ Key terms

Open skill: skill affected by the environment, or performed in a dynamic changing situation or environment.

Closed skill: skill performed in a stable, unchanging environment, where the environment has little or no impact on the performance of the skill.

▓ Activity

Draw a continuum line for the Open-Closed continuum and using the criteria in the boxes place five skills (other than those given) at different places on the continuum line. For each skill you must be prepared to justify why you have placed it in the position that you have.

Open   Closed

Unstable, changing environment	Stable, unchanging environment
e.g. *opponents, teammates, flight of the ball*	e.g. *athletics area – shot putt, gymnastics performance area – vaulting horse*
Performance highly affected by changing environment	Performance not affected by environment
e.g. *required to actions of other players, ball flight, etc.*	e.g. *no/little need to pay attention to the actions of others – e.g. gymnastics competition*
High level of cognitive/ perceptual skill	Low level of cognitive/ perceptual skill
e.g. *acquiring and using external information, high levels of decision making*	e.g. *little decision making required, little information needs to be processed prior to or during the skill action.*
Skills involved in invasion games, strike and field, etc. Any activity where the performer has to attend to a changing environment, decide upon a course of action and be prepared to modify it as the skill action is carried out. Typically externally paced.	Skills involved in activities such as gymnastics, explosive athletic events, weightlifting. The actions are habitual, stereotyped, require little/no decision making. Typically self paced.

Fig. 7.4 *The Open-Closed continuum*

Externally Paced-Self Paced continuum

The pacing continuum is concerned with:

- What controls the rate or pace at which a skill is performed?
- What controls the start of the movement?

Fig. 7.5 *Where would you place these on the Externally Paced-Self Paced continuum and why?*

Externally paced   Self paced

The rate of movement is controlled or influenced by external factors (environment) *e.g. opponents – receiving a tennis serve*
The initiation of the movement is controlled by external factors (environment) *e.g. hockey defender reacting to an attacker*

The rate of movement is controlled by the performer *e.g. speed of rotation in a gymnastic somersault*

The initiation of the movement is controlled by the performer *e.g. start of a dive*

Fig. 7.6 *The Externally Paced-Self Paced Continuum*

Key terms

Externally paced skill: a skill that is initiated by something other than the performer. The pace at which the skill is performed is dictated by factors other than the performer.

Self paced skill: the performer decides when the movement is begun and the pace at which the movement is performed.

Activity

Draw a continuum line for the Externally Paced–Self Paced skill continuum and, using the criteria in the boxes, place five skills (other than those given) at different places on the continuum line. For each skill you must be prepared to justify why you have placed it in the position that you have.

Gross-Fine skill continuum

This is whether the large gross muscle groups in the body are being used or whether the smaller muscle groups, capable of more delicate muscle control, are being used.

Fig. 7.7 *These would go where on the Gross-Fine skill continuum . . . and why?*

Key terms

Gross skill: a strong powerful movement requiring the use of the major muscle groups. Where fine control is not possible or required.

Fine skill: small, precise movement showing high levels of accuracy and coordination, using small muscle groups.

Gross   Fine

Major body movements involving large muscle groups	Intricate, fine movements using small muscle groups
Associated with strength, power and endurance	Associated with accuracy, precision
Little fine control required	Requiring good hand-eye coordination
Often a fundamental motor pattern	*e.g. tennis drop shot*
e.g. kicking, throwing a ball, shot putt, long jump	

Fig. 7.8 *The Gross-Fine skill continuum*

Activity

Draw a continuum line for Gross-Fine skill continuum and using the criteria in the boxes place five skills (other than those given) at different places on the continuum. For each skill you must be prepared to justify why you have placed it in the position that you have.

Discrete-Serial-Continuous continuum

This is concerned with whether or not an observer can see a definite beginning or end to the movement, whether it is composed of a number of separate elements, or whether the movement has no clear beginning or end.

Fig. 7.9 *Place these on the Discrete-Serial-Continuous continuum and justify their position*

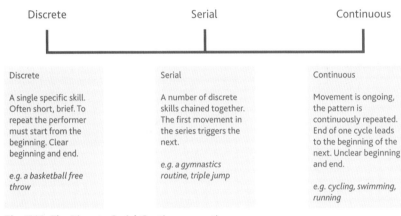

Discrete   Serial   Continuous

Discrete

A single specific skill. Often short, brief. To repeat the performer must start from the beginning. Clear beginning and end.

e.g. a basketball free throw

Serial

A number of discrete skills chained together. The first movement in the series triggers the next.

e.g. a gymnastics routine, triple jump

Continuous

Movement is ongoing, the pattern is continuously repeated. End of one cycle leads to the beginning of the next. Unclear beginning and end.

e.g. cycling, swimming, running

Fig. 7.10 *The Discrete-Serial-Continuous continuum*

Activity

Draw a continuum line for Discrete-Serial-Continuous skills and using the criteria in the boxes place five skills (other than those given) at different places on the Discrete-Serial-Continuous continuum. For each skill you must be prepared to justify why you have placed it in the position that you have.

✔ *You should now be able to:*

- use the terms *skill* and *ability* accurately when discussing a performance
- evaluate if they are performing skilfully and identify the underlying abilities when observing a performer
- recognise the part that cognitive, perceptual and psycho-motor skill plays when analysing a performance
- accurately place a range of skill performances on a range of skill classification continua.

Key terms

Continuous skill: no clear beginning and end, one end phase of the movement blends into the start phase of the next cycle.

Serial skill: series of specific movements (often discrete) chained together in a sequence.

Discrete skill: a movement with a clear beginning and end.

1   You and a friend are watching basketball being played on the school playground.

    (a)   Describe three criteria that you would use to decide if the players are performing skilfully.   *(3 marks)*

    (b)   Some of the players are better than others. If the weaker players practised more explain why they would not be guaranteed to become as good as the better players.   *(3 marks)*

2   The player with the ball receives a call from a teammate, they pass them the ball.

    (a)   Describe the elements of skill that have been used in this situation.   *(3 marks)*

    (b)   What perceptual skills have been used?   *(3 marks)*

3   Describe the passing action in basketball in terms of the Open-Closed, Gross-Fine, Externally Paced-Self Paced continua.   *(6 marks)*

4   In an invasion game like hockey describe a situation where a player would have to use perceptual, cognitive and psycho-motor skills.   *(6 marks)*

8 Information processing

AQA Examiner's tip

Using the analogy of a computer makes information easier to understand. You will not have to name different information processing models, rather you will be asked to explain what happens in the different stages of information processing.

Activity

Think of when you are playing basketball or netball. Write down what information you might be thinking about prior to receiving a pass.

You learned about skills and skilled performance in Chapter 7 – Skills (page 78). Now we need to understand how we go about choosing what skill to perform in which situation. We don't simply do skills. We decide what skill to perform. When performing a skill you have to make decisions such as exactly how to perform the skill. Good sports people tend to perform skills correctly; bad sports people may think they are performing a skill correctly, but often a coach can highlight their mistakes and try to correct them. Even good performers do not perform skills correctly all of the time. Professional sports people are not perfect. The bowler at cricket does not take a wicket with every delivery. The football player does not accurately pass to a member of their own team every single time he attempts to do so. The long jumper does not improve on their personal best with every attempt that they make. We also have referees and umpires whose job it is to judge whether skills were performed correctly and/or accurately.

You also have to decide when to perform a skill. Good performers will attempt a skill at the appropriate time; weaker performers will often attempt a difficult skill when a simpler skill would have produced better results. Think of a golfer faced with a difficult shot from a difficult position. Good golfers will carefully choose how to play their next shot so as to make the chances of success high, and therefore which skill to use. The weaker player is often inclined to play a rash shot in the hope that it might work, rather than playing the sensible shot that offers the best chance of success and therefore the least chance of failure.

We also have to decide at what speed to perform it. Think of the golfer again. The good golfer will swing the club at a speed that allows them to maintain control of the club. The weaker golfer will often swing the club too fast in the hope that the club head will connect with the ball perfectly.

All of these decisions depend on what is going on around you, what you are capable of actually doing and these may well need adjusting from the normal way you perform the skill.

Performing skills is a complex business and requires you to analyse lots of bits of information often in a very short space of time. This information can be what you can see, hear, feel or remember. What you have to do is to analyse all this information before deciding what to do and performing the skill. Psychologists say that this information has to be processed; hence they talk about information processing. Information processing is like looking at the brain as if it were a computer.

Fig. 8.1 *A simple information processing model*

Input

Information can include the pictures, sounds and feelings that convey information to you. In other words your senses provide you with information. This is called the **input**.

Back to the basketball/netball pass. You, the receiver, must take in all that is going on around you, through using your eyes (seeing your teammates and the opposition players, seeing their and your own position on court, seeing the ball, seeing how close players are to you and each other, seeing which players are open/available for a pass, seeing where the net is), ears (listening for calls from teammates, listening for the sounds made by opposition players close to, but behind you, listening for instructions from the coach, listening for whistles from the referee/umpire), as well as your hands (feeling the ball). You must also be aware of the positions of your arms and legs. All this is information.

The information comes from the environment that surrounds the performer. This particular information is sometimes called the **display**.

The brain has to decide what the information being received from the environment represents. In terms of psychology this information is sensory information because it comes to us through our senses. Hence this, the first stage of information processing, is sometimes called the **stimulus identification stage**.

The other stages in decision making are response selection – deciding how to respond, and response programming – selecting a response. We will deal with these other stages in more detail later in this chapter.

Fig. 8.2 *Simple IP model including the three aspects of decision making*

Perception

Stimulus identification is primarily a sensory (sense organs) stage, involving the analysis of all the various bits of information about the surrounding environment that is received from a variety of senses. As part of this process the performer must also make sense of this information. This is the idea of **perception**.

Information is defined as that which enables a performer to decide how to act. In sport, information comes from the specific environment that we are concerned with, but it also comes from the memory of previous relevant situations.

We use two types of environmental information: that from the external environment and that from the internal environment. Information from the external environment includes vision (the most important sense in sport) and hearing. Vision defines the physical structure of our environment (tells us where things are!) and therefore allows us to anticipate. Vision also provides information about movement of objects in the environment, including your own movement. For example, vision helps us with timing of the interception of a pass.

Information from the internal environment is called **proprioceptive** information (body awareness).

Proprioception has three components:

- touch
- equilibrium
- kinaesthesis.

Touch is our tactile sense; it detects pressure, pain, temperature. It is used in many sports.

Equilibrium is balance, tipping, turning, inverting. This sense is important in many sports.

Kinaesthesis is the sense that provides information about the state of contraction of muscles, tendons or joints. When a performer becomes highly skilled, they instinctively know if a movement was performed correctly; this is due to kinaesthesis.

All these senses convey information to our brain. Whether it is the correct information depends upon perception.

These factors are all **stimuli**. A stimulus is any item of information which stands out from the background (the **noise**). Stimuli in a game situation include things like the ball, but also include opponents, conditions, teammates, etc.

It is usually easier to sense and identify things if they are loud, bright, large, contrasting, fast-moving, or unusual. Hence, your team-mates wear the same kit as you, not to look good, but to make identification easier.

During perception, identification of a stimulus occurs. This involves three elements: Detection, Comparison and Recognition.

Hence perception involves the **Detection, Comparison and Recognition (DCR) process**.

- Detection is the process of the registering of the stimulus, by the sense organ.
- Comparison is the process of referring the stimulus to the memory, to compare it to previously stored stimuli.
- Recognition is the process of finding corresponding stimuli in the memory.

During a sporting activity, we will be receiving a tremendous amount of information from our senses. There is so much that we cannot detect, compare and recognise all of it. The vast majority of it is ignored. For example, during a game such as basketball or netball, we tend to be unaware of many stimuli, such as the temperature, the touch of our clothes on our skin, the noise of the crowd, buses passing outside the hall, the firmness of the ground beneath our feet, etc. We regard this information as largely irrelevant.

We try to be solely concerned with the activity in question, and more importantly, those aspects of the game that are directly our concern.

The amount of information received during a basketball game demands that we have to learn to concentrate on the stimuli that are important. This is called **selective attention**.

Certain stimuli attract our attention better, for example, loud, bright, fast, contrasting, unusual, but so do stimuli which we are expecting. A demonstration of an overhead clear in badminton would present much more information to somebody who had never seen it performed before, than it presents to an expert.

Activities

1. List four examples of situations from sport where tactile senses are important.

2. List four examples of situations from sports where equilibrium is especially important.

Key terms

Kinaesthesis: a sense that tells the brain about the movement of muscles, tendons and joints; it is our sense of body-awareness or the position of various limbs in space.

Detection, Comparison and Recognition (DCR) process: involves detecting the stimulus, comparing that stimulus to information stored in the memory, and recognising and identifying that stimulus.

Selective attention: the process of picking out and focusing on those parts of the display that are relevant to our performance.

Activities

1. Imagine you are playing in a game. You are waiting to receive a pass. List the things that your senses have to detect, in order for you to be able to perform the skill of receiving the pass.

2. Obtain a variety of balls – hockey, tennis, cricket, airflow, lacrosse, squash, table tennis, etc. Without allowing a partner to see which ball you are going to throw, throw one of the balls to your partner. Describe the stages that have to occur in order to identify what ball is being thrown.

Thus the amount of information, as used in this context, is directly proportional to the amount of uncertainty an event holds for a given individual. If the situation presented to you is novel, it is the first time you have been in this particular situation, then there is considerable information to be taken in, and you can easily suffer from trying to perceive too much information. This is called information overload.

If however, you are an expert, then there is less information to be concerned about. You will filter out the unnecessary junk that is part of the environment to leave yourself with just the relevant information to concentrate on and deal with.

Selective attention allows us to focus on just a few of the millions of stimuli that are arriving. This is helpful in a game situation. It enables the elite performer to not bother with information that is irrelevant, so as they get better at a skill, they are increasingly able to analyse important patterns of sensory information.

Consider a batsman facing a bowler in cricket or rounders. The experienced performer ignores the majority of sensory information and just concentrates on the relevant information such as the flight of a ball automatically, and thus detects relevant stimuli quicker and without any cognitive (thinking) involvement. In other words, their stimulus identification improves.

The learner will be taking in loads of irrelevant stimuli (the bowler's arm action, the noise from the crowd, the feeling of the bat in their hand, etc.) before thinking about the flight of the ball. All this extra information means that the actual processing of the relevant stimuli – the flight of the ball – becomes a relatively slow process.

■ Memory

All information being received by the senses is stored in the **memory**. In sport, perceiving the flight path of a ball, or knowing which muscle commands to use to be able to perform a somersault, require that remembered information be used in the execution of the action.

There are three stores in memory:

- ▨ short-term sensory stores (STSS)
- ▨ short-term memory (STM)
- ▨ long-term memory (LTM).

There are three processes within memory:

- ▨ **encoding** (putting information into a store)
- ▨ maintenance (keeping it 'alive')
- ▨ retrieval (finding encoded information).

Short-term sensory stores

All the information coming in from the environment can be stored in the **short-term sensory stores**. This means that these stores must have a huge capacity, but these memories only last for about half a second or less. It is the first 'compartment' of memory. Separate STSS compartments are thought to operate for each form of sensory information. It is subconscious, and if not immediately attended to, is lost. In other words, selective attention takes place in the short-term sensory stores. If the information is considered useful it will be encoded.

Short-term memory

Only information that is attended to is moved from STSS to the **short-term memory** (STM). That is why it is important in sport that attention is maintained whilst performing a skill, e.g., keep your eye on the ball until you have caught it before attending to the next skill of moving another part of your body.

The capacity of the STM is limited. Information can be retained for up to 60 seconds, but the capacity is limited to 5–9 items. 'Chunking' helps. This is the idea of storing not single items like letters, but groups of items as single pieces of information. For example, the letters 'b d e' make up three items of information while the word 'bed' represents one item even though it is composed of the same number of letters.

Information remains in the STM only as long as it is attended to, for example by rehearsal. This rehearsal can be imagining an action, or by sub-verbal repetition (talking to yourself). If attention is directed elsewhere, information in the STM is lost within 30 seconds. STM is very important when learning motor skills. You need to be able to recall information about a performance so that you can compare it to previous performances.

Hence, all the information involved in the learning and performing of skills is compared to existing information via the STM, and for this reason it is sometimes called the 'working memory'. The DCR process occurs within the short-term memory.

STM is also important for the coach. The limited capacity of the STM means that instructions to learners should be:

- brief
- to the point
- given when learner is paying attention.

Otherwise the information will be lost from the STM before the learner can use it. Selective attention is really just another form of rehearsal, in that it lengthens the time that a stimulus remains in short-term memory. In other words selective attention keeps the information alive in STM. This is the idea of maintenance.

Long-term memory

All information that enters the STM is rehearsed and is stored. All information in the STM is either stored in the **long-term memory** (LTM) or lost. The LTM is therefore a store of well-learned past experiences. It has almost limitless capacity and items may be stored for dozens of years. The information held in the LTM is used to compare against new experiences. The LTM also stores responses used in these different situations. Using LTM involves the process of retrieval of information and passing it into the STM.

Retention and retrieval of information from LTM is influenced by:

- rehearsal – the more a memory is rehearsed, the more likely it is that it will be remembered
- meaningfulness – the more meaningful a memory is, the more likely it is to be remembered
- speed of learning – the quicker a process is learned, the more likely it is to be remembered
- overlearning – the more a skill is practised, even when perfected, the better it will be remembered.

Key terms

Short-term memory: also called 'working memory' – relates to what we are thinking about at any given moment in time. This is conscious memory. It is created by our paying attention to an external stimulus, an internal thought, or both.

Long-term memory: a store of past experiences of almost limitless capacity and long duration.

All of the processes discussed so far involve information that appears to be stored in some way within the Central Nervous System.

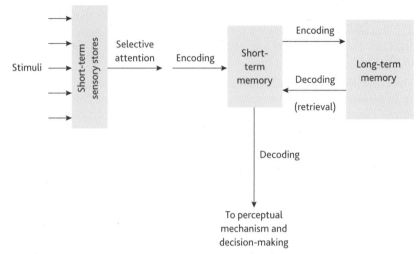

Fig. 8.3 *Model representing the memory processes*

Short- and long-term memory work together. When a batsman is facing the bowler, they know by experience (LTM) that they must focus on the ball (STM). Once the ball leaves the bowler's hand (STM), the batsman will have experience of the flight of balls (LTM) to be able to predict the flight of the ball. They can then refer to his store of information (LTM) as to how that ball might bounce. They may then select an appropriate response (LTM) about what stroke to play. In other words the batsman is continuously moving from using information from his senses to information that he has stored so that he can play the correct stroke.

The better the player, the quicker they are able to process the information and the greater the capacity (or the less that is cluttered up!) to deal with it.

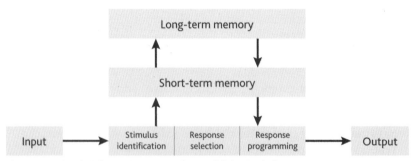

Fig. 8.4 *A simple information processing model that includes memory*

💡 Strategies to improve memory

There are various ways that we can improve our memory to help our sports performance. The first is practice. Continually performing a skill will help you be able to know how it should feel. This is rehearsal and helps make information in LTM fairly permanent. While you are learning a skill you should avoid providing conflicting, but similar information that would interfere (avoid interference) with learning and could cause transfer of learning.

Link

For more information on transfer of learning, see Chapter 9 – Learning and performance (page 102).

If new information is linked to previous learned information it will be more easily and better remembered. Hence coaches often remind their performers of previously and recently learned skills before developing them to another level. This definitely aids storage in memory. So if you can perform a backward roll first and then add a handstand onto the end of the roll, you will find it easier to remember the information required to perform the whole sequence – a backward roll through handstand. This is called association. Similar to this is organisation, where a gymnast will find it easier to remember the information required for a sequence of movements if they learn the first move fully before adding the second move. This links to progressive part learning.

Another way of improving memory is through **chaining**. Chaining involves breaking a complex action down into a series of simpler actions that may then be linked together to form a chain of actions that forms the whole complex action.

We have already discussed 'chunking' as a means of improving short-term memory. In sport, this is where the experienced player has reduced information such as the dimensions of a tennis court into a single piece of information, rather than the many bits of information that the same court represents to a novice. The experienced player thus has more 'space' or capacity for other information. Finally we remember images far better than any other piece of information. Therefore creating a mental picture of what is required to perform a skill will help us to remember it and the skills associated with it more easily. This is the idea of **mental rehearsal**. Much evidence exists to show that mentally rehearsing a skill is almost as beneficial as physically practising a skill, and the greatest gains in learning occur when both physical and mental rehearsal are used.

Skill acquisition emphasises that motor skills are to a large part cognitive in nature. It follows therefore, that in the same way as people can logically think through an intellectual problem, so they can also think through a movement sequence, without actually physically moving.

Mental rehearsal is far easier for closed skills. In open skills, part of the plan for action must also include knowledge about the relevant environmental cues with which the movements must be matched. Mental rehearsal is defined as the improvement in performance that results from an individual either thinking about a skill, or watching someone else perform it (live or recorded), or even reading or listening to instructions.

How to make mental rehearsal effective

1 Before mentally rehearsing you must relax; perhaps a sauna or muscle relaxation technique but don't go to sleep!
2 Create a mental picture of what needs to be done. Use all your senses to develop what you hear and feel when you carry out the movement.
3 See yourself through your 'mind's eye'.
4 Evaluate the movements and mentally experience the consequences.

Mental rehearsal actually causes motor neurones to send impulses to appropriate muscles. These impulses cause the firing of motor units resulting in a small contraction in the muscle. This simulation of the real thing helps to establish movement patterns, as per schema theory, see Chapter 9 – Learning and performance (page 102).

Link

Linking new information to help remembering is elaborated upon when progressive part learning is covered in Chapter 16 – Practical skill acquisition (page 250).

Key terms

Chaining: simplifying an action by reducing it into smaller links in a chain of events.

Mental rehearsal: 'running through' a performance in one's mind.

Link

Mentally rehearsing a skill is itself a learned skill and involves cognitive processes, as discussed further in Chapter 9 – Learning and performance (page 102).

Uses of mental rehearsal

▨ Mental rehearsal has an important role in the acquiring of skill.

▨ Mental rehearsal (sometimes called imagery) is often used by elite performers in controlling their arousal.

▨ Mental rehearsal can be used to practise when the performer is unable to undertake physical practice due to physical fatigue or being injured.

▨ Mental practice can be used to reduce psychological refractory period (see page 96).

▨ Imagery can be used to help develop confidence.

All sports people can use mental rehearsal if it becomes part of their training sessions. It is an excellent activity for the rest periods during distributed practices. Elite performers could use the technique to refine skill and manage their thoughts whilst novice performers may acquire the basic action. Mental rehearsal is less effective for novice performers as they may be unsure of the correct technique.

Experiments have regularly shown that mental rehearsal is far better than doing nothing. The most effective learning comes from situations where physical and mental practice are combined, such as mental rehearsal before and interspersed with physical practice.

💡 Decision making

Having used memory to identify a stimulus that comes from our sense organs, the next stage in information processing is to make a decision about how to respond to the information that has been received. This is the **response selection** stage. The activities of the response-selection stage begin when the stimulus identification stage provides information about the nature of the environmental stimulus. The response-selection stage has the task of deciding what movement to make, given the nature of the environment.

It is here that the choice of what movement to do is made from a store available, e.g. in basketball, should I catch the ball, and if so how? These types of decisions are part of the central mechanisms in the information processing model and contain many processes which when added together produce decision making.

Decision making, sometimes called the translation process, can be thought of as taking place within a tube. Once entered it cannot leave the tube until it has been completed. This is known as the single channel hypothesis. It explains that until one stimulus has had a decision made about it, another cannot be acted upon.

The decision-making process can become overloaded. The decision-making process becomes more efficient if the tasks can be dealt with free from other matters. You must not 'clog up the system'.

The depth/wealth of the performer's 'knowledge' of the relevant signals (cues), and his/her ability to detect these cues early, influences the time spent making a decision. As skill levels increase, outside interference to the decision-making process is ignored. This is one reason why the skilled performer is better than the novice. The novice is trying to take in too much information at once, and because of this their decision-making process is slow.

Decision-making time is therefore improved by practice, and is speeded up through coaching, where the relevant 'cues' can be 'highlighted'. In

Key terms

Response selection: deciding how to respond; deciding what to do.

sport, many of our actions depend on a fast decision-making process. The time spent making decisions is called **reaction time**. It is measured from the point in time from when the stimulus was given to the point in time where the response is initiated. It is, in reality, the time taken to process stimulus information.

 Activity

Watch some inexperienced performers playing a team game such as netball or basketball. When in possession, the players have to make a decision about what to do with the ball – pass (and who to), shoot, dribble, etc. Notice how long it often takes to make these decisions. Now watch some more experienced performers. Their decision making is much quicker. Can you explain why this might be?

Reaction time is to a large extent genetically determined, although it is influenced by the uncertainty of the stimulus to the performer, i.e. his lack of knowledge. Reaction time is also influenced by the intensity of the stimulus (selective attention), and anticipation. Males tend to have a faster reaction time than females, and reaction time slows as you get older. More practice gives more knowledge, which in turn reduces uncertainty and hence reduces reaction time.

 Activity

The 100-metre sprinter has to make the decision when to push off from the starting blocks. Who is quicker at deciding, the sprinter or the basketball player? Explain your answer.

The time from when the movement is initiated to the point when the movement is complete is referred to as the **movement time**.

Movement time is determined to a large extent by the muscle-fibre type and strength, as well as the level of learning of the motor programme involved, all of which can be improved by training/practice.

Once our 100-metre sprinter has finished the start, the response is complete. The time from the signal being presented to the response being completed is the **response time**.

Response time = Reaction time + Movement time.

 Reaction time can be divided into two types:

- **choice reaction time**
- **simple reaction time.**

Choice reaction time is the time taken for an individual to respond correctly from a choice of several stimuli each one demanding a different response. For example, the basketball player deciding whether to shoot, pass or dribble.

Simple reaction time is quicker than choice, and simple reaction time becomes even quicker when attention is given to it. Experiments have shown that audible stimuli produce quicker reaction times than visual stimuli. Choice reaction time is far commoner in sport. Performers have to make a choice about what to do. The skilled performer has a much quicker choice reaction time than the novice.

 Key terms

Reaction time: the time taken to make a decision.

Movement time: the time from the start of the response or movement to end of movement.

Response time: the time from stimulus being given to the end of the response.

Choice reaction time: the time taken between stimulus and action which requires a choice.

Simple reaction time: the time taken to start a single response to a single stimulus.

Activity

Using the skill of a sprint start, describe the beginning and end of each of response, reaction and movement times.

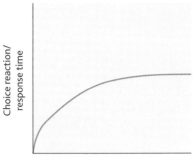

Fig. 8.5 *Hick's Law*

Key terms

Hick's Law: the more choices there are, the slower will be your reaction time.

Spatial anticipation: is guessing a movement that will be needed.

Temporal anticipation: is guessing what is about to happen.

Psychological refractory period (PRP): the delay in the response to the second of two closely spaced stimuli. Ball players often attempt to increase the PRP in their opponents by disguising a shot or 'selling a dummy' (i.e. feinting to go one way and then going another). According to the single channel hypothesis, the PRP is due to the inability of the brain to deal with two stimuli simultaneously.

The more choices that are available, the slower the choice reaction time. This is **Hick's Law**. As the number of choices increases, so does reaction time.

Choice reaction time is affected by 'stimulus-response compatibility'. This is the extent to which the stimulus and response are connected in a 'natural' way. For example, if a subject has to respond to two lights, by pressing one of two buttons, the subject has a quicker choice reaction time if he can use his right hand to press a button for the light on the right-hand side.

If you reverse the procedure, so that the subject has to press the left-hand button as a response to the stimulus of the right-hand light, the choice reaction time is slower. Choice reaction time also improves with practice, even when there is a low stimulus-response compatibility.

In competition the athlete should avoid making the same response, or presenting the same stimuli, all the time. This leads an opponent to treat the situation as simple reaction time, and thus allows him to minimise the time taken to respond. Hence the athlete should try to give his opponents as wide a variety of stimuli as possible to increase their opponent's choice reaction time.

The athlete should practise to develop as wide a range of new movements as possible, so as to increase the number of possible stimulus alternatives to present to an opponent.

Spatial and temporal anticipation

Skilled performers appear to have more time in which to complete their skills. The skilled performer uses their past experiences to anticipate what is going to happen and actually processes information before the event, thus saving time. **Spatial anticipation** is when the performer programmes a pattern of movement prior to the movement being needed. **Temporal anticipation** is when the performer predicts what is about to happen.

The value of anticipation is that it gives the performer more time to complete a skill; however anticipation can be less helpful, as when a performer anticipates a move, and their opponent then fakes the move. We shall look at this process next.

Psychological refractory period

When responding to a stimulus there is a short delay while the performer decides how to respond to the stimulus and initiates the appropriate movement. During the time that this deciding and responding takes, the performer, because of the limited capacity of the brain to deal with the processing of information, cannot produce a response to any other stimulus. If a second stimulus is given, the reaction time is much slower than normal. This is called the psychological refractory period.

This **psychological refractory period** serves to illustrate the single channel theory of information processing.

The psychological refractory period is used in sports by performers who 'dummy' or 'fake' their opponents. The performer pretends to move one way. Your opponent perceives these signals and decides to block your move and begins to initiate a response to these signals. Meanwhile the performer starts to move the other way. Your opponent cannot immediately respond to your change of movement because of the single channel hypothesis. They must complete their response to the first signal before they can attend to the second signal. Even when they do respond the response is slower because of the psychological refractory period.

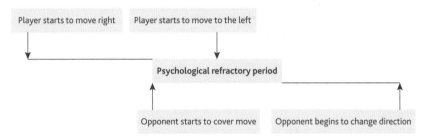

Fig. 8.6 *Psychological refractory period*

Motor programmes

Once the performer has decided which response to select, they must then choose a movement or skill to perform. This is the **response selection** stage of information processing.

Motor programmes are a generalised series of movements stored in the long-term memory. Motor programmes are developed through well-guided and well-informed practice over a long period of time. These programmes can be simple or complex.

Part of the decision-making process is the selection of the motor programme that is to be used for the movement. Motor programmes are retrieved from the long-term memory by a single decision. The motor programme thus governs which muscles contract, in what order and with what timing. Motor programmes are selected from the long-term memory, but then run by the short-term memory.

Practice helps us to develop new, more effective, more stable, more precise or longer-operating motor programmes. Practice makes complex motor programmes simpler to use and reduces the amount of information processing that is needed for them to run. Thus practise more conscious control for other details of the movement.

Highly skilled performers seem to be able to perform motor programmes while attending to other, peripheral stimuli. This is achieved through complex skills being broken down into their component parts (**sub-routines**). These sub-routines are so well learned that the performer does not need to think about how to perform them. Well learned sub-routines are organised and stored as executive motor programmes.

Key terms

Response selection: choosing a motor programme.

Motor programme: a series of muscle contractions that produce a movement; stored in long-term memory.

Sub-routines: separate movements that make up a whole skill.

Link

Motor programmes are learned. The ways we learn these programmes are described in Chapter 9 – Learning and performance (page 102) as Schmidt's schema theory.

Activity

Watch a novice basketball player dribbling the ball and compare their performance to that of an expert basketball player. Can you see that the novice uses up most of their information processing by trying to dribble the ball, and this leaves them with little processing capacity to see what is happening in front of them; whereas the expert player seems to perform dribbling automatically, leaving considerable processing capacity for seeing who is free to pass to.

A tennis serve is an example of a motor programme. The sub-routines within a tennis serve would include the feet position, body position, the preparatory arm action, the racket swing, the follow through and the recovery to a ready position.

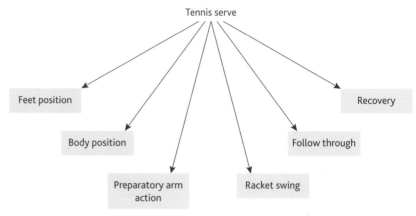

Fig. 8.7 *Sub-routines of a tennis serve*

You learn a motor programme as a response to a certain situation and then remember that programme and repeat it if the situation arises again. The long-term memory thus has a store of muscle commands in the form of a motor programme that can be put into action. A motor programme is simply a sequence of muscle contractions. These commands can be stored in the brain or spinal cord, and once a programme is 'run', muscles receive impulses in a pre-determined sequence, at pre-determined intervals and with pre-determined strength.

When this motor programme produces a response that matches the requirements of the situation, then skilled performance results. Performers can initiate inappropriate motor programmes. They may not have learned the appropriate programme and therefore produce unskilled movements.

■ Factors affecting the efficiency of the components of the information processing system and strategies for improvement

You should now be able to appreciate that information processing is a complex system with several parts that, with help, can be improved to aid a performer's decision making and performance.

Improving selective attention

Sports performers are bombarded with information, and one of the differences between good and not so good performers is their ability to selectively attend to the most appropriate stimuli. Selective attention may be improved by practice. Experience of the situation will enable performers to pick out the appropriate cues from the display. Coaches can assist this process by making the cues more obvious. The more 'stand out' a cue is the more it attracts our attention. Similarly, the more unusual or contrasting a cue is, the more likely we are to attend to it. When we need to attend to a ball in a game it helps if the ball contrasts with the background and so is easy to identify. Coaches can therefore help selective attention by highlighting the cues and directing

Examiner's tip

Questions on ways of improving information processing will tend to be specifically related to one aspect of information processing, such as how to improve selective attention or how to improve reaction time.

the performer's attention to the important cues. Hence the often-used expressions 'watch the ball' or 'look where I place my feet'. Performers are also able to identify appropriate cues quicker if they are expecting those cues. Anticipation improves selective attention and reduces decision-making time. Coaches should not only direct performers to the correct cues, but should also encourage performers to ignore inappropriate or distracting stimuli. These improvements may be achieved through physical practice, but may also be assisted by mental rehearsal, and like all practice, the more alert, aroused or motivated the performer, the better they become, even at selective attention.

Improving retention in memory

Performer use their memory to assess the information that is available about a particular situation and compare that information to that available through experience before selecting from a range of alternatives what to do in the situation as a response. The selective attention we have previously discussed is largely the role of the short-term sensory store. The short-term memory is the working memory that receives the selected information. It may be improved through repeated practice and rehearsal to get the performer used to dealing with the information. This is the idea of over-learning. The more the performer practises the more responses they will develop. It may also be improved by associating pieces of information with other, previously gained pieces of information. This is the idea of chaining that forms the basis of progressive part practice.

It is also important for the coach to make the information more meaningful for the performer by being related to past experiences rather than completely novel. The coach should also attempt to encourage retention in memory by reinforcing success to again make the response meaningful. Research on memory has identified its limitations and therefore 'chunking' information into larger units is helpful. The performer is better able to remember whole scenarios such as set plays than the individual roles of their teammates. Memory may also be improved by mental rehearsal.

Improving reaction time

Improving the speed of the decision-making process is important in sport as so many activities require speed of thought. Once again, the best way to improve this aspect of information processing is through practice. Practice gives the performer experience of detecting cues earlier and so speeding up the decision-making process. Practice will strengthen the stimulus-response bond. Psychologists talk about 'grooving the response'. Performers may anticipate a cue and so provide themselves with a warning signal that something is about to happen, and this improves the expectancy of the signal which means they no longer have to concentrate on alternative cues, so improving reaction time. There are limits to reaction time however. In general, reaction time deteriorates after a certain age, and men tend to have faster reaction times than women. A heightened sense of expectancy often leads to higher arousal levels and this too improves reaction time. This expectancy may also come from mental rehearsal.

Why skills break down

When beginners perform skills they often break down and they are unable to repeatedly complete the skill successfully. This may be due to the fact that beginners are unable to identify the appropriate stimuli

Link

Chaining is discussed further in Chapter 16 – Practical skill acquisition (page 250).

from the display. They may also suffer from information overload and have insufficient processing capacity to complete the whole skill. Even if they correctly identify the skill required, they may lack the range of responses to deal with the situation. They may also find that because of the demand for rapid decision making, they are unable to concentrate on the response and the skill breaks down as they are unable to decide on a response. They will also have a limited range of responses, which are often not able to be adjusted to suit the demands of the situation.

✔ *You should now be able to:*

- describe the process of the input of information through the senses and the process of selective attention
- describe the role and characteristics of memory
- describe decision making in sport
- describe how performers may use response time – anticipation, Hick's Law and the psychological refractory period
- describe the concept of motor programmes and sub-routines
- describe the factors that affect the efficiency of information processing systems.

AQA Examination-style questions

1   During a team game such as volleyball, performers will use their senses to detect stimuli. Figure 1 shows an information processing model.

The model suggests that sense organs receive information from the display.

    (a)   State three of the major senses used in volleyball. *(3 marks)*

    (b)   Briefly explain the three processes that occur as part of the perceptual mechanism. *(3 marks)*

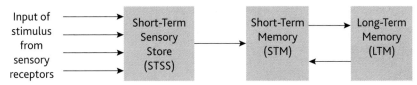

Fig. 1

2   (a)   To be effective, games players will need to use selective attention. Explain the term 'selective attention' and give examples of its use from a game of your choice. *(3 marks)*

    (b)   How can a coach improve a player's selective attention? *(3 marks)*

3   A basic information processing system consists of perception, translation and effector control. Explain what you understand by these terms, using appropriate examples from a named game. *(6 marks)*

4   Figure 2 shows the relationships between the memory stores in a simple information-processing model.

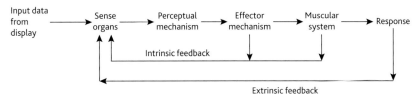

Fig. 2

Using Figure 2, describe the main functions of the:

    (a)   Short-term memory *(2 marks)*

    (b)   Long-term memory *(2 marks)*

    (c)   Suggest how a coach might help the retention of newly learned skills by a sports performer. *(2 marks)*

Learning and performance

Key terms

Learning: learning can be defined as the relatively permanent change in behaviour brought about as a result of experience or practice.

Maturation: the natural progression of physical development with age. We are not able to perform a skill until we have the physical, anatomical and psychological maturity to do so.

From the moment we are born we begin to acquire and develop psycho-motor skills. From being able to stand, to completing a double back somersault or hitting a top spin forehand, all are acquired skills, developed as a result of **learning** as well as **maturation** (growing up).

Fig. 9.1 *From toddler to tennis player – maturation and learning*

Skill development is therefore a product of learning plus maturation. This chapter will focus on the forces that drive us to learn new skills, how we acquire skills, the stages we go through as we become more skilful, and how we can make the process of skill acquisition as effective and as efficient as possible.

Psychologists have been investigating the process of learning for many years and many general learning theories have been adapted and applied to the learning of motor skills. More recently specific research into motor skill learning itself has been conducted and theories put forward as to how we make that progression from unsteady toddler to skilled performer. A new theory is developed because an existing theory is disproved or it does not account for all the variables in a situation.

Early motor skill learning theories focused on conditioning theories, also known as stimulus-response theories. Dissatisfaction with those led psychologists to develop cognitive and observational theories of learning. Although an earlier theory might be considered to have been superseded it is most likely that in making the progression from unsteady toddler to skilled performer an individual experiences a range of learning processes, and that learning is multi-threaded.

What drives us to acquire psycho-motor skills?

In general we only spend time and energy doing something if it brings us a benefit, an advantage or some form of reward. Psychologists call this drive **motivation.** Motivation may be defined as the biological, emotional, cognitive or social forces that activate and direct behaviour. Although these forces may be powerful they are also moderated by individuals so that they generally lead to appropriate behaviour – although there are some performers who lack this necessary element of control.

Psychologists have identified two basic types of motivation – intrinsic and extrinsic.

Intrinsic motivation is that drive that comes from within, the need to achieve something for personal satisfaction, a sense of mastery, a sense of accomplishment. The reward for such mastery may well be feelings of greater self-worth, status, etc.

Extrinsic motivation is the drive we experience if we are offered an external reward – a prize, a medal, money or praise from another individual, etc. External rewards may be further divided into tangible and intangible. Tangible rewards are those rewards that can be touched, held or have physical substance – for example, medals, trophies, money. Intangible rewards are external rewards that cannot be touched, for example the cheers of a crowd, congratulations from teammates or the coach.

It is of course true that the receiving of a medal or a prize may also bring feelings of self-satisfaction and pride. It would be a mistake to consider that extrinsic and intrinsic forms of motivation are independent of each other; there is a great deal of overlap. Why for example would the elite performer in Fig. 9.2 keep on training and competing?

The vast majority of research into motivation has concluded that intrinsic motivation is far better than extrinsic. There are a number of reasons for this:

- Extrinsic rewards can lose their power – if you are a multi-millionaire sports performer one more prize pay packet will make little difference to you.
- If the focus is solely on external rewards then the enjoyment of the activity may be lost and intrinsic satisfaction will not be developed or maintained.
- The extrinsic reward may not be valued by the performer (another certificate!) and motivation is lost if there is no intrinsic motivation present.

Although external rewards may play a part in motivating learners they should always be linked to feelings of accomplishment, success and increased self-worth so that intrinsic motivation is developed.

Theories of how we learn

Learning is defined as a permanent or semi-permanent change in behaviour or changed behaviour that remains stable over time. For example after many attempts a child may learn to ride their bicycle and can then do so again the next day. If their bike is broken for a few weeks and then repaired they may experience some initial difficulty in riding the bike but this is only temporary. We could infer from this that learning has occurred.

Psychologists have devised a number of theories of how we learn, each successive one being a reflection of dissatisfaction with the previous one, a feeling that the theory does not adequately explain the full variety of ways in which we learn.

Link

For an understanding of the nature and characteristics of skill, see Chapter 7 – Skills (page 78).

Key terms

Motivation: internal states and external pressures that direct an individual towards a goal or a course of action.

Intrinsic motivation: the most enduring form of motivation. Drive that comes from within – personal satisfaction, a sense of mastery, a sense of accomplishment. Leads to greater sense of self-worth. Supported by extrinsic motivation but should be not replaced by it.

Extrinsic motivation: the drive to perform to win or gain tangible or intangible rewards.

Learning: a permanent or semi-permanent change in behaviour as a result of teaching, coaching and practice.

Activity

Using the following terms, construct a mind map to show the essential features of motivation:

- Crowd acclaim, Extrinsic, Intangible, Intrinsic, Money, Praise from coach, Satisfaction, Self-worth, Tangible, Trophy.

Fig. 9.2 *Intrinsic or extrinsic motivation . . . or both?*

Activity

What forms of motivation may be occurring in the situation shown in Figure 9.2?

Key terms

Operant conditioning: manipulating behaviour to shape the correct response thought the use of reinforcement.

In this section we shall be considering three theories of learning:

- Conditioning theories such as **operant conditioning**.
- Cognitive theories such as **schema theory**.
- Social learning theories such as **observational learning**.

Conditioning theories

There are three different types of behaviouristic or conditioning theories of learning – contiguity, classical conditioning and operant conditioning. We are only concerned with operant conditioning.

Operant Conditioning

Operant conditioning is an example of an associationist or connectionist theory of learning, relying upon the connection between a stimulus and a response. These may also be known as *S-R theories*. This theory states that we become **conditioned** to give a particular **response** to a particular **stimulus;** that we have learned to act in a certain way given a certain stimulus. The likelihood of the response is dependent upon the strength of the bond between the stimulus and the response as shown by the diagram below.

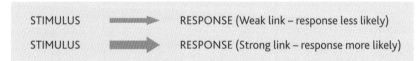

STIMULUS ⟶ RESPONSE (Weak link – response less likely)

STIMULUS ⟶ RESPONSE (Strong link – response more likely)

Fig. 9.3 *The stimulus-response link*

Having understood the nature of the S-R relationship two questions now need to be answered:

- How do we get the performer to give the desired response?
- How is the link or bond between the stimulus and the response created?

Getting the performer to produce the desired behaviour

In the context of physical performance the 'desired behaviour' is a particular technique or movement that we wish the performer to learn and reproduce.

One method is to rely upon trial and error. The objective is explained to the learner and then the learner is allowed to experiment with different ways of achieving the objective.

Activity

A class of children are being introduced to basketball. The teacher explains that to score, the ball must go through the ring from above (the objective). The children are then left to experiment to find ways of achieving the objective. Eventually a number of baskets are being scored with the children using a variety of methods for doing so.

1. What problems may arise through using this trial and error learning?
2. Is it an effective method of learning?

Alternatively the teacher may show a demonstration of a method of shooting a basketball and then ask the children to go and try this for themselves. This is more likely to lead to the desired performance. This will be more fully explained when we look at observational learning later on in the chapter. The combination of these two learning processes supports the view that learners will experience a range of learning processes as they acquire motor skills.

Creating the link or bond between the stimulus and the response – reinforcement

We create the link between stimulus and response by using a process of **reinforcement.**

Having got the learner to perform the desired action we must then reinforce the link between the stimulus ('score a basket') and the response (use a particular physical action or technique).

Reinforcement may take one of three forms:

- positive reinforcement
- negative reinforcement
- punishment.

Positive reinforcement is achieved by rewarding the correct response. Rewards are generally **extrinsic** and may be **tangible** or **intangible** (look back at the earlier section on motivation). Given that we are all motivated to receive rewards we experience a drive to repeat the action to gain the reward. Performing an action that leads to success will also give us an 'internal reward' – feelings of satisfaction, success and improved self-worth. This also motivates us to repeat the action that led to that feeling.

> **Key terms**
>
> **Reinforcement:** a process by which a connection (bond) between a stimulus and a response is established and developed.
>
> **Positive reinforcement:** a process by which the performer associates the correct response to a stimulus, strengthening the S-R bond.

Fig. 9.4 *Positive reinforcement*

Fig. 9.5 *Negative reinforcement*

Key terms

Negative reinforcement: the process by which an aversive or unpleasant stimulus is withdrawn when the correct response is given. The S-R bond is strengthened.

Punishment: giving a stimulus to prevent a response occurring, breaking the S-R bond.

Cognitive: the process of thinking and understanding.

Negative reinforcement also seeks to create or strengthen a link between a stimulus and a response. It does so by giving an aversive action (something the learner does not like) when they give the wrong response and then stopping the aversive action when the learner gives the correct response.

Punishment seeks to break the S-R bond – the link between a stimulus and a response – because the wrong response is given to the stimulus.

Fig. 9.6 *Punishment*

AQA Examiner's tip

To avoid confusion between reinforcement (positive or negative) and punishment remember that punishment weakens the S-R link whilst reinforcement strengthens the link. Do not confuse negative reinforcement with negative feedback.

Another aspect of operant conditioning is **shaping**. Shaping is where an action that is closer to the desired action is rewarded by positive reinforcement but an action that is further from the desired action receives negative reinforcement. The learner gradually moves closer to the desired action.

Criticisms of operant conditioning and psycho-motor skill learning

There are a number of criticisms and evident weaknesses of the operant conditioning approach to learning.

- The learner is not required to understand why they should do something. A lack of understanding may be de-motivating.
- Trial and error learning may lead to the wrong technique being adopted by the learner if it leads to initial success. This may require 'unlearning' and will waste time.
- The learner may not know how to react when the stimulus is slightly different from those already experienced. Due to their lack of understanding the learner may not know which response to use.
- This form of learning implies that for every skill or performance situation a stimulus-response bond has been created. Given the vast number of S-R links this would require this seems an unlikely scenario.
- Beginners do not react well to negative reinforcement and the use of punishment hardly seems appropriate in a skill learning situation! Shaping requires a learner to act as an automaton, reacting without understanding.

AQA Examiner's tip

Just because conditioning theories have been criticised as not giving the complete answer as to how we learn motor skills they can account for some learning experiences. You should therefore have some examples of how skill can be learnt through operant conditioning to use in an exam.

Cognitive theories of learning

Cognitive theories of learning developed as a result of the criticisms and perceived weaknesses in conditioning learning theories. Cognitive theories of learning stress the importance of what the brain does with the information (stimuli) that it receives. Cognitive theories reject the concept that we merely respond to a stimulus in an unthinking way. Cognitive theories of learning require the learner to understand where they are starting from and their objective – where they need to be, what they are trying to achieve.

We shall be looking at three cognitive learning theories which although different are all interrelated and based upon the notion of 'understanding' – Adams' Closed Loop theory, Insight Learning and Schema Theory.

Adams' closed loop theory

This was an early attempt at a cognitive explanation as to how we learn motor skills. Adams' theory states that:

- Movement is initiated by a **memory trace**. The memory trace of the motor programme is stored in our long-term memory and is developed as a result of experience and external feedback.

- Once initiated, movements are controlled by the **perceptual trace**. Skill learning requires the development of this perceptual trace through using a wide range of feedback both internal (kinaesthetic) and external (auditory, visual, etc.).

- The perceptual trace acts as an ongoing comparison for the performer to compare and evaluate the correctness of their movements – compare what you should be doing to what you are actually doing.

- If there is a mismatch between what you are supposed to be doing (memory trace) and what you are actually doing (perceptual trace) the performer attempts to eliminate the error by changing the movement.

- Learning therefore becomes a process of eliminating errors.

Key terms

Memory trace: chooses the initial motor programme to achieve the goal, then taken over by the

Perceptual trace: which uses feedback to refine the movement and eliminate errors.

Activity

Practise taking shots at a netball or basketball ring from in front of the ring. Then put on a blindfold and repeat the exercise. After each shot get a partner to tell you how successful you are being in terms of direction and length. They should only provide you with feedback about the shot (knowledge of results) not what you should correct – that is up to you.

1. Can you identify the memory trace and the perceptual trace?
2. How were they developed?
3. How were they used?
4. Having completed questions 1–3, can you interpret what you did in terms of the flow chart shown below in Figure 9.7?

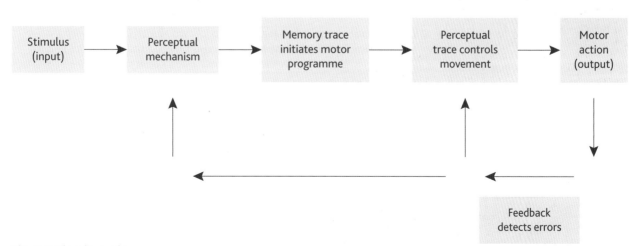

Fig. 9.7 *Closed Loop Theory*

Closed loop theory has weaknesses as a theory of learning but is also used to explain how we adapt a movement to achieve a goal, for example running to catch a ball. You need to remember closed loop control in terms of a possible explanation for learning and as a motor control process.

Schmidt's schema theory

Schmidt developed his theory as a result of his criticism of earlier theories such as Adams' closed loop theory. Schmidt's criticisms of closed loop theory were:

▓ To carry a separate memory trace for every single movement or technique that we perform would place too great a burden on our memory storage capacity – also a criticism of stimulus-response theory.

▓ Schmidt considered that every movement we make is unique in some way, due to a slight change in the environment, such as our opponent's actions or our own objectives.

▓ For example an overhead clear in badminton is never performed in exactly the same way but will be dependent upon our position on court, where we wish the shuttle to go, the size of our opponent, the movement of our opponent and tactical considerations.

▓ Neither closed loop theory nor stimulus-response theory give an explanation of how the performer manages the problems of storage capacity and unique responses to unique situations.

Schmidt's **schema** theory states that we develop and store in memory a set of schema which can then be adapted or refined to deal with a new situation. A schema is defined as a set of relationships involving joint actions and muscular contractions which produce a movement.

Schema theory states that we develop two different forms of schema – **recall schema** and **recognition schema**.

▓ Recall schema consists of two elements – **initial conditions** and **response** (movement) **specification.** Recall schema is used prior to movement.

Initial conditions are the knowledge we have of the environment, body position, limb position, muscle tension, etc. before we start.

Response (movement) **specification** – the motor programme (limb action, forces, speed, timing, etc.) and the movement objective (what we are trying to achieve).

▓ Recognition schema also consists of two elements – sensory consequences and movement outcome. Recognition schema is used during and after movement.

Sensory consequences are the internal (kinaesthetic) feedback we receive as we undertake the movement.

Response (movement) **outcome** is the result of the movement compared to the objective.

▓ Key terms

Schema: a set of relationships between joint action and muscle contractions that can be adapted to produce a new technique or skill.

Recall schema: stored information about how to produce a movement, made up of the initial conditions and the response specification.

Recognition schema: information that allows the performer to evaluate their movement – made up of sensory consequences (knowledge of performance) and response outcomes (knowledge of result).

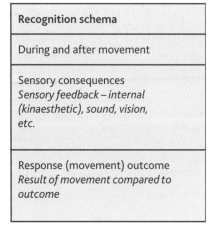

Recall schema	Recognition schema
Before movement	During and after movement
Initial conditions Knowledge of environment Body position Limb position Muscle tension	Sensory consequences *Sensory feedback – internal (kinaesthetic), sound, vision, etc.*
Response (movement) specification *Motor programme (limb movement, forces, speed, timing, etc.)* *Movement objective*	Response (movement) outcome *Result of movement compared to outcome*

Fig. 9.8 *Schema Theory*

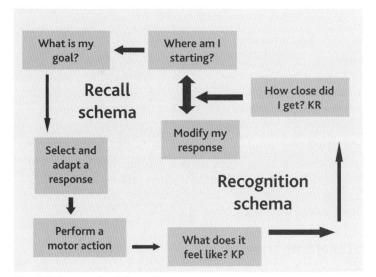

Fig. 9.9 *Interpreting Schema Theory*

Insight learning

Cognitive theories are also known as **insight theories** of learning. In these instances the learner suddenly gets an insight into the task as a whole, puts connections together and experiences a dramatic change in performance. A good example would be when learning to ride a bike. You struggle for a while to get the combination of balance, steering and forward motion in the right combination, then all of a sudden it 'clicks' and off you go. You have suddenly acquired the 'knack'. Insight learning occurs when the individual is able to combine together both the internal information about joint position, muscle tension and external information about the bike, road direction, etc. into an integrated model of what is required to ride the bike.

This appreciation of the problem as a whole is also connected to Gestalt theories which consider that the 'whole is greater than the sum of its parts'. In relation to skill learning this would mean that that although a movement can be broken down into component parts the relationships between the parts, the timing and transition between one component

Key terms

Insight theories: where the learner has a sudden leap of understanding and experiences a rapid improvement in performance.

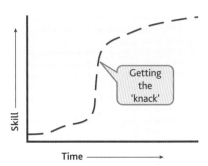

Fig. 9.10 *Insight learning – getting the knack*

Activity

The 'throw the ball between the legs into the waste bin' game

Try this as a class activity. It involves getting a performer to learn a new skill.

Equipment – waste bin and a soft ball or table tennis ball. Prepare some pieces of paper or card with the words 'initial conditions', 'response specification', 'sensory consequences' and 'movement outcomes' on them. These will need to be held up during the learning process.

Explain to the volunteer that you want them to stand with their back to the waste bin, and then throw the ball into the bin from between their legs, using their non-dominant hand. (Observers hold up a card.)

- Let them have an attempt.

- If they missed ask them where the ball landed in relation to the bin – front, behind, left, right and by how far. (Observers hold up a card.)

- Give them another attempt but tell them that you are going to ask them how the movement felt after they have performed it.

- After the second attempt ask them about the outcome as before. Also ask them about muscle tension, limb action speed, etc. Give them a third attempt. (Observers hold up a card.)

- After the third attempt ask them what they need to modify to be more successful, etc.

During this learning process the rest of the class must be holding up one of the four schema cards.

They should also write on each of the schema printouts what is actually happening.

Questions to the class:

1. What is the general schema that is being modified here?

2. What other feedback could be provided? What difference might it make?

3. What might happen if you allowed the performer to have some attempts with the other hand first?

and another is an integral part of the whole movement. Learners need to be able to experience and understand the skill as a whole before it can be correctly performed. It is also the case that this form of learning will occur at different time scales for different learners and requires coaches and teachers to provide a range of learning situations to allow performers to gain an insight into what is required.

Key terms

Social learning theory: learning by copying others because we wish to be socially accepted.

AQA Examiner's tip

Remember that social learning theory can apply to the formation of habits as well as skill learning.

Social learning theories

Social learning theory is based upon the concept that we learn by copying or mimicking others. It is most commonly applied when we are considering how we acquire attitudes and behaviours that help us become socialised into a group, accepting its norms and conventions. For example young performers will often copy the attitudes and behaviours that are displayed by elite performers or that are demanded or displayed by the coach or captain. It is not uncommon to see young players, particularly at school, change their sport behaviour when they change from one sport to another. Actions that are acceptable in one sport are not displayed or are punished in another so the player's behaviour changes accordingly. To be accepted into a group means acquiring the norms and behaviours of that group and the desire for acceptance is a powerful motivator of our behaviour – we all want to be accepted.

The methods by which we acquire such attitudes or social behaviours are explored in more depth in Unit 3 of the A2 course. We are concerned with the process of skill acquisition and common sense tells us that it is possible for us to learn a skill by copying somebody else. This process is known as observational learning and it shares many of the same processes as social learning. Although different from conditioning and cognitive methods of learning, observational learning will often be used as part of both of those approaches.

Observational learning

Much of our understanding of how observation of others can help us to learn and acquire skills stems from the work of Bandura. His focus was primarily on how we acquire general behaviours rather than skill acquisition but he identified a range of factors that affect how well we learn from observing others. The process of learning through observation most often occurs when we use a **demonstration** in a teaching or coaching session.

In a demonstration we wish the learner to copy or model their behaviour on what they see demonstrated – **observational learning** is also known as **modelling**. For a demonstration to be an effective method of skill learning a number of factors need to be considered:

- the attributes and characteristics of the model
- the physical and psychological readiness of the learner
- the motivation of the learner to attend to the model and to practise.

The four stages of the process – attention, retention, motor reproduction and motivation – link observation to performance.

Attention – the performer must attend to the demonstration. How much attention is paid to the demonstration will be affected by points 1 and 3 below (relevancy and status of the model).

Retention – the visual model must be retained otherwise performance is not possible. It helps if the learner can create a 'mental picture' of the skill by using a process known as imagery. Imagery can be enhanced by using mental rehearsal.

Having achieved attention and retention we move from the perceptual side to the psychomotor side of the process.

Motor reproduction – the learner must have reached a stage of sufficient physical development so that they can actually perform the skill.

Motivation – the learner will not perform the skill unless they are motivated to do so. External rewards may help in the early stages but intrinsic motivation is far better.

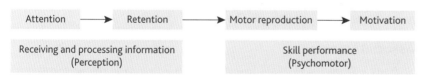

Attention → Retention → Motor reproduction → Motivation

Receiving and processing information (Perception) | Skill performance (Psychomotor)

Fig. 9.11 *Observational learning – perceptual elements*

For the process to be successful the coach or teacher must ensure that the characteristics of the model and the situation are appropriate. The appropriateness of the demonstration or the model is determined by:

- Relevancy to the learner – particularly to the existing skill level of the learner. To use an elite performer to demonstrate to a beginner may set too high a standard and the learner may feel that it is unattainable.
- The accuracy of the demonstration – if the learner views a flawed model they may acquire a faulty technique.

The status of the role model. If the role model has high status in the eyes of the learner they are more likely to attend to and be able to mimic the demonstration (but bear relevancy in mind).

Point of observation – can the learner see the relevant and key points – the 'cues'. For example the learner may be told to look at the movement of the arm during the shot putt. The coach may use cue words such as 'extension'. It is important however to allow the learner to watch the demonstration with full attention – too much verbal guidance.

Key terms

Stages of learning: the stages a learner goes through from a beginner to mastering a skill.

From beginner to expert – the stages of learning

It should be clear from your own observations that individuals rarely go from an inability to perform a motor skill to being an accomplished performer instantaneously; it is a gradual process. It is possible to see three distinct periods and these are known as the **stages of learning** – cognitive, associative and autonomous.

Cognitive stage

Learner is still trying to understand the demands of the task; they are putting together a mental model of what is required. This is sometimes known as the pre-practice stage.

The coach/teacher must ensure that they acquire the mental image through the use of demonstrations, guidance and use of key words or cues.

The learner needs to give all of their attention to the performance of the skill. For example the young basketball player watches when dribbling.

As they begin to attempt the skill based on the new mental model and their existing skills the learner makes many gross errors.

Learners in the cognitive stage are not able to pay attention to outside stimuli – any feedback must be after the performance (terminal feedback). Feedback must also be clear, simple and limited.

The cognitive stage is primarily a stage of gaining information about the skill model and organising the cognitive processes to produce a movement as close to the desired movement as possible. Little or no practice occurs except towards the end of the stage.

Associative stage

This stage is normally longer than the cognitive and the performer gradually becomes more successful and makes fewer gross errors.

This is normally a stage of rapid improvement. The skill actions become smoother, more accurate, better timed and more efficient. They begin to demonstrate the characteristics of skill that we looked at in Chapter 7 – Skills (page 78).

The learner begins to be able to make use of some intrinsic or kinaesthetic feedback and begins to compare the performance to the mental model.

Performers in the associative stage can also begin to pay attention to concurrent feedback given during the performance. They begin to use more complex and detailed cues.

The learner performs and practises (or should practise) the skill under a wider variety of situations. For example the coach may introduce an element of competition, add a defender or an extra attacker.

▓ It is a period of consolidation of correct or nearly correct movement responses.

Autonomous stage

▓ Skill improvement continues but at a less rapid rate.

▓ The performance of the skill displays very high levels of smoothness, efficiency, accuracy (almost always achieves the objective) and is performed without stress.

▓ The performer pays even less conscious attention to the performance of the skill – it has become habitual. They are increasingly less affected by outside distractions.

▓ The performer can pay attention to increasingly complex tactical and situational considerations.

▓ Increasingly the performer can analyse their own performance and adjust their own actions.

▓ Progress results from attention to fine details of technique and performers are increasingly involved and responsible for their own skill improvement through self-evaluation, mental practice and self-motivation.

Stages of learning and types of feedback

Feedback is the information that a performer receives during and after a performance, both from within and externally. There are a number of different forms of feedback – terminal, concurrent, positive, negative, intrinsic, extrinsic, knowledge of performance, knowledge of results and each form should be appropriate to the learner and the learning situation.

Forms of feedback

Intrinsic/internal/inherent feedback

This is feedback that the performer receives from their proprioceptors (state of muscle contraction, speed of contraction, joint position, etc.). In essence the performer can 'feel' the movement. This forms part of the information processing model covered in Chapter 8 – Information processing (page 87). It is also known as kinaesthetic feedback and is linked to knowledge of performance.

Extrinsic/external/augmented feedback

Feedback that is received from outside through vision and hearing, and often given by a coach, teacher, teammates, etc. It is linked to knowledge of results.

Positive feedback

Feedback received when the performer or performance was successful. This may be in the form of practice and strengthens the likelihood of the action being repeated.

Negative feedback

Feedback received after an unsuccessful performance and again can be in either an internal or an external form.

Terminal feedback

Feedback given (therefore predominantly external) after a performance has been completed. This form of feedback may be delayed.

AQA Examiner's tip

Do not make the assumption that the stages of learning are like a flight of steps, it is more of a continuum with the end of one stage blending into the next.

▓ **Key terms**

Feedback: the information a performer receives during and after the performance of a movement.

▓ **Activity**

In the classroom bounce a sponge ball on the edge of your hand or juggle it on the foot. The test is to count the number of consecutive bounces gained in a minute. Working in coach/learner pairs each coach should be assigned a different type of feedback to use.

After five minutes practice and feedback test whch juggler is best. Ask each peformer about how valuable they found the type of feedback they were receiving. Keep the data – you will need to use it later.

Concurrent/contiguous feedback

Feedback being received during performance. Most often internal feedback from the proprioceptors but can also be from a coach as the performer is undertaking the performance.

Knowledge of results

This form of feedback is external and usually terminal. **Knowledge of results (KR)** involves the performer seeing the results of their action or receiving that information from another person – normally the coach or teacher. This form of feedback is vital to learning; little progress will be made without the learner receiving this information and feedback.

Knowledge of performance

This form of feedback involves receiving information about the movement pattern rather than the outcome. It can be internal with the performer feeling how close the movement was to the perfect model, or can be provided by the coach. The external provision of this form of feedback involves giving information about small errors in technique – angle of release, foot position, etc. that the performer may not be able to detect for themselves. The use of high definition slow motion cameras and movement analysis software has made the use of this form of feedback increasingly important and available.

The type of feedback that should be used is highly dependent upon the learner and the stage of learning they have achieved. These can be seen as a series of continua.

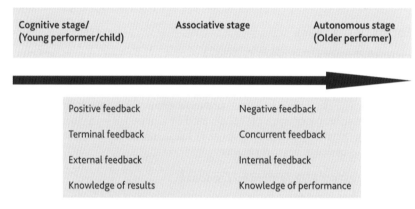

Fig. 9.12 *Feedback and stages of learning*

As the performer becomes more independent from the coach, more able to evaluate, analyse and alter their own performance the form of feedback that is used changes. Having said that, most performer/learners and performance situations require a sensitive blend of feedback. Too much negative feedback can be de-motivating but too much positive feedback does not give the learner a clear idea of where they are and what they need to do. Too much feedback from a coach during a performance can be very irritating and off putting for any performer.

💡 Skill development and performance curves

It is possible to represent the progression that a performer or learner is making in the development of a new skill as a performance curve or graph. The vast majority of these performance curves show levels of success over time and can give an impression of progress.

■ **Key terms**

Knowledge of result (KR): feedback about the outcome of a movement – its success or otherwise. External feedback gained via our senses or given by others.

Knowledge of performance (KP): internal feedback (kinaesthesis) about a movement, the feel of the movement.

Performance curves are sometimes incorrectly called learning curves because it is assumed that a change in performance is due to learning. Our definition of learning stated that 'learning is a relatively permanent change in behaviour brought about as a result of experience or practice'. Unfortunately merely measuring performance cannot tell us why that performance has changed – but it is a reasonable assumption that some of the change will be due to learning and practice, we just don't know how much.

There are four basic types of performance curve:

Positive performance curve

As shown in Figure 9.13, a positive performance curve indicates that progress is quite slow at the beginning but then rapidly improves.

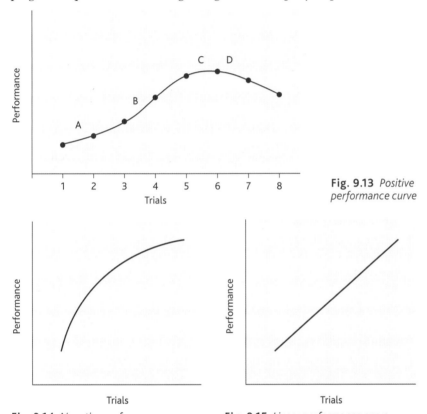

Fig. 9.13 *Positive performance curve*

Fig. 9.14 *Negative performance curve*   **Fig. 9.15** *Linear performance curve*

Negative performance curve

As shown in Figure 9.14 a negative performance curve shows that the performer improves rapidly at the beginning, has much early success but then the improvement slows down and may eventually stop.

Linear performance curve

If performance keeps on improving at a steady rate it is shown as a linear performance curve. This cannot go on indefinitely as at some stage the performance is either perfect or the learner has reached their limit. Figure. 9.15 shows a linear performance curve.

S-shaped performance curve

Learners frequently experience periods of improvement and progression and then times when they seem to make no improvement for while, never mind how well they practise. Then all of a sudden they take

Activity

Either observe live, or from a video, a class of badminton players attempting to use an overhead drop shot. Observe and using the criteria, place the players in the appropriate stage of learning. Place the players on a labelled performance graph.

Activity

Take the data from the hand juggling experiment on page 113 and plot it on a graph to show performance over time. What kind of curve do you get?

another step forward and experience a period of improvement. This leads to the S-shaped curve in Figure 9.17. The place where performance improvement stops is known as a learning plateau.

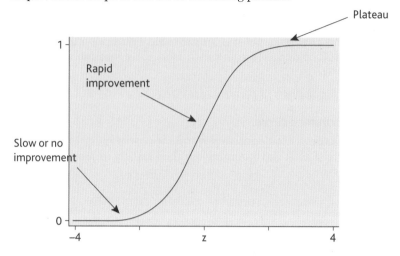

Fig. 9.16 *The S-shaped performance curve*

Key terms

Learning plateau: a period of time during which there is no change in performance – a levelling off.

Learning plateau

A **learning plateau** occurs when the learner stops progressing and no improvement in skill is evident. This may also be known as a performance plateau.

Studies suggest a number of reasons why a learning plateau may occur:

- The learner is physically not ready to make further improvement or go to the next stage.
- Learner lacks the ability to develop or modify current skills.
- Earlier faulty skill learning means that the learner is unable to master the next step.
- Fatigue – the learner is simply too tired to make any further progress.
- Moving from a simple skill to a more complex skill may take more time to assimilate the mental model and cues involved in the more complex skill.
- The next stage is too high or complex for the learner.
- Boredom due to lack of variety or length of practice.
- Motivation – the performer lacks the desire to move on, maybe as a result of boredom. Goals are being set too high, leading to fatigue and boredom.
- Poor coaching or teaching.

Overcoming a learning plateau

There are a wide range of strategies that may help a learner overcome a performance plateau:

- Ensure that the learner is physically ready for the next step.
- Reset the goal to an achievable level.
- Avoid fatigue and boredom by breaking the practice session into shorter or distributed time periods.
- Break the skill down into component parts if possible (see transfer of learning).
- Allow time for mental rehearsal.
- Try to generate more motivation and enthusiasm by providing external rewards or by providing some opposition.

AQA Examiner's tip

Questions will frequently ask you why the plateau may have occurred and how a coach or teacher can help a learner/performer overcome the plateau and move on.

▩ Ensure that the performer is receiving the correct feedback.

▩ Make practice enjoyable; add variety by changing team roles.

Not all the factors that can affect learning progression and improvements in performance are within the control of the teacher or coach – fundamental abilities and the ultimate demands of the situation or task are not alterable. Many factors are, and the teacher or coach must be aware of these factors and take note of them when planning practice sessions.

▩ The transfer of learning

The learning and acquiring of skills is a process that begins with a baby learning to sit up, stand, grasp, walk and run. Each of those skills is based upon some previous skill learning or element of body control and will form the basis of further skill development. Something we have already acquired will transfer or be adapted as we acquire further skills. This is known as **transfer of learning**.

Transfer of learning is likely to occur in situations other than the **basic to complex** scenario outlined above. It is also the case that transfer need not always be positive or beneficial; it may be quite the reverse.

Many practice activities assume that a transfer of learning will take place. For example when a coach breaks down a skill into its component parts and asks the learner to practise each component separately or when a simpler version of the skill is taught first it is being assumed that the learner can transfer it back to the performance situation. The relationship of transfer to the skill being learnt and practice conditions will be explored more fully in the next section.

> ▩ **Key terms**
>
> **Transfer of learning:** the application of previous experience to present learning. The effect on the performance of practising one skill or learning another.

> ▩ **Activities**
>
> **Transfer of learning experiment**
>
> 1. In the classroom bounce a sponge ball on the edge of the hand or juggle it on the foot. The test is to count the number of consecutive bounces gained in a minute.
>
> 2. Learners (swap round after using this experiment for feedback) should use a different practice strategy prior to the test – some juggle with other hand/foot, some undertake mental practice, some do practice after the test then retest (no practice before test), some juggle with flat of hand not edge, etc.
>
> 3. Undertake the test. Is there any difference in the outcome against a control group who did no practice?

You need to know the meaning of, and be able to give examples of, the following forms of transfer.

Positive transfer

Where the effect of a previously learned or practised skill has a beneficial effect upon another – for example using an overarm throwing technique to help learn a tennis serve, or to throw a javelin.

For there to be positive transfer there must be **similarity** in the structure of the skill components. Positive transfer can also be enhanced if these similar elements are shown to learners. It is also helpful if the context or situation is similar although this is not critical if the situation is clear and not confusing for the learner.

Negative transfer

This is where the effect of the previously learned or practised skill is damaging to the learning or performance of the new skill. The classic example is the tennis player who spends the winter playing badminton and then finds that their tennis techniques are not as effective. It is rare that the effects of negative transfer last for very long. In the tennis-badminton example although the contexts may be similar – they are both court/net games with serve and response and other similar tactical elements – the skill components are quite different.

Short-term negative transfer can also occur when a skill is transferred into a new situation – for example when going from an outdoor to an indoor version of the game. A change of tactic from the ones that players are habitually used to may cause short-term negative transfer – for example change from man to man defence to zone defence in basketball. Players may exhibit moments of confusion until their cognitive processing has readjusted.

Finally, negative transfer can occur if the practice situation does not demand the same response as the playing or competitive situation. For example only practising set moves or plays without defenders or just passive defenders, swimmers doing land drills.

Zero transfer

This is when there is no effect on current performance or learning from previous learning. This will occur when there is little or no similarity between the tasks or skills, when the situations are dissimilar or when the cognitive and information processes are also different.

Bilateral transfer

When there is a transfer from one limb to another – for example helping a player kick a ball with their non-dominant foot by relating it to the more skilful performance of the dominant foot.

Proactive transfer

Proactive transfer of learning occurs when what the learner is practising has an effect on a later skill or performance. Many teachers and coaches attempt to use proactive transfer when they set up skill improvement practices.

Retroactive transfer

This is the opposite of proactive and is said to occur when current learning or practice of a skill is affecting a skill that was learned in the past.

▉ The effect of practice on learning

You may well have heard the term 'practice makes perfect' or 'perfect practice makes for perfect performance'. This means that what you do in practice, how you construct and use practice time has a fundamental effect on the progress you make as a performer.

The most important variables involved are:

▉ how practice time is structured – massed, distributed or variable the form of guidance that is used – verbal, visual or mechanical

what teaching style should be used – command, reciprocal, guided discovery, problem solving

how the skill is presented to the learner – whole, part, progressive part, whole-part-whole.

A successful practice session takes into consideration these factors in the light of:

the learner's current stage of learning

the learning situation

the task or skill to be learned.

Skill learning and teacher guidance

How the teacher guides the learner can have a significant impact on progress. What follows is a brief overview of **guidance** – there is a much fuller explanation in Chapter 16 – Practical skill acquisition (page 250).

There are three forms of guidance – visual, verbal and manual/mechanical.

Visual guidance

The teacher provides a range of visual images – demonstrations, pictures and video to allow the performer to see what the skill looks like – this helps build a cognitive model of the skill. It is often used with beginners.

Verbal guidance

The teacher uses verbal descriptions, cue words or phrases to help the learner understand what is to be achieved. It is often used in conjunction with visual guidance and is better for more advanced learners.

Manual/mechanical guidance

The teacher physically moves the learner's limbs through the movement to enable them to feel the correct action. The teacher may also help the learner produce the correct movement by physically restricting the movement.

Now that you have completed this chapter you should have a much better idea as to how skills are learnt. This knowledge will be useful to you when you suggest ways to improve your own or another performer's performance in the practical work of Unit 2.

 You should now be able to:

identify the different forms of motivation that drive us to learn motor skills

quote examples of things that motivate us and their relative importance

help a performer achieve more by applying your knowledge of motivation

apply theories of learning to help a performer acquire or develop a new motor skill

Link

The design and conduct of successful practice sessions is considered in much more depth in Chapter 16 – Practical skill acquisition (page 250).

Key terms

Guidance: method by which a teacher/coach transmits the information necessary to help a performer to develop a new skill.

AQA Examiner's tip

Questions on skill learning/ acquisition will normally require you to describe the theory, apply it to a learner or learning situation and for the most marks be able to critically analyse the theory in a skill-learning context.

- recognise that motor skill learning is a continuous process and that learners will learn in a variety of ways, using all of the theories that you have studied

- identify the stage of learning that a performer has reached and know how this would help a performer overcome a plateau

- use the concepts of transfer to assist a learner in acquiring a new skill or developing an existing skill

- use performance graphs to show the rate of progress made by a learner.

AQA Examination-style questions

1   Operant theories of conditioning (learning) are based on the use of reinforcement.

   (a)   Briefly explain the terms positive reinforcement and negative reinforcement giving examples from a game such as basketball.   *(4 marks)*

   (b)   Give an example of how you would use operant learning methods in the coaching of a game such as basketball.   *(2 marks)*

2   Schmidt's schema theory is based on four sources of information.

   (a)   List three of the four sources of information.   *(3 marks)*

   (b)   How should a coach organise practices to enable a schema to develop?   *(3 marks)*

3   Transfer is an important process in skill development.

   (a)   Explain the concepts of postive and negative transfer.   *(2 marks)*

   (b)   How can a coach ensure that the transfer from practice to the competitive situation is as effective as possible?   *(4 marks)*

4   Performers vary in the rate at which their performance progresses.
   Figure 1 shows a performance graph.

   (a)   Name the part of the curve labelled A.   *(1 mark)*

   (b)   What may have caused this?   *(2 marks)*

   (c)   What steps would you take as a coach to either prevent this stage occurring or help the performer overcome it?   *(3 marks)*

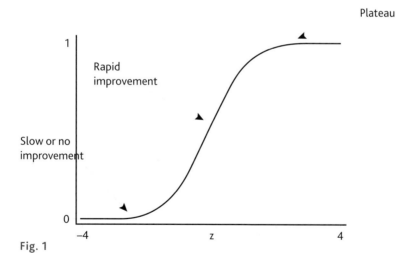

Fig. 1

Opportunities for participation

Introduction

The third part of the AS Physical Education theory is the study of opportunities for participation. Many of the terms that are used in describing physical education are part of our everyday language, but for the purposes of this course these terms need to be clearly defined as they each have a distinguishing role in physical activity. For example, we may play a game, but play and game have distinct meanings when it comes to the study of physical education, as does the term 'physical education' itself!

Involvement in any physical activity is rarely done in isolation. There are often teammates, opposition, supporters and officials, and the activity needs to take place at some fairly specific location such as a pool, court or pitch. The provision of the facilities and opportunities to take part in physical activities is studied, looking at who provides the facilities and the different ways these providers work.

In a similar way, there is a need to understand the role of schools, clubs and other agencies in providing opportunities for physical activities and the reasons why these opportunities exist as they do. Many of the physical activities that you take part in have been around for well over a hundred years and many aspects of our current sporting opportunities are remnants from long ago, and so a study of some of the history of how physical activities came into existence in both schools and clubs explains why we do things in certain ways.

Finally, one of the problems within our society is that not everybody has the same opportunities as others. There can be many barriers to participation in physical activity, and so we look at some of these barriers and how they can be reduced so that we provide equal opportunities for everybody to become involved in physical activity.

10 Concepts and definitions

One of the central objectives of physical education programmes is to encourage young people to develop a lifelong engagement with physical activity. As people develop from young children to adults they have the opportunity to participate in an ever increasing range of physical activities. A young child's first experience of physical activity is through the medium of play and then through experiences at school and finally in an increasingly independent choice of physical recreational activities. For a few talented individuals their ability in a physical activity may give them the opportunity to play professionally or at an elite level.

Fig. 10.1 *From play to sport*

In this chapter we examine different types of physical activity an individual may engage in – from sport to play, from gentle recreation to the risk taking involved in many adventurous activities. Firstly we analyse and define the characteristics and objectives of the physical activities that an individual may be involved in from infancy to adulthood. We shall see that although there is a huge diversity of physical activity they all have some shared characteristics and they form a continuum from play to professional sport. Having analysed and identified their characteristics and objectives we look at the hugely varying experiences that individuals receive when they participate in physical activity and whether or not these can be shared with others. Finally we look at the benefits that individuals and society gain from being involved in physical activity.

The socio-cultural elements of the AS Level course require a greater degree of debate and argument than the other topic areas. Socio-cultural topics cannot have the same level of factual certainty as anatomy and physiology. Social research cannot be as reliable and valid as that carried out in the laboratory. To become the social scientist this element of the course demands that you look at the contrasting and often conflicting evidence, debate the issue and then reach a conclusion. To successfully answer questions from this part of the course you will need to argue based upon knowledge, value judgements and beliefs. You are then able to make reasoned judgements about whether or not your government should be spending millions of pounds a year of your taxes on sport and physical recreation, and whether it was justified in spending billions of pounds on the 2012 Olympics.

The characteristics and objectives of physical activities

If you look at any school playground, the local playing fields, street, lake, beach, sports centre or back page of a newspaper you will see people from the ages 3 to 83 engaging in physical activity. Some activity will be highly strenuous, some much less so, some participants will be highly competitive but others will be engaging in a more light-hearted way. Some will be participating alone whilst others will be running with 50,000 others in an event such as the London Marathon and many millions more watch on television (the TV audience for the last Olympics was 34 billion people in 55 countries).

Some of the activities we are about to study will be very familiar to you – certainly sport and play. Others may be less familiar – adventurous activities for example. As part of the AQA specification you are required to understand the following types of activity:

- play
- leisure and recreation
- active leisure
- outdoor and adventurous activities
- sport
- physical education.

You will have had no difficulty with matching many of the photographs to the categories in the list, but some could have fitted into one or more category or it was not clear which category they should be allocated to. In fact it is impossible in many cases to decide where one category ends and the other begins – they form a continuum. You will be asked to repeat this activity later on.

Play

The word 'play' is used in a very wide range of contexts. 'I play a game of football', 'you should play fairly', 'the children are playing'. At first we are concerned with children and play. It is often assumed that **play** is something that only children engage in, and that play is childlike or childish. Whilst there is some truth to those assumptions we shall see by the end of this section that play is something that we can all engage in – whatever our age!

Key terms

Play: an activity that is undertaken purely for enjoyment or amusement and has no other objective.

Activities

If possible, go and observe a group of children playing in a playground or watch a younger brother or sister and their friends.

Whilst you are watching ask yourself the following questions:

1. Why are the children playing? What immediate benefit might they be gaining?

2. Do the children seem to be obeying any rules?

3. Is it always the same group or individual children that are participating?

4. Are there any limits or boundaries to the space in which they are playing?

5. How long do the children play for, are there any constraints or limits on their time?

6. Do you observe any changes to the game or the rules as the children play? If so how did those changes arise?

7. Think back to yourself as a child – what do you think you gained or learned from play? How would you, or the children you have been observing, have been different without engaging in play?

8. Do you think play is important for a child?

Characteristics of play

From your observations and answers to the questions in the last learning activity you should have discovered that play has a number of very important characteristics:

- Play is fun.
- Play can be **spontaneous**, it requires little pre-planning or organisation.
- **Rules** are changeable, **negotiated** and freely accepted.
- Play is not strictly structured, participant numbers can vary, physical boundaries can be negotiated or adapted to fit local conditions, the length of the play activity is flexible or constrained by outside influences (mum calls you in for tea!).
- Play is undertaken for its own sake, it has **intrinsic value**, there are no external rewards, it has no purpose.
- Play, despite being fun and purposeless can nevertheless be serious – watch the arguments that can break out when children play.
- Play allows an individual to be in a fantasy world, to be self-fulfilled outside of their normal life.
- Play can be childlike.

Fig. 10.2 *How many of the listed characteristics of play can you identify in the picture?*

Do not fall into the trap of saying that play has no rules – this is not true. Rules can be complex and binding, but are negotiated and changeable.

Activity

A group of children meet during break-time. After some discussion they decide to play hide and seek. They agree that the catcher will hide their eyes and count to 50, that everybody has to stay within the playground, the dustbins are out of bounds and that the netball post is the home base. The most popular child is the first catcher. She hides her eyes and the others scatter and hide. The catcher gets to 50 and yells 'coming, ready or not'. She begins to search; quickly she finds all of the children.

The children complain that it was too easy for the catcher so it is agreed to extend the hiding area. A few more children ask to join in and they do. The next catcher hides their eyes, gets to 50 and then starts to search… he screams with laughter when he races another child to the home base and catches the person who has been told by the lunch-time supervisor that they 'can't hide there, it's against the school rules'.

Key terms

Spontaneity: unplanned behaviour, unconstrained behaviour.

Rules: codes of behaviour, conditions that govern behaviour or action.

Negotiation: reaching an agreement through discussion and compromise.

They are about to play again when the bell goes for afternoon school. As the children walk in a child tells the lunch supervisor 'that's not how we played hide and seek at my other school'.

How many of the characteristics of play can you identify in that passage?

What if the Case Study on page 125 had been describing a game of football played on the local park after school by a group of children, using coats for goals, teams picked by self-nominated captains, (one of whom owns the ball), no referee but taking corners, free kicks and penalties? Would this still have been play? Clearly there would be elements of play, but also elements of more formal sport coming in – use of standard rules for example, or keeping the score. We would probably agree however that it has enough of the characteristics of play to still be classified as play. So when does play end and sport begin? In reality there is no clear boundary and even in a highly competitive, professional sport match there can be elements of play evident – the players may still be having fun for example. As an activity becomes more formal, more serious, less spontaneous, more structured, then it moves from play into the arena of sport.

Is play therefore only for children? You will be able to answer that question after the next section.

The objectives of play

What we are really asking is 'what is the value of play?', 'what purpose can it have in the lives of people?' Human beings, even under the harshest conditions find ways to play – why?

For children play allows them to learn the structures and etiquette of social interaction, to learn to accept rules, to understand that they can change a situation by imposing their own ideas, but also learn that they must also accommodate the situation and fit in, to learn to share, negotiate and sometimes to not agree. Through play children can learn about dominance and leadership. Play therefore has a **socialisation** purpose, in simple terms children learn about life through play.

Play is deemed so important for children that it is an important part of what is offered to children in nurseries, play groups and early years classes. Local authorities are responsible for installing and maintaining children's play areas. Children's play schemes and other initiatives receive government funding.

> ■ Key terms
>
> **Socialisation:** acquiring the skills and rules to enable an individual to successfully interact with other individuals or within a community.

For adults play allows them to escape the pressures and formality of their working lives. Play offers an opportunity to be something other than your usual self – seeing teachers on ski trips involved in snowball fights for example! Play offers the opportunity to be in 'another world', to be spontaneous and not worry about the outcome. Play allows adults to construct their own reality and their own rules. Play allows adults to be 'childlike'.

The objectives of play for children and adults are summarised below.

For children:

■ allows a child to test boundaries

■ allows a child to experience risk whilst keeping them safe from harm

- enables a child to learn social 'rules' (socialisation) – team work, sharing, the nature or rules and authority
- fosters independence and self-esteem
- develops children's respect for each other
- offers opportunities for social interaction.

Adults can also experience all of these but play has other outcomes for adults:

- adults play to escape **reality**
- adult play is about being childlike
- adult play gives opportunities for creativity and fantasy.

Leisure and recreation

The characteristics of leisure

Leisure is a concept that has moved from being something engaged in by a privileged few, or as a reward, to something which is deemed to be essential for normal human life and development. In our day-to-day lives we spend differing amounts of time on work, looking after our own basic needs, or fulfilling our responsibilities to something other than ourselves.

Work is something that we have to do to enable us to gather the resources to maintain life. The term 'work' encompasses paid work, housework, school or college work, etc. We also spend time meeting our physical needs, for example eating and sleeping. We also may have duties or responsibilities to other people or things – children, parents, the local community, pets, etc. The time we have left over after fulfilling all those roles, needs and responsibilities is time that when we can choose to do as we please – our free time. Leisure may therefore be defined as a time during which you have no obligations, work or family responsibilities, and therefore are free to engage in enjoyable, self-chosen and self-directed activities.

Leisure can therefore be summarised as:

- something that is engaged during free time – free from obligations
- a time when you engage in freely chosen activities
- used for ease and relaxation
- done for enjoyment.

It is quite possible of course for somebody to freely choose to do nothing during their leisure time and they may find this perfectly enjoyable. Given that it is freely chosen and self-directed this would fulfil the criteria of leisure. But would it be recreation?

Fig. 10.3 *Urban relaxation!*

www.cartoonstock.com

Key terms

Recreation: engaged in activities that refresh, relax or enable the recreation of oneself after the rigours of work or day-to-day life.

Recreate: to make anew, to go back to an earlier state.

Physical recreation: engaged in physical activity to refresh, relax or to recreate after the rigours of work or day-to-day life.

Link

How we make provisions for physical recreation and what is being increasingly referred to as 'active leisure' is covered in more depth in Chapters 11 – Leisure provision (page 146) and 12 – National Curriculum PE and school sport (page 164).

The characteristics and objectives of recreation

The word **recreation** brings to mind something active, positive and beneficial. The dictionary defines recreation as 'the refreshment of the mind and body after work, especially by engaging in enjoyable activities'. Recreation implies relaxation – escaping or freeing oneself from the efforts of day-to-day life. It also implies recuperation or recovery – this could be from stress, or physical and mental fatigue. Recreation would also suggest the act of **recreating** oneself, to be creative, to do things that reflect your interests and personality. Recreation of course has all the characteristics that we defined for leisure.

Recreation has all the features of leisure but has some additional characteristics:

- to refresh the mind and/or body
- recuperating, recovering from a stressful work life or other obligations
- recreating – being creative, activities for self-fulfilment.

However we are more interested in the more active forms of leisure that are known as physical recreation.

Physical recreation is physical activity that fulfils all the characteristics and objectives of recreation – relaxation, recuperation and recreation.

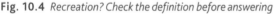

Fig. 10.4 *Recreation? Check the definition before answering*

Active leisure

The term 'physical recreation' is normally linked with sport of one kind or another, from team games to athletics, from water sports to racket sports. Although sport is a positive and beneficial use of leisure time there would always be some people for whom sport would hold no interest. Many people do not wish to be competitive, or believe that sport is only for those who can excel, or that sport is only for the young. However our knowledge of the link between an active lifestyle and health (see Chapter 1 – Improving fitness and health, page 2) and the unhealthy effects of a sedentary or pressured lifestyle means that ways had to be found to encourage individuals to become more active in their lives. This has led to the development of the concept of active leisure.

Activity

Using the physical activity that you are developing for Unit 2, discuss with a partner how it can fulfil all the characteristics for leisure and physical recreation.

Active leisure is precisely what it sounds like – being physically active in one's leisure time. This does not need to be sport-based or competitive – jogging, cycling, gardening, swimming, water aerobics, walking, bird watching, use of home gym equipment, rambling all fall into the category of active leisure. They do not require you to join a club, take part regularly or at set times, buy expensive specialist equipment or reach a certain standard. The emphasis is on flexibility and enjoyment, participation when and where you like. More emphasis is being placed on **'lifetime sports'** – activities that can be participated in throughout one's life.

One method of being engaged in active leisure is through outdoor recreation and adventure activities.

💡 Outdoor and adventurous activities

Over the last 70 years there has been a huge increase in interest in outdoor and adventurous activities and this has been accompanied by a range of government legislation to give people more access and opportunity and a growth in both social and commercial providers of outdoor and adventure opportunities.

Fig. 10.5 *A lifetime sport*

Activity

Research the London Marathon. Just over a million people took part in this event – why? What did they gain from it? What did the spectators gain from it?

1. How many ran? Were all the participants motivated to participate in the same way?

2. How many applied to run?

3. How many lined the route to watch? Why?

4. Why did so many watch the event on television?

5. Does the country gain from this activity/event?

Key terms

Active leisure: being physically active in leisure time.

Lifetime sport or activity: activities that can be undertaken in their normal form, or sometimes as an adapted form, all the way through an individual's lifetime.

Activities

1. List any outdoor recreation or adventure activities you have experienced – this could be with family, school or youth groups, scouts, guides, etc.

2. List any local providers of outdoor and adventure activities in your area.

3. Are there any areas near to you that can provide the environment for these kinds of activities?

4. Does your school or college provide such opportunities? Do they find it easier or more difficult to do so than in the past?

Key terms

Outdoor recreation: recreation (see earlier definition) that takes place and uses the natural environment.

Adventure activity: a form of outdoor recreation that involves a degree of challenge and risk. The level of challenge or risk is determined by the nature of the environment and the experience of the participant.

Characteristics of outdoor recreation and adventure activities

Outdoor recreation and **adventurous activities** are similar but different. Outdoor recreation includes undertaking an activity in the natural environment – in woods, on lakes, up mountains, over moorland, on the sea or on rivers. Adventure activities use the same natural environment

Adventure education: an adventure activity that is undertaken as part of a school or educational programme, with educational objectives.

Outdoor education: school work, lessons or curriculum activity that takes place in the natural environment.

Perceived risk: the participant believes themselves to be at risk or in some form of danger. Linked to the performer's level of experience and skill. Sometimes known as subjective risk/danger.

Actual risk: the situation carries a level of risk or danger regardless of the skill or experience of the participant. Sometimes known as objective risk.

but also include an element of challenge and risk. Not all outdoor recreation would be classed as adventure activities but all adventure activities would be considered to be outdoor recreation.

A third classification would be **adventure education** or **outdoor education**. This is where the natural environment is used as a classroom and children experience those feelings of danger and risk but in a controlled and safe manner. It is believed that by doing so children will receive educational experiences and undertake learning that would not be possible, or not as effective, in the classroom. Children may learn about the natural environment, outdoor adventure skills such as map reading, and also experience social learning opportunities such as leadership and team work.

Finally some outdoor and adventure activities have a competitive, sport-based format, for example canoeing.

▓ Activity

Copy and complete the following table. List all the outdoor recreation activities you can think of in the left-hand column, then put a tick if you consider them to be an adventure activity, state which part of the natural environment is used, and finally put a tick in the last column if you think it has a sport or competitive format.

Outdoor recreation activity	Adventure activity	Location	Sport?

Due to the terrain and climate of our country we have many outdoor recreation opportunities. Over the years we have enacted laws to give greater access to open countryside, moorlands, mountains, rivers and our coastline. Through the work of bodies such as the National Trust, Open Space Society and Natural England a great deal of our countryside is open and accessible. The latest objective from the Government is to ensure that our entire coastline is open for the public to walk around. As a nation we have a great love of the outdoors and have produced many of the world's greatest mountaineers, sailors, canoeists and explorers.

Earlier on, a distinction was drawn between adventure activities and outdoor recreation. The essential difference lies in the concept of challenge and risk. Adventure activities carry with them an element of either perceived or actual risk.

Perceived risk is where the participant believes that there is an element of danger and thinks that they are at risk when they undertake the activity. They perceive that their safety is dependent upon their skills and the actions they take. **Actual risk** is quite simply a situation in which there is an element of real danger, there is a real risk and it may not be eliminated no matter how experienced or skilful you are.

Risk relates to the element of predictability in a situation. Where a situation is predictable and therefore avoidable any danger is subjective – it is connected to an individual's level of knowledge and experience. An inexperienced person with an experienced leader may think that the situation is dangerous and will feel at risk, but due to the leader's experience they are in a predictable and therefore relatively safe position. At the other end of the spectrum a situation can have so much unpredictability that the situation has high levels of objective and non-avoidable danger, no matter how experienced the participants.

Figure 10.6 below illustrates this relationship.

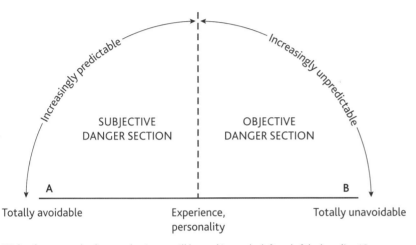

Increasingly predictable

Increasingly unpredictable

SUBJECTIVE DANGER SECTION

OBJECTIVE DANGER SECTION

A

B

Totally avoidable

Experience, personality

Totally unavoidable

With reference to the diagram, beginners will be working at the left end of the base line AB, Committed experts will be taking on challenges at the right end of the base line

Fig. 10.6 _The Mortlock experience-risk continuum_

The two examples below will exemplify the combination of danger, risk and experience that goes to make up the adventure experience.

Activities

Consider the two situations given below:

Situation 1 – A group of 13–15 year olds on a mountain walk with an experienced teacher. They are well equipped. During the day they encounter mist, steep and rocky ground and learn how to do an emergency bivouac.

1 How would the children be feeling as the day progresses?

2 Would their pre-trip preparations have increased or decreased their feelings of fear, danger, and apprehension? Give reasons for your answer.

3 Looking at Mortlock's diagram, where would you have placed the group on the inexperience-experience continuum, and the avoidable-unavoidable continuum?

4 Are they in subjective or objective danger?

5 Suppose the group lost the leader – how would that change the positioning on the continua?

6 Why would schools think it a good idea to include such an experience as part of a child's curriculum?

Situation 2 – A highly experienced and talented climber has decided to scale an 8,000 metre Himalyan peak, solo and without oxygen.

7 What risks is the climber taking?

8 Why attempt it solo and without oxygen?

9 Place the climber on the experience-inexperience continua and the avoidable-unavoidable continua.

10 What facts in the passage have helped you determine the positioning on the continua?

11 What elements of real danger are present?

12 Why has this highly experienced and knowledgeable performer decided to undertake this challenge?

To gain a better understanding of the motivation of individuals who pursue adventure activities to a high level watch films such as *Touching the Void* or read books by Rheinold Messner, for example *The Crystal Horizon*.

The objectives of outdoor recreation, education and adventure activities

This section explains why individuals engage in these activities and why schools or colleges include them in their curriculum.

Outdoor recreation involves a vast range of activities, can be as physically demanding as an individual chooses, and can be undertaken with little or no equipment, experience or skill, with minimal objective risk. Experience and knowledge will allow for a greater range of outdoor recreation opportunities to be engaged in. Taking part in outdoor recreation can provide opportunities for:

- engaging with, learning about and enjoying the natural environment
- being involved in active leisure, physical exercise and a lifetime sport
- extending an individual's experiences beyond their everyday life or environment
- becoming involved in adventure activities
- **escaping** from day-to-day life.

Adventure activities have risk and challenge at their heart. Individuals participate because they wish to challenge themselves, to take on the challenge that the changing environment poses. What is a pleasant walk in summer can become a high risk activity in the depths of winter. Such activities give rise to feelings of fear, exhilaration, apprehension and excitement – sometimes all in the space of a few minutes. Taking part in adventure activities can provide opportunities for:

- experiencing fear, excitement, and exhilaration
- developing self-reliance
- developing self-knowledge
- experiencing the problems and satisfaction of leadership and decision making
- the development of team work and trusting others
- accepting the trust of others.

Outdoor education

Since the early part of the twentieth century taking children into the 'great outdoors' has been seen as a valuable method of education. Schools and a host of other organisations (Scouts, Guides, Boys Brigade, Outward Bound, YHA, etc.) have provided opportunities for children to learn about the natural environment and the challenges it can provide. Many young people, particularly those from less advantaged backgrounds, have been given opportunities and experiences that would have been far out of their reach. In the past much of this provision was organised through experienced and enthusiastic adults, keen to pass on to children their enthusiasm for their own activity. Schools and the other organisations began to develop and run their own **outdoor activity** centres in the remoter parts of the country. During the latter part of the twentieth century a range of commercial providers also sprang up, offering schools and families the opportunity to undertake these activities either during holiday time or as part of the school curriculum.

Activity

Debate the following motion: 'Schools have a duty of care towards their pupils and it is not acceptable to offer adventure activities within the curriculum due to the extra risk that the children would be exposed to.'

You may be asked to speak for or against the motion. With a partner prepare a bullet point list supporting or disagreeing with the motion.

Outdoor education embraces activities and experiences that:

- normally take place in the outdoors
- frequently have an adventurous component
- generally involve a physical activity
- always respect the natural environment.

Urban adventure

Whilst the benefits of outdoor and adventure education have been recognised for many years, budget constraints have meant that many local education authorities cannot maintain an outdoor education or adventure programme that takes young people to residential accommodation in wild areas.

To overcome this problem there has been a development of urban adventure – using local facilities to provide adventure opportunities, for example using local parks, canals, indoor climbing walls, rivers, school playing fields and lakes in towns or cities. It has been possible to provide a whole range of adventure activities without the need to travel.

Urban adventure has now moved from being a means to give children in towns and cities an opportunity to experience adventure activities, to an activity in its own right with the development of activities such as Free Running (parkour), and the Rat Race urban adventure series. It could also include activities such as paintballing and adventure playgrounds.

Fig. 10.7 *An urban adventure – parkour*

Adventure activities as sport

A whole range of outdoor and adventure activities now have a competitive form: skiing (downhill and cross-country), sledging, rock climbing, canoeing, sailing (from dinghy to solo round the world), mountain biking, surfing and orienteering. Like all sports they have competitive rules, local, national and international competitions, and methods of talent identification and development.

Although these activities in their sporting guise are very popular there are those who feel that to have a sporting format takes away an essential element of the activity. Adventure activities are about using skills to overcome the challenge that the environment poses. Adventure activities are often collaborative, with a sense of looking out for each other. In the

UK, mountain rescue teams are manned by volunteers, fellow walkers, mountaineers and climbers who willingly put themselves at risk to rescue others who have been unlucky or made the wrong decision. Adventure activities are not bound by rules and governing bodies, each participant decides for themselves when and where to participate, and how much risk to accept. For many the addition of a competitive format with all the trappings of the professional and elite sporting world degrades the purity of the activity.

Sport

Sport is one of the most significant social phenomena in the world. Millions of people participate on a regular basis, many more pay significant sums of money to watch sport either live or on television. To support their participation people will give up large amounts of their leisure time to practise and train and use a significant amount of their income to equip themselves and travel to perform. For some, sport has become the new religion.

Outside of actually playing or competing many people give up their time, on a volunteer basis, to run clubs, sport events, to be coaches, managers, minibus drivers, scorers, referees, etc. Sport England estimates that in 2006, five million people gave one billion hours to sport on a volunteer, unpaid basis. Economically sport is a billion pound industry, allowing an elite few to be professional sportsmen and sportswomen, but many more to make their living as coaches, trainers, commentators and other TV professionals, manufacturers, salesmen, providers of medical support, sport event managers and staff, etc.

Such a level of interest and passion in what, from a dispassionate viewpoint, must seem to be a pointless and trivial activity must mean that there is something fundamental about sport that makes it so attractive. Sport as a word is often used loosely, inaccurately or in a variety of contexts. For example – is darts a sport? What is the 'sport of Kings'? What do we mean by 'international sport – war without the weapons'?, What is meant by 'being a good sport'? and so on. We need a more precise definition.

Characteristics of sport

With a partner write down a list of buzzwords that describe sport for you. When you have completed your list put them in rank order of importance in terms of how well they express your view on what sport is, and why people do it. As a group get your words up on the board and see how much agreement there was in your rank order.

You probably had all or some of these words – **competitive**, winning/losing, team work, physically hard, physically talented, skilful, training, chance, clear outcome (win, lose or draw) and probably many more. Many writers have tried to define sport. One of the most used definitions was given by Coakley.

> Sports are institutionalised competitive activities that involve vigorous physical exertion or the use of relatively complex skills by individuals whose participation is motivated by a combination of intrinsic and extrinsic factors.

Coakley, Sport and Society: Issues and Controversies, *1982*

Activity

Prepare a presentation of three slides.

- The first slide should detail your sporting history.
- The second slide should describe how you became involved in sport.
- Finally, the third slide should cover why you play the sport.

Key terms

Competitive: wanting to win, to defeat others.

Fig. 10.8 *It's not just about winning…*

How many of those words or concepts had you already identified? A more romantic, philosophical view of sport was given by Inglis:

> sport is a scrapbook of memories which defines life. It involves a peculiar and intense awareness of yourself, a self-consciousness, in which the point awareness is to get something right which is quite outside of yourself . . .

Inglis, The Name of the Game, *1977*

We need to explore in more depth what Coakley means by 'institutionalised activities' and 'motivated by intrinsic and extrinsic factors'.

Institutionalised activities

- fixed set of competitive structures – leagues, cups, competitions organised by some regulatory body
- set of standardised rules that governs each competitive encounter, set by the regulatory, governing body
- rules enforced by officials
- range of strategies for play, specialisation of players (forwards, backs, etc.), training schedules and development of specialist equipment
- codes of conduct (written and unwritten) that govern player or participant behaviour.

Intrinsic and extrinsic factors

This relates to what drives people to participate in sport.

Intrinsic factors are factors that are internal to you and would include self-satisfaction or fulfilment, fun and enjoyment, personal choice, the element of 'play', the desire to win.

Extrinsic factors are those things that come from outside of the individual and would include – medals, prizes, money, fame, praise, the demands of the job (for the professional).

Most sport participants are motivated by a combination of these factors

Link

For a more detailed discussion on motivation see Chapter 9 – Learning and performance (page 102).

although the amateur or less gifted performer is more likely to be motivated more by the intrinsic than the extrinsic. Professional players, those who make their livelihood from sport, are of course driven by the rewards they receive – they have to feed themselves and their families. But many will say that what keeps them training hard, pushing their bodies, keeping going when results are going against them is their inner drive to win, to compete, to be the best. This would also explain why those who are highly successful, millionaire professional sports performers still train hard and compete.

Categories of sport

There have been many attempts to group sports into categories linked to their essential characteristics. The AQA specification uses the following categories of sport, based upon the National Curriculum for PE:

- dance activities
- games activities
- gymnastic activities
- swimming activities and water safety
- athletic activities
- outdoor and adventurous activities.

Games are often sub-divided into a number of sub-groups, the most common of which are given below:

- invasion
- striking and field
- combat
- target
- net sports
- athletic.

We can now prepare a checklist of what constitutes a sport.

- competitive
- selective by ability and excellence
- is serious, requires commitment
- requires physical endeavour
- has organisational stringency – space and time restraints, rules, competitive structure
- involves elements of sportsmanship, team spirit, fair play, etc.

Now we know what sport is we can discuss the benefits it is believed to bring. It is clear that many people believe that 'participating in sport is good for you'. In the UK we spend £262 million (from taxation and National Lottery) providing sporting opportunities. Sport England is tasked with getting more people involved in sport. Schools are encouraged to offer sport opportunities for all pupils (Sportmark and Sportmark Gold). Why do we spend that amount of tax revenue and lottery money on sport? What are the expectations of sport – why is it good for us?

The objectives of sport

Sport is considered to have the potential to achieve a wide range of social and individual developmental objectives. For individuals it can offer opportunities for:

- fulfilling individual potential and talent
- challenging oneself to strive to be as good as you can, discovering personal strengths and weaknesses

Activity

Using these lists find two examples of each of the sport groups and the games sub-groups. Compare with others in your group and compile a master list.

1. Were there any disagreements over how an activity should be categorised?

2. Were there any activities that could have been placed in more than one group?

▦ release of tension and stress

▦ developing health, fitness and skills

▦ achieving success, building self-esteem

▦ learning to accept rules and decisions of others

▦ working with others, leading others

▦ showing determination, perseverance and courage

▦ developing a sense of fair play, consideration for others in the context of competition, winning and losing.

For society at large it can provide opportunities for:

▦ socialisation of individuals, helping them learn the norms of a society

▦ prevention of **anti-social behaviour** by producing worthwhile activities

▦ development of economic benefits to individuals and society through sport related business and business activity

▦ reducing social unrest by diverting people's attention and passions into sport rather than politics – a form of social control

▦ improvement in international relationships – sport acting as an opportunity for recently warring countries to come together

▦ improvement in social morale, the feelgood factor when we win gold medals at the Olympics, or World Cups.

Fig. 10.9 *Building esteem for all*

Fig. 10.10 *Good for society*

Sport can and has produced all of these benefits for individuals and society. That is why schools, youth clubs, local government, national government give time and money, and why in 2006 five million volunteers gave one billion hours to sport.

💡 *Sport has its problems*

It is not a completely positive picture however. Sport has suffered from a number of problems that diminishes its power for social or individual good.

▦ The rise in commercial and monetary rewards in elite professional sport can result in an over-emphasis on winning at all costs.

▓ Media interest in elite sport can mean that sporting contests become more related to entertainment than sport, and the influence of the media through financial pressures can change the nature and structure of sport competition.

▓ Sport, but particularly football, has suffered from problems relating to hooliganism and crowd violence.

▓ Crowd violence on the international sport scene can damage a country's reputation.

▓ Elite sport is waging a constant battle over the use of performance-enhancing drugs.

▓ Younger sport performers' behaviour can be over-influenced by the excesses and bad example of some elite performers.

▓ With the advent of 24-hour sport on cable and satellite and the interest from terrestrial TV there is a danger that people will play sport less but watch sport more.

Most of these problems are associated with elite, commercial, professional sport. The positive impact that sport has on the millions of people who play and perform below the elite level, especially young people, is clearly a positive one.

Sport is believed to have such a positive impact upon the lives of young people that PE has been a compulsory element of the school curriculum since 1944, and there have been a stream of initiatives since 2000 to ensure that children have opportunities for sport outside the curriculum. In the following section we shall examine physical education, its characteristics and its objectives.

Key terms

Physical education: a formalised body of knowledge and experience taught within educational establishments (but see text).

💡 Physical education

So what is **physical education** and why has it been an element of school curriculum since the late nineteenth century? In this section we shall be concentrating on the nature, characteristics and objectives of PE.

Fig. 10.11 *PE – a compulsory part of education. Why is this?*

Characteristics of physical education

If you were to ask a random sample of people 'what is physical education' you would get a wide variety of answers even though for the vast majority of them their knowledge of PE would have been shaped by what they experienced at school or college. Some would say 'it's sport that you do at school' or 'it's about learning the rules of sport'. Others might say 'it's about how to get fit' while a rare few would say 'it's **learning through the physical**'. Whilst all those things are true it is interesting that after some 20 years of the national curriculum there is a very diverse understanding of what PE is.

Rather than attempt to give an all-encompassing definition it would be better to list the characteristics of physical education.

- It is a formal body of knowledge with a clear educational philosophy.
- It is learnt through undertaking physical activity and experiencing physical activity.
- It is concerned with learning fundamental physical/motor skills that may develop into sport or physical recreation-specific skills.
- It involves learning the rules, tactics and etiquette of a diverse range of sports and other physical activities.
- It is a vehicle for developing desired personal and social attitudes and values.
- It enables the appreciation and critical evaluation of movement and skill performances of yourself and others, and how to improve that performance.
- It enables an understanding of **health-related fitness** issues and how to support health maintenance through exercise and physical activity.
- It attempts to develop a lifelong love and engagement with exercise, physical activity or sport.

Some of these require further explanation. For example what do we mean by 'developing desired personal and social attitudes and values'?

In our society, and many others, there are certain values and attitudes that we believe to be essential for living a civilised life and being part of a community. These might include:

- a sense of fair play and keeping to the written and unwritten rules or codes of an activity voluntarily, showing self-control and self-discipline
- acceptance of rules that govern the activity and the authority of those empowered to enforce them or judge actions within an activity – umpires, judges, referees, etc.
- consideration of others – being a good winner and a graceful loser
- being able to work with others, accept and give leadership
- be able to make independent moral judgements based upon personal values even when situations or others pressure you to act differently.

It is worthwhile looking at the objectives for the National Curriculum. In each of the Key Stages pupils should:

- acquire and develop skills
- select and apply skills, tactics and compositional ideas
- evaluate and improve performance
- develop a knowledge and understanding of fitness and health.

Key terms

Learning through the physical: being educated through the use of physical activity.

Health-related fitness: fitness activities that contribute to improvements or maintenance of health.

Activities

1. Compare the objectives and characteristics of PE and sport.

2. Given your knowledge of sport, particularly elite high level sport, are there any conflicts between the objectives of sport and the objectives of PE?

3. Would those conflicts mean that school sport and club sport should be approached in a different way?

During each of the key stages, pupils should be taught about a range of activities – dance, gymnastics, games, water-based activities, athletics, outdoor and adventurous activities.

These National Curriculum objectives mirror many on the list we developed earlier but a significant omission would seem to be any mention of development of attitudes and values.

Physical education is not of course the only physical activity that you may experience in school or college. The diagram below shows the separate yet overlapping areas of physical education, school sport and recreation.

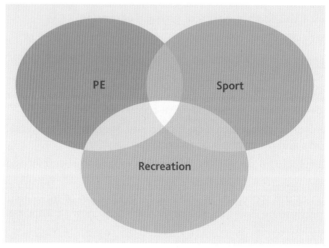

Fig. 10.12 *Venn diagram showing the overlap between PE, sport and recreation*

Activity

Using the diagram in Figure 10.12 determine with a partner examples of each of the three categories.

Notice that the categories overlap.

What occurs in these overlapping areas – can one activity fulfil the objectives of two or more areas?

You may have thought of some of the following:

■ PE
  ■ working with a partner perfecting a gymnastics routine
  ■ learning how to jump shoot in a basketball lesson
■ Recreation
  ■ playing on a basketball court with friends during the lunch break
  ■ watching a school or college match
■ Sport
  ■ playing in an-inter-house or inter-form match at lunchtime
  ■ training for the school/college team.

It should have become clear from your discussion that PE, sport and recreational activities can share many of the objectives of each other. For example, a PE lesson may well involve the playing of a sport for part of the time. It is possible for a PE lesson to be recreative, to recreate oneself. But it is not being done in free time, free from obligations – you have to be there!

Key terms

Extra-curricular activity: a physical activity undertaken in school outside of curriculum time.

Taking part in sport at school commonly takes place as an **extra-curricular activity** – it falls outside curriculum time, being done at lunchtimes, after school, Saturday mornings, etc.

It can be seen that physical education is designed, and has the potential to be, an important and influential part of a young person's education and development. How well that is achieved is of course dependent upon a whole host of factors – school expectations, curriculum time, physical resources for PE, quality of teaching and learning, etc. Governments, since the turn of the twentieth century, have periodically redefined the aims and objectives of PE and expressed concern over the amount of time and resources available for PE.

Recognise when individuals are engaged in these activities

You should now be able to recognise and categorise which activity an individual is engaged in by simple observation.

> Two families are on the beach playing cricket with each person taking a turn at bowling, batting and fielding. Rules are developed as they go along. One of the parents shows the children how to bowl correctly and helps one of the adults with their throwing. Every now and again one of the participants gets a drink or something to eat. During a time when everybody goes for a swim the cricketing adult decides to have some throwing practice. The children also award each other points for successful throwing, catching and bowling.

1) What elements of play, leisure, active leisure/physical recreation, sport or physical education are evident in this situation?

2) Is the experience the same for all of the participants – thinking of the children, the cricketing adult, the parents, etc.?

Physical activity situations can rarely be simply categorised as just one form. There are forms of play here (rule development, lack of seriousness), of leisure (they are on holiday, there is no obligation to play with the child of another person), elements of active leisure and physical recreation. There is what could be considered sport practice going on and even some elements of PE with the children showing good skill.

The overlapping of the forms of physical activity seen in the learning activity scenario leads us into a discussion as to whether or not they are a continuum.

Are these activities interrelated? The physical activity continuum

The interrelationship of the forms of physical activity should now be apparent. The factors that enable us to most readily distinguish between them is their:

- level of organisation
- amount of competition.

By level of organisation we mean the amount of pre-planning an activity requires, the amount of structure and regulation that is involved, the level of involvement by regulatory bodies such as sport national governing bodies and how much an individual's involvement in the activity is controlled by all of these factors.

A **physical activity continuum** based on the level of organisation might look something like Figure 10.13.
This shows that play has a loose structure, is very flexible and is very much controlled by the participants.

| Play | Leisure | Physical rec/active leisure | Outdoor rec/ adventure act | PE | Sport |

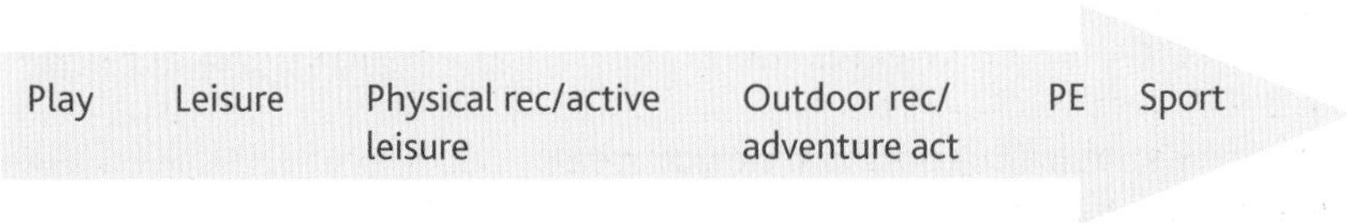

Fig. 10.13 *Physical activity continuum based upon level of organisation*

Liverpool Community College

AQA Examiner's tip

If a scenario is given in an exam, it is likely that it will be predominantly one of the forms of physical activity. Try to think more widely, as it is likely that some of the marks will be given for spotting the characteristics of other forms of physical activity that may be present.

Key terms

Physical activity continuum: the range of physical activities from play to sport, determined by level of competition or level of organisation.

The opposite would be true for sport of course. The position of the other forms of play on such a continuum is open to debate and discussion and it is possible to find examples of any of the activities that alter its place on the continuum but that is not the purpose of such a continuum – merely to show the interrelatedness and what distinguishes them.

Similarly for the continuum shown in Figure 10.14 based upon level of competitiveness:

| Play | Leisure | Outdoor rec/adventure act | Physical rec/active leisure | PE | Sport |

Fig. 10.14 *Physical activity continuum based upon level of competitiveness*

▥ Activity

Recall a children's game you may have played – 'kinger', stuck in the mud', 'catch ball'. Think about and discuss the following:

1 Agree the rules. Play the game.

2 Adapt the play activity for it to be considered active leisure or physical recreation. Adapt it and then do it.

3 What changes would you make to enable it to be played as a sport between groups of children at different schools across the country? Adapt it. Play it.

4 What changes would you make so this inter-school sport could now be played at national and international level?

Again the extremes of the continuum are play and sport. PE has been removed as PE is a structured experience where none or high amounts of competitive activity may be planned to take place. The bunching of physical recreation/active leisure and outdoor and adventurous activities indicates that generally there is no formal competitiveness in adventure activities although sometimes it is described as competing against the challenge of the environment or competing with oneself.

The characteristics of each of the activities, their inherent objectives and their place on the continua will enable you to compare and contrast any one of the forms of physical activity with another.

▥ Understand the benefits of participating in physical activity

The specification requires you to understand the benefits that each of the forms of physical activity may bring to either individuals or to wider society. Many of the perceived benefits have been discussed when looking at the objectives of each of the forms of activity so this section will focus on the more general benefits to either individuals or wider society.

Benefits to individuals

Individuals who participate in physical activity may gain many benefits:

▥ reduction in stress, opportunities to step outside one's obligations and work

▥ improvement in fitness and health

▥ development of social relationships, an understanding of social conventions and rules, socialisation

▥ Activity

Return to the pictures used at the start of the chapter for the first learning activity. Decide which order the pictures would appear on either of the continua.

- opportunities for socialising (making and meeting friends)
- being challenged, stretched, opportunities for self-development, for acting creatively
- opportunities for self-fulfilment and the building of self-esteem
- developing team working skills and team leadership
- learning about the natural environment.

Benefits to wider society

Any benefit to individuals represents a benefit to wider society. Government, both local and national, consider it the state's responsibility to ensure that individuals are able to benefit from participation in physical activity and active leisure. This is achieved through legislation – laws that ensure that workers and employees can only have reasonable work demands made upon them, with time left over for recreation and leisure and through the provision of resources derived from local and national taxation.

Given this expenditure and the impact of legislation you would expect there to be clear benefits to society from the provision and subsequent uses of recreation time and resources and these are summarised below.

- Improvements in mental and physical health, reduce the burden on the national health service and make for a healthier society and enhanced feelings of wellbeing.
- The spending on leisure and recreation creates other economic activity which enhances employment opportunities and national wealth.
- Opportunities for **personal development** lead to the development of excellence and the creation of role models within society.
- The existence of national role models, successful individuals and teams, enhances feelings of national self-esteem.
- The shop window effect – successful high level performers act as advertisements for the nation, with possible economic benefits.
- It is hoped that enhanced opportunities for physical activity, particularly in less advantaged communities, will reduce levels of anti-social behaviour and crime, especially amongst the young.

Many of these benefits can be demonstrated empirically – through economic data for example, or from simple observations or qualitative research in what people feel. Some benefits though are harder to prove and seem to be based upon belief rather than evidence. Both national and local governments have policies that are designed to increase the level of opportunity for participation in physical activity for young people in disadvantaged areas and communities with the objective of reducing youth crime and anti-social behaviour.

However recent research has concluded:

> The reviews suggests that there are some areas for which there is a considerable amount of evidence in favour of a positive relationship with participation in this activities (such as physical and mental health), and others for which rigorous research remains necessary (such as cognitive and academic development, crime reduction, truancy and disaffection).

R Bailey, 'Evaluating the relationship between physical education, sport and social inclusion', Education Review, Feb 2005

 Examiner's tip

Be sure not to confuse socialisation – learning the rules and conventions of a society, and socialising – enjoying time with friends and family.

Activity

Research how much your local council spends on leisure and recreation each year, and the plans they have for future developments. You will probably find this data in public documents on their website, or you may also find it useful to talk to your local leisure and sport development unit.

Key terms

Personal development: to progress as an individual, using one's abilities more effectively.

It has also been reported that schools which have introduced a higher level of sport and physical education are experiencing an improvement in examination results and a reduction in truancy and other poor behaviour. Unfortunately no research has yet established why this is the case and it is too early to state that there is a causal link between those two factors.

The objectives of this chapter have been to introduce you to the various forms of physical activity, consider their characteristics and objectives, how they are similar and how they differ. You should also now be able to apply a level of critical awareness to the many and varied social and educational policies and projects linked to physical activity and the benefits they are believed to bring.

✔ *You should now be able to:*

- identify and describe the different types of physical activities and be able to recognise when individuals are engaged in a specific activity

- describe the objectives of each of the different types of physical activity and how these objectives are linked to the nature of the activity

- show an understanding of the different experiences that individuals gain from participating in physical activities and how these can be shared or experienced by the wider community

- discuss, debate and justify the provision of physical activity opportunities on the basis of the benefits received by individuals and wider society.

1   A parent and a child are using two badminton rackets and a shuttlecock in their back garden.

    (a)   Discuss the forms of physical activity they are engaged in. *(3 marks)*

    (b)   What are they gaining from engaging in this activity? *(3 marks)*

2   Schools are one place in which young people can participate in physical activity.

    (a)   Schools today are being asked to provide at least two hours of PE per week for every pupil and a further three hours of extra-curricular sport. Why is the Government asking schools to do this? *(3 marks)*

    (b)   Adventure activities carry an element of risk. Is it justifiable to include adventure activities in the school curriculum? *(3 marks)*

3   Many people take part in physical recreation as a form of leisure activity.

    (a)   Define the term 'leisure'. *(2 marks)*

    (b)   What do you understand by the term 'physical recreation'? Comment on its benefit to individuals. *(4 marks)*

4   Many people engage in sport at both school and club level.

    (a)   Discuss the similarities or differences in characteristics and objectives between school and club sport. *(4 marks)*

    (b)   Explain why outdoor recreational activities, such as cycling and rambling, are considered 'lifetime activities' compared with many team sports in today's society. *(2 marks)*

Leisure provision

Link

This inequality of provision is studied in more depth in Chapter 13 – Equal opportunities (page 186).

In Chapter 10 – Concepts and definitions (page 123) we examined the different forms of activity in which individuals could participate. Many activities require groups of individuals to cooperate together or require the use of specific facilities. The provision of those opportunities is crucial to us becoming a more active nation.

Over the last 100 years a tripartite system of provision has developed, with a combination of opportunities provided by local or national government, opportunities that come from a commercial leisure industry and finally opportunities provided by individuals voluntarily coming together to form clubs, teams and the infrastructure of managers, officials and coaches, etc. for the benefit of each other.

Although such a diversity of provision has produced a very wide range of opportunities it is the case that the provision is uneven and not everybody has equal access to physical activity opportunities. It has become a matter of national concern that certain individuals or communities are relatively poorly provided for and are unable to gain the benefits of regular physical activity.

In Chapters 1– Improving fitness and health (page 2) and 10 – Concepts and definitions (page 123) you learnt about the individual and social benefits that regular participation in physical activity can bring. It is not reasonable therefore that certain members of our community are unable to benefit due to a lack of provision and all governments of recent times have introduced a range of policies and objectives to reduce inequalities in provision. From the days of 'Sport for All' in the 1960s to the current 'National Framework for Sport' a huge amount of money, time and energy has been expended in raising levels of active participation.

In this chapter we shall be looking at the characteristics of each of the three sectors – public, private and voluntary and their objectives. Each of the three sectors is quite distinctive and each plays a vital role in the provision of physical activity opportunities. We have developed this tripartite approach because each form of provision has its advantages and disadvantages and if opportunities were only available from one of the sectors then we would not have the range of opportunity that we currently enjoy. We shall also be studying how efficiently the public and private sectors provide opportunities and what steps have been taken to ensure that money provided from the Lottery and the Government is used effectively.

We saw in Chapter 10 – Concepts and definitions (page 123) that participation in physical activity varies enormously from the youngster playing with their parents, to Sunday morning hockey leagues, those out rambling and those playing elite level sport either on an amateur or professional basis. Due to the way that sport and recreation had developed during the twentieth century, providing for such diverse levels was the responsibility of a whole range of bodies – sport national governing bodies, national sports councils of England, Scotland, Northern Ireland and Wales, representative organisations such as the CCPR, professional clubs. This led to a lack of clarity as to who was responsible for what, much duplication of effort and subsequent wastage of resources. In recent years the Government has separated responsibility for the provision of grass roots opportunities for all from the responsibility for the development of high level performers. At AS level you are mostly concerned with looking at how grass roots opportunities are provided so we shall be examining closely the role of Sport England.

This is an important chapter as exam questions frequently ask you to describe and discuss the provision of physical activity opportunities. It is also an area where you can make use of examples local to you, or use your own experience to help you answer exam questions.

💡 Characteristics and goals of each of the sectors

The three sectors – private, public and voluntary – share some characteristics, objectives and goals. All three are concerned with the provision of physical activity opportunities to individuals or groups of people, all three hold the belief that physical activity is worthwhile and is beneficial to the individuals they serve. But once we move beyond those basic similarities we will see that they are quite different in their approach, although it is true to say that the public and the private sectors are more similar now then they would have been 25 years ago.

Public sector

In the United Kingdom the term **public sector** means any services that are provided from taxation – local and national or through some other means of government or public support such as the Lottery. Although national government provides funds from central taxation, either distributed directly as local authority grants, or via Sport England (along with Lottery funding), local authorities (your local council) have the responsibility for building and maintaining physical recreation and sport facilities for their local community. How and where facilities are developed is decided after estimation is made of the level of **public good**. They are also charged with ensuring that the facilities they provide are managed effectively, although they may not have responsibility for day-to-day management (see section on Best Value). In general this means that the capital funding for the building of facilities, such as sports centres, is provided from public funds (taxation or Lottery) and the users are charged when they use them. Some user groups are subsidised, in that they may pay a lower charge, or have free access depending upon their circumstances. Such groups might include those who are unemployed, single mothers, those in receipt of a pension, those with a disability, under 16s, those who receive family credit, etc.

The range of facilities provided within the public sector is extremely wide:

▦ large multi-sport centres
▦ swimming pools
▦ sport pitches
▦ parks
▦ adventure playgrounds
▦ leisure pools
▦ nature trails
▦ skateboard parks
▦ local sports halls.

▦ Key terms

Public sector: services that are provided by national or local government, funded from taxation, provided and managed for the good of the local community.

Public good: an action by national or local government that is deemed to meet the needs of the national or local community.

Activity

Research your local authority leisure services department and compile a structure diagram.

Key terms

Educational sector provision: facilities and opportunities that are provided via school facilities.

Dual use: a school sport and physical recreation facility that is used by the school during the day for curricular and extra-curricular use, and by the local community outside those times.

Joint use: an extension of dual use, where a sport and physical recreation facility is planned and built to be used by a school and the local community.

AQA Examiner's tip

Remember that you can (and should!) make use of local examples within your examination answers.

Activities

1. Make a list of a range of examples of physical recreation and sport facilities that are provided by the public sector in your area.

2. Research the leisure and recreation plan for your local authority. This information can usually be found on your local authority website.

Local authorities attempt to make provision for everybody within the local community. Most councils will have a leisure services department and sport development officer and they will be responsible for ensuring that the council's recreation and leisure development plan becomes a reality.

Recreation and leisure development plans normally include the following:

- development of new facilities
- refurbishment of old facilities
- targeting under-represented groups in terms of participation (see sports equity)
- where recreation and leisure provision and opportunity can make contributions to improvements in community health.

Fig. 11.1 *Public provision for the local community*

Provision by schools

Opportunities that are provided by the **education sector** are an increasingly important element of public sector provision. Schools will often have excellent sport facilities which are used for curriculum physical education and extra-curricular sport. In many areas a **dual use** agreement is in place where the local community makes use of these facilities in the evenings, weekends and during school holidays. This often has the benefit of improving the facilities available to the school but can cause problems when local community use impinges on school use, particularly if the school is extending or developing their evening extra-curricular provision.

Joint use is an extension of dual use where the facility is planned in the first instance to be a resource shared by the school and the local community, and it is financed from both the education and leisure budgets. This results in schools getting a more extensive and well-equipped sport and physical recreation facility.

In summary the characteristics of public sector provision would be:

- Capital funding for building and maintenance is provided by national and local taxation, and the Lottery.
- Facilities are to financially break-even, not to make a profit.
- Local authority will have a sport and leisure development plan, paying particular attention to encouraging under-represented groups to participate more.
- Local community pays for entrance and use.
- Use is subsidised for less well–off groups within the local community.

- Management policies are set by local authority to ensure that facilities and services are managed for the good of the community.
- Day-to-day management of facilities may be by a private sector company but they must adhere to community provision constraints within the contract.
- There is a range of methods of provision including joint use and dual use.

Private sector

The **private sector** consists of primarily commercial companies who provide physical recreation and sport opportunities and facilities as a business venture, and for profit. This is a large and growing sector and provides very many employment opportunities as well as adding to the country's economic activity. Private enterprise now provides opportunities for the following:

- squash and tennis
- fitness and conditioning
- outdoor and adventurous activities
- children's play facilities
- health and spa facilities
- golf.

Over the last twenty years there has been a rapid expansion in the private sector. This is due to increasing national wealth, increased awareness of the exercise and health link (See Chapter 1 – Improving fitness and health, page 2). The primary purpose of the private sector is to make a profit and although they provide facilities of a very high quality, this is reflected in the admission and membership charges. There is a fear that the private sector will cherry pick the best recreational opportunities and users leaving the public sector to provide the more expensive facilities such as large swimming pools for the less well-off members of society.

Fig. 11.2 *Should all physical recreation opportunities be provided by the private sector?*

The other phenomenon that has changed the relationship between the private and public sectors has been the Government's insistence that local councils manage their leisure and recreation facilities efficiently and

Key terms

Private sector: active leisure and recreation facilities and services provided as a commercial venture, where the prime objective is making a financial profit.

effectively. This began in the early 1990s with the policy of 'Compulsory Competitive Tendering', through to the current 'Best Value' system, and the use of Private Finance Initiatives (PFIs). The effect of all of these policies was to introduce to the public sector the standards of management and service evident in the private sector. Private sector providers have to view their users as customers, and if they do not provide a high enough level of service they will not return and profits will fall. This whole process is covered in more depth in the section on 'Best Value'.

The characteristics of the private sector are:

- Their foremost objective is to make a profit.
- They provide high quality facilities.
- Their membership and admission charges are higher than the public sector.
- They target high value goods and services for better-off members of the community.
- They do not have a public service commitment or remit.

Voluntary sector

The voluntary sector is the biggest sector in terms of the range and amount of provision that is made. The voluntary sector comprises all the opportunities for sport and recreation that are provided by people on a voluntary basis for themselves or for others. It includes all the sports and clubs and teams where the participants and the administrators either pay to play for the team through subscriptions and match fees, or give up their time to be coaches, fixtures secretaries, bar managers, grounds staff, referees and umpires, kit washers, team bus drivers, etc. For every professional club or team there are hundreds of amateur ones. For every paid professional player there are thousands of players who pay to play.

It is estimated by Sport England that over five million people volunteered one billion hours to sport in 2006 and it is their ambition to see this figure rise.

What kinds of physical activity are provided through the voluntary sector?

- sports clubs and teams – almost any sport you can think of
- countryside activities via groups such as the Ramblers Association and Community Service Volunteers who provide opportunities for walking and environmental conservation work
- local jogging, recreational cycling or fitness groups.

The amount of resources such groups require will depend upon the nature of their activity. Sports teams will need a playing facility, changing rooms, kit, match and training equipment, etc. Rambling groups require little more than an individual willing to pick a location, decide a time and inform others.

How does the voluntary sector find the resources to run its activities?

- grants from local authorities, councils, parish councils, etc. (remember that local councils get their funding from government grants and local taxes)
- grants from the National Lottery – these will either be Awards for All (up to £10,000) direct from the Lottery or Community Investment Fund (above £10,000) from Sport England

- annual subscriptions and match fees from participants
- fund raising activities by individual clubs or teams
- income from social activities, club bar, etc.

Fig. 11.3 *The National Lottery has provided £2.2 billion for sport and physical recreation since 1996 including the 2004 Track Cycling World Cup*

Local sports clubs will either own their own facility or will hire from local authorities, councils and parish councils. All the other roles that are required in a club will be filled by volunteers.

In sports where there is a professional layer there will be clubs who have ambitions to move up the league or the sport's competitive structure and they introduce some paid roles. They may for example employ a professional coach, a professional business manager to raise money for the club, and some or all of the players will move onto professional contracts. It is quite possible that this club will also have purely amateur teams and a whole range of individuals still in voluntary roles.

The characteristics of the voluntary sector would be:

- It operates on a not-for-profit basis.
- Players and participants pay to play through match fees or subscriptions.
- The support roles within a team or club are filled by volunteers.
- Clubs and teams receive grant aid support from the National Lottery, Sport England and their National Governing Body.
- Clubs and teams will raise funds through social activities, raffles, etc.
- Any surplus from income generation will be retained within the club to enhance facilities or provide more or better services for members.
- The sector encompasses the whole range of sporting and physical recreation activities.

▦ Equality of opportunity – the advantages and disadvantages of each of the sectors

The reason that we have our tripartite system of public, private and voluntary is that not one sector can provide the necessary or appropriate facilities to satisfy the needs and demands of all those that wish to participate in sport and physical recreation. It has long been government policy to increase the number of people that regularly participate in sport and physical recreation and you will recall from Chapter 10 – Concepts and definitions (page 123) that this is for three reasons – improvement in physical and mental health, reducing anti-social behaviour, improvements in individual and community self-esteem. If government policy is to be met it is vital therefore that there is an equality of opportunity for all groups and individuals in society.

Inequality of opportunity exists because:

- Some local areas are poorly provided for in terms of facilities because of local economic circumstances.
- Some individuals do not have the personal resources to be able to participate.
- Not everybody is aware of the benefits of regular participation in sport or physical recreation, nor of the opportunities available to them.
- There may be an element of social exclusion or discrimination and individuals feel unable or are discouraged from joining local clubs.

In this section we shall be considering how well each of the three sectors is able to support an objective of sport and recreation for all.

Private sector

The private sector exists under a business imperative. Each facility has to attract enough paying customers to make a profit. This means that the private sector will react quickly to fulfil a demand, and it can move more quickly than the public sector where the proposal, planning and building phase takes longer. It means that the private sector can provide opportunities flexibly and rapidly. For example there has been an upsurge of interest in individual health and fitness. There was a rapid response, firstly by people seeing an opportunity to become private fitness trainers, or by large companies building health and fitness centres. If there is a rapid increase in interest in a sport then the private sector can react as it did with squash in the 1980s by quickly building squash clubs.

Can we say though that this is providing equality of opportunity? Privately run facilities are usually of a very high quality and numbers are restricted to ensure that members can have the use of the facility without feeling crowded out. This all comes at a cost and membership and subscription fees are high and therefore a disincentive to those on lower incomes. It is also the case that many private facilities may have a degree of social exclusivity and some individuals may feel that this is not a club for them, or indeed may be actively discriminated against.

The advantages and disadvantages of the private sector in terms of equality of provision may be summarised as below:

Advantages

- It can react quickly to meet a demand as demonstrated by market research or generated by government policy.
- The private sector can meet individual needs.
- The private sector can restrict membership so that all those that use a facility do so unhindered by too many other people being there at the same time.

Link

You will be studying the topic of equality of opportunity in a more detailed way in Chapter 13 – Equal opportunities (page 186).

Disadvantages

- Costs of joining the club or facility and fees for using the facility are relatively high and therefore out of the reach of those with insufficient income.
- A restriction on numbers will mean that some people are unable to join – gold clubs and tennis clubs frequently have long waiting lists.
- There can be a degree of social exclusivity or actual discrimination against certain groups in society. Whilst actual discrimination would be illegal it is quite possible for private clubs to have rules, or hidden criteria to maintain social exclusivity.
- A sport may suffer from an image of exclusivity and therefore people may not wish to join or participate – tennis in the UK would be a good example of this.

It should be clear therefore that although the private sector can meet a need and a demand quickly and with a high quality of provision it can never provide equality of opportunity for all. For that we must look to public and voluntary sectors.

Voluntary sector

As we have seen earlier the **voluntary sector** is huge both in its diversity and in its sheer numbers. It can range from large clubs with many teams, perhaps owning their own facilities to small groups of enthusiasts out for a Sunday morning ramble. Every single sport or physical recreation activity will have some provision made by the voluntary sector. Indeed there are many activities where almost all the provision is made by the voluntary sector. Can we therefore assume that the voluntary sector is able to provide for all and that it can genuinely provide equality of opportunity?

Like so many questions that may be raised in the socio-cultural elements of this subject the answer is 'yes . . . but'.

The voluntary sector is dependent upon a range of factors before it can provide an opportunity to participate. There must of course be individuals prepared to undertake the many and varied jobs that have to be done to so that others can participate. Somebody has to book the fixtures or location, arrange transport, inform those that are participating of the arrangements, sort out the playing facility, refreshments, kit if required and so on. There needs to be financial support from those bodies able to give grants – National Lottery, Sport England, local councils, possibly even a local benefactor from the business community. There may not be a playing facility available at this stage and will need to be provided for.

The principal problem with thinking that the voluntary sector can provide equality for all is the fact that it is voluntary. If some provision does not exist, if there is not an opportunity available then you cannot plan for or make the voluntary sector provide that opportunity. It is possible to suggest, ask or support but the provision cannot be guaranteed. In terms of equality of opportunity therefore the voluntary sector has the following advantages and disadvantages:

Key terms

Voluntary sector: the provision of active leisure, recreation and sport opportunities by individuals without receiving payment. The provision is made by the members for the members.

Activities

1 Write a letter to your local leisure services department asking for a grant for your new club/activity/group. Justify why they should consider giving you taxpayers' money – in essence what is the 'public good' that is being provided?

2 Imagine that you have just moved to a new town or area. You have an enthusiasm for an activity and cannot find anywhere in the locality where you can engage in that activity. You decide to set up the opportunity for yourself and others. How do you do it? As a group decide upon an activity (try and avoid the obvious ones!) and then think of:

a How you find others who already share your interest?

b How do you get others to know about your activity and want to come and try it?

c How do you determine what physical resources you need?

d How do you get those resources? Bear in mind that no authority or body hands out hard cash without a clear rationale.

e What needs to be done before you can actually participate in that first opportunity, and who needs to do it?

3 Prepare bullet points on each of the above as a PowerPoint. presentation.

Advantages

▥ As it is based upon the enthusiasm of individuals, a whole range of activities, at all kinds of levels, is already available.

▥ If an opportunity is lacking then one or more persons, with enthusiasm and drive can provide that opportunity.

▥ The voluntary sector exists for the benefit of the people who choose to become involved and support it though their labours or their money costs are kept low, so there is rarely an economic disincentive for most people.

▥ There is a lot of financial support for the sector from local and national government, and often the business community through local sponsorship.

Disadvantages

▥ The sector is unplanned and relatively uncontrolled. People can be encouraged and supported in organising activities for others but it cannot be demanded.

▥ It does not have an equal opportunities remit – the sector does not have a responsibility for provision.

▥ Continuity cannot be guaranteed. It only takes the enthusiast who has been the stalwart of the club to move away and the club collapses.

▥ Financial support from national and local bodies cannot be guaranteed, and if there is a change in economic climate then grants may be reduced.

▥ It can still be socially exclusive.

In summary, whilst the voluntary sector does provide a huge range of opportunities it does not have an equal opportunities remit. If we are serious in our belief that participation in sport and physical recreation is valuable for all members of the community then we need to look to the public sector to provide that equality of provision that is essential for that belief to become a reality.

Public sector

As we have already seen, the public sector has a responsibility to act in the 'public good'. Whether this is at national or local level the use of resources must meet a public good criteria. It has been national and therefore local policy that participation in sport, physical recreation and active leisure is good for individuals and good for communities. It must therefore be the responsibility of national and local government to provide equality of opportunity.

Each year national government will determine how much money will be allocated in the national budget to spend on sport, active leisure and physical recreation (alongside the arts and other leisure activities). This money is then allocated via Sport England for both national and local projects. We shall be looking at the role of Sport England later.

The government also sets a local authority grant which is added to the money that is collected via local taxation. Each local authority then decides how much of that budget is allocated to local provision for physical recreation, active leisure and sport. Local authorities do not have a completely free hand as there will be national polices they will be responsible for implementing at local level. Local authority development plans are driven by two prime objectives – 'public good' and 'equality of opportunity'. Examples of the development objectives in relation to sport and active leisure are:

- Improve participation by under-represented groups.
- Improve access to parks and open spaces.
- Extend the number of people volunteering to help young people participate in sport.
- Increase the range of summer holiday sport and recreation schemes for young people.

They may also have broader objectives linked to the beneficial effects of sport and active leisure:

- improvements in local community health through a more active population;
- reduction in youth crime linked to greater provision of summer holiday activity programmes.

The advantages and disadvantages that the public sector has in ensuring equality of opportunity may be summarised as:

Advantages

- The public sector has an underpinning requirement to act in the public good for the national and local community. It cannot be in the public good for some members of the community to have a reduced or poor access to sport and physical recreation facilities.
- The public sector has resources allocated from local and national taxation for this purpose.
- The public sector is not driven by the need to make a commercial profit – it can engage in non-profit making or indeed loss-making activities if these are thought to be in the public or community interest.

Disadvantages

- The funds for capital projects or improvements to services are limited by national and local taxation policies and may be insufficient to provide sufficient or good quality facilities.
- Local authorities in economically disadvantaged areas have less money to spend on recreational facilities.
- Local authorities do not have the same financial freedom as the private sector to borrow money to invest in facilities for the future.

Local authorities have provided sport and physical recreation opportunities for many years. About 20 years ago concerns were raised about how effectively local authorities were using their resources. To encourage a more effective use of money, raise the quality of facilities and to improve customer services, local authority facilities were audited more and opened up to competition with the private sector. Private sector companies were invited to bid for the right to manage local authority facilities. The private sector bidder had to meet certain public benefit requirements such as having cheaper entrance charges for less advantaged groups in the local community, and the facilities were still owned by the local authority.

💡 'Best value' – improving the public sector

In 1980s the '**Compulsory Competitive Tendering**' policy was introduced. This compelled local authorities to ask companies in the

Activity

Research your own local authority development plan and identify:

- Objectives linked to improvements in physical resources.
- Objectives linked to participation.
- Objectives linked to broader social objectives – health, behaviour, etc.

Key terms

Compulsory Competitive Tendering (CCT): a system whereby local councils must invite private sector companies to bid for the right to manage a local authority leisure facility.

Best Value: a system of national performance indicators that show the quality of active leisure and physical recreation provision provided by your local council.

▓ Activity

Research the Best Value criteria and prepare a mind map to summarise them.

▓ Activity

Visit and then make a comparison of the quality of provision between a local public sector facility and a private sector facility. Research by question and answer session with the centre manager the effects of Best Value inspection and grading system.

On return prepare a PowerPoint presentation – three slides: who owns and manages the centre, what are its objectives and how they evaluate provision to meet Best Value criteria.

private sector to make a bid to run local authority leisure facilities such as leisure centres in competition with local authority leisure services departments. This forced local authorities to look at how well they were using their facilities, the kind of service they were providing for the local community and whether they were able to run their facilities within budget guidelines. Many local authority leisure departments made an in-house bid to manage their facilities in competition with private sector companies and were successful. There is no doubt that the Compulsory Competitive Tendering (CCT) process improved the quality of local authority provision. Concerns were raised that private sector companies would not pay enough attention to the less profitable areas where there was a public benefit requirement because of their need to make a profit but generally these fears proved to be groundless.

CCT was replaced in 2000 by a system known as **Best Value**.

Best Value is a government regime aimed at improving the quality of local government services including leisure and recreation. The emphasis is on continuous improvement. If a council has improved its performance from poor to average it will get a better report than a council whose performance has stayed at average. The system works around a set of Best Value Performance Indicators and council leisure services are judged on a range of criteria including customer satisfaction.

Councils are regularly inspected and are required to apply a system known as the four Cs to all of their leisure and recreation services. The four Cs are: challenge, consult, compare and compete.

▓ Challenge – the council has to ask themselves whether they are doing as well as they can, compared to the best councils.

▓ Consult – they must consult with local communities and monitor customer satisfaction.

▓ Compare – councils have to compare their services against other councils, and the private and voluntary sectors. They also have to show how well they are doing against national Best Value performance indicators, and have an improvement plan. If performance does not improve the Government has the power to switch control of a service away from council control.

▓ Compete – councils have to show that in-house services are the best way of managing their leisure and recreation provision by subjecting them to external competition (like CCT). If in-house services are more expensive councils may have to switch management of some or all of their active leisure and recreation to a private firm or the voluntary sector.

Many councils disliked the Compulsory Competitive Tendering system and have reservations about the Best Value system of monitoring. There is no doubt that since 1985 the quality of local authority provided active leisure, physical recreation and sport provision has improved significantly. It is also the case that the relationship between the public and the private sector has become closer. Local authority leisure managers are more conscious of the need to provide value for money, to get local people to keep returning to their facilities by providing a high quality experience, and if possible generate a surplus to be ploughed back into maintenance or improvements to the facility.

We have been focussing on the role played by local councils and authorities as public sector providers. Local authority resources are partly determined by the local taxes that they collect. In areas of lower socio-

Fig. 11.4 *The relationship between the public, private and voluntary sectors*

economic level less revenue is collected and therefore fewer facilities may be provided. It is also less likely that private sector providers will be interested in investing in such an area and so we must now consider the impact of the role played by national government. National government policy for the provision of sport and recreation opportunities is delivered through the Department of Culture, Media and Sport and more specifically Sport England and the Sports Councils for Northern Ireland, Scotland and Wales.

The role of National Government

The Department for Culture, Media and Sport is the government department responsible for policy and funding for all sport, physical recreation and active leisure. It has a wide-ranging remit 'from the playground to the podium'; from supporting talented performers to ensuring that there is equality of provision for all. The national Sports Councils and UK Sport are primarily responsible for putting DCMS policy into practice and allocating funding.

At AS level we are primarily concerned with the role of **Sport England**. The original Sports Council was established in 1965 and received its charter in 1972 alongside the Sports Councils for Wales, N. Ireland and Scotland with an overarching GB Sports Council.

In 1972 the English Sports Council's main objectives were to:

▪ Increase participation in sport and physical recreation.

▪ Raise standards of performance.

▪ Increase the quality and quantity of sports facilities.

▪ Act as an information centre for sport and physical recreation.

The National Lottery came into being in 1994 and National Sports Councils were responsible for the distribution of the sports component of the 'Good Causes' fund, along with GB Sport Council.

In 1996 the GB Sports Council was transformed into the United Kingdom Sports Council (known as UK Sport). Its objectives at that time were to:

▪ Support winning athletes.

▪ Stage world-class events in world-class style.

AQA Examiner's tip

Although the specification focuses on the role of Sport England it is recommended that students in Northern Ireland and Wales research the work of their own Sports Councils and use those as their examples in examination answers.

Key terms

Sport England: government agency responsible for advising, investing in and promoting community sport.

Activity

Using the DCMS website prepare a mind map of the main policies and areas of interest of the DCMS in relation to sport. Discuss with your group how many of those policies and objectives have been reflected in your own local council leisure department plans or objectives.

■ Promote ethically fair and drug-free sport.

■ Represent the UK on the international stage in terms of sporting relationships and policies.

Since the mid-1990s the division of responsibilities between Sport England, the other national sports councils and UK Sport in terms of developing grass roots participation in sport and the development of elite performers was complex and unclear. Therefore in 2006 the Government through the DCMS redefined the roles of Sport England and UK Sport.

UK Sport's role is now focused on development of elite performers and sports excellence, whilst still retaining the UK-wide role it was originally given in 1996. Sport England is now primarily focused on developing grass roots participation.

Sport England's role

Sport England's objectives are now to advise, invest in and promote community sport to create an active nation.

Its focus is to sustain and increase participation in a wide range of community sport including fitness activities such as aerobics and gym-based work, newer activities such as skateboarding; and traditional team sports such as rugby, hockey and netball. The ways in which individuals might participate in sport are identified by Sport England as 'sports pathways'. Sport England develops these sports pathways by promoting, advising and investing in the following:

■ community sports activities

■ sports clubs

■ coaching and officiating

■ player pathways

■ volunteers

■ sports facilities.

Sport England works in partnership with national governing bodies of sport (NGBs), Sport England's regional sports boards (RSBs), county sports partnerships (CSPs), community sports networks (CSNs) and of course all those involved in the voluntary sector.

Two of the most significant partnerships are with the Youth Sports Trust and UK Sport. Between them they cover the range from what happens in schools to the development of an elite gold medal winning performer. The Youth Sport Trust (YST) is primarily responsible for improving the quality and quantity of school sport. Sport England is responsible for participation at the grass roots level in community sport and UK Sport is responsible for elite sport and world-class events.

Sport England works alongside the YST from the ages of 14 to 16 to help in the transition from school sport to community sport at the age of 16. To help develop the future elite Sport England is working with sport NGBs to help them develop effective pathways that take talented athletes from club to UK Sport's World Class Performance Programmes.

Sport England's own research, along with other government analyses of participation has enabled a much more detailed understanding of under-participation. It is clear that certain groups within society are under-represented in terms of participation. Sport England has formed an alliance known as the **Sporting Equity** Alliance, which brings together the Women's Sport Foundation, English Federation of Disability Sport

Link

You will look at the role of the Youth Sports Trust in more detail in Chapter 12 – National Curriculum PE and school sport (page 164).

Key terms

Sporting Equity: a policy designed to ensure that everybody, regardless of ethnicity, gender, disability, age or social background has an equal opportunity to participate in sport and to fulfil their potential.

and Sporting Equals (an organisation dedicated to achieving racial equality in sport) to address those issues.

The structure of Sport England

Sport England has a central executive based in London which looks after relationships with government policy development and provides human resources, legal and ICT services for the regions. Sport England has nine regions which are responsible for providing regional advice and allocating funding based on regional plans. Each region is run by a regional director who is guided by a regional sports board (RSB). Regional investment is undertaken via the Community Investment Fund (CIF). The Regional Sports Boards meet several times a year to assess CIF grant applications against criteria laid down in each region's regional sports plan.

Sport England's funding

The money that is used to develop sports participation comes from two sources – the Government and the National Lottery. Government funding is known as '**exchequer funding**' and between 1994 and 2006 Sport England received £550 million exchequer funding. Since the inception of the National Lottery, Sport England has invested £2.2 billion **lottery funding** into community sport. Sport England works with a range of other bodies including the Women's Sports Foundation, English Cricket Board, has funded or part funded some large national projects such as Wembley Stadium and provides funds to sport national governing bodies to help them invest in grass roots sport and provide the routes to the elite level where they are then supported by UK Sport.

The National Sports Foundation exists to encourage private finance into local community sports facilities. It is attempting to attract investment into three key priority areas:

- 2012 Kids – getting more children and young people playing sport
- Women into Sport – involving more women in playing sport
- Fit for Sport – investment in clubs, coaches and volunteers in local communities.

Sport England's policies

Sport England has developed a wide range of policies and activities to help it fulfil its primary objective of getting more people in England involved in sport. These are often national policies designed to be implemented at local level. In 2004 Sport England published the 'National Framework for Sport' with the objective of making England, by 2020, the most active and successful sporting nation in the world. The three main objectives were:

- making England active – increasing community participation
- making England successful – building on the success of the England rugby team in the 2003 World Cup
- backing the bid for the 2012 Olympic and Paralympic Games to help develop the sporting infrastructure.

Sport England links to other national policies by showing how sport can contribute to general social policy. The report 'Sport Playing its Part' describes how sport can play a role in urban renewal, improvements to community physical and mental wellbeing and a reduction in crime.

Link

In Chapter 13 – Equal opportunities (page 186) you will study issues of sports equity and under-representation in more detail.

Key terms

Exchequer funding: funding that comes directly from central government, from national taxation.

Lottery funding: grants that come from the National Lottery's good causes fund.

Activity

Research your regional sports plan and prepare a one-page summary including a mind map to show the principal objectives and methods for achieving them.

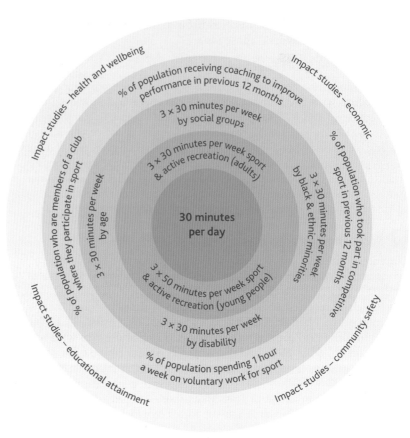

Fig. 11.5 *National Framework for Sport – the bullseye targets*

Sport England also carries out extensive research to establish how many people are regularly involved in sport and also to monitor how effectively their policies are working. For example the 'Taking Part Survey' looks at levels of participation on an annual basis and through the use of 27,000 questionnaires.

The following are some examples of these policies and activities. You should check on the Sport England website for their current policies and activities as they will change over time.

- *Promoting Sport Toolkit* – a collection of simple-to-use tools to help local communities and sports bodies promote sport and active recreation to the public.
- *Active Places* – a database on the Sport England website which gives details of sports clubs, ways to get into active leisure or physical recreation in an individual's region (www.activeplaces.com).
- *Community Investment Fund* – grants over £10,000 for projects included within a regional development plan. Sometimes involving Partnership Funding where other contributors (a sports club, local council, private sponsor, etc.) contribute up to a 2:1 ratio.
- *National Sports Foundation* – responsible for getting private investment into grass roots sport in England.
- *Community Club Development Programme* – helps sport national governing bodies to develop sport clubs in the community. Sport England operates this programme in collaboration with the

Department for Culture, Media and Sport, and National Governing Bodies of Sport (NGBs).

▥ *Step Into Sport (SIS)* – focuses on young people aged 14–19 years and aims to encourage them to undertake an involvement in sports leadership and volunteering that will continue into later life. It is linked to the PE and School Sports Club Links (PESSCL).

▥ *PE and School Sport Club Links (PESSCL)* – this initiative forms part of the government programme to provide each child with a minimum of five hours per week high quality PE or extra-curricular sport each week for 5–16 year olds, and three hours for 16–19 year olds. Step into Sport and Club links are linked to this programme.

▥ *Active Communities Development Fund (ACDF)* – grants of £500 to £5,000 to local communities for projects designed to encourage people to be more active.

▥ *Sport Action Zones (SAZ)* – launched in 2000 in order to combat low levels of participation in sport in deprived communities. By 2007 12 Sport Action Zones had been created.

▥ *Community Sports Coach Scheme (CSCS)* – designed to provide the resources to fund coach education courses to people wishing to get involved in sport from local communities. It is partially funded by the Department for Culture, Media and Sport and is managed nationally by Sports Coach UK and Sport England.

▥ *Sporting Champions* – taking world-class athletes from a diverse range of sports into schools and local communities to inspire and motivate young people to take part in sport. The main goal of the scheme is to show young people that sport can and should be fun and to encourage them to get the sporting habit.

Sport England – a summary

Sport England is the single most important organisation for sport in England. The part it plays is summarised below:

▥ Sport England is the government agency responsible for developing local community sport and increasing sport and physical recreation nationwide.

▥ Sport England has produced an overarching policy, the National Framework for Sport.

▥ Sport England works with national partners such as sport NGBs, Sport Equity Alliance, National Sport Foundation and others to improve participation and to address under-representation.

▥ Sport England liaises with the Youth Sports Trust and UK Sport to provide the 'sporting landscape' – ensuring that there is a structure to take an individual from their first experiences of sport and physical recreation to possibly fulfilling their potential as an elite performer.

▥ Sport England achieves its objectives by developing locally based initiatives to put into action the objectives of the National Framework.

▥ Locally Sport England works with local councils, voluntary sector clubs and groups, schools and other youth organisations.

▥ Sport England allocates exchequer and lottery funding to help achieve its objectives.

▥ As well as providing funding Sport England also provides advice to local and national providers.

AQA Examiner's tip

You will not be asked to discuss or describe specific Sport England policies or projects. You will be asked about Sport England's general objectives and then to give *examples* of how these are to be achieved.

Activities

1 Using the notes above and the Sport England website prepare two spray diagrams/ mind maps.

   a Show the national policies of Sport England and the links to other national bodies.

   b Show the local community initiatives that are being used to increase community participation in sport.

2 In groups of two or three prepare a bid as a PowerPoint presentation, from a local sports club for a Sport England grant. Use the notes in this chapter and the Sport England and National Lottery websites to help prepare the bid. You must meet as many of the Sport England and Lottery criteria as possible if you are to be successful.

▨ Sport England undertakes research into levels of participation and the reasons why individuals participate in sport or not.

▨ Sport England works with other government agencies to assist with wider social policies for community wellbeing and safety.

✓ *You should now be able to:*

- describe the characteristics and objectives of each of three different types of provider

- show an understanding of who are the characteristic users whose needs are met by each sector

- understand that through the policy of Best Value the difference between public and private is less distinct

- understand that the inequalities within provision, especially in the public sector, has an impact upon rates of participation of different socio-economic groups.

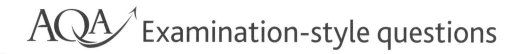

1   The government provides a large amount of money from taxation to fund the
     provision of physical recreation and sport facilities. Sport England is the agency
     responsible for determining priorities and allocating funding to local communities.

     (a)   What are Sport England's main objectives?   *(3 marks)*

     (b)   What strategies is Sport England using to try to meet those objectives?   *(3 marks)*

2   'It would be better to allow the private sector to provide sport and physical
     recreation facilities for all, as it would do so more efficiently and with higher quality'.
     Discuss this statement.   *(6 marks)*

3   Individuals have a range of opportunities to participate in sport and physical
     recreation.

     (a)   Explain the terms public, private sectors and voluntary sectors.   *(3 marks)*

     (b)   How and why has the relationship between the public and private sectors
              changed in recent times?   *(3 marks)*

4   The provision of sporting and physical recreation activities is the responsibility of
     a variety of organisations in the United Kingdom.

     What advantages arise, in terms of equality of provision, from having many
     different providers for sport and physical recreation?   *(6 marks)*

12 National Curriculum Physical Education and school sport

Activity

Physical Education takes place in schools, but so does sport. Explain how school sport differs from school Physical Education.

In Chapter 9 –Learning and performance (page 102) we defined Physical Education as a formalised body of knowledge and experience taught within educational establishments. In other words Physical Education only takes place in schools, colleges and universities. It will always involve a teacher who will be trying to pass on their knowledge to their pupils. Physical Education is also almost always concerned with bodily movement. Yet even though all pupils follow the same National Curriculum for Physical Education, there is a wide variety of experiences available and it is probably correct to say that no two schools teach exactly the same Physical Education programme.

Physical Education activities vary, because teachers and schools are able to choose which activities to teach based on their own expertise, but the major part of a pupil's experience in Physical Education will tend to centre on traditional team games. The most commonly taught individual activities are swimming and athletics. However, with ever-changing developments there are now more 'health-related fitness' and 'lifetime activities' being taught in schools such as aerobics, badminton and table-tennis.

Physical Education is both a popular subject in schools and an important one. It is popular because of the variety of experiences available to pupils and because it takes place in a different environment from other lessons. Physical Education often serves as a break from those other lessons. But Physical Education also has a purpose – it has values that are of benefit to the individual. There are those practical skills that you might develop as part of a Physical Education programme. You learn simple skills; often called fundamental motor skills that you develop to enable you to participate in sports and activities. What other school subject can save your life? Physical Education can when you learn to swim! Physical Education also instils social skills such as leadership, cooperation and discipline which helps people develop into more rounded humans, better able to cope with a modern society.

Physical Education is not a new subject, it has been around for about 100 years or more, but it has changed considerably from its earliest days. Modern Physical Education is an amalgamation of two distinct strands of educational provision that were both present in nineteenth century England; the public schools and the state elementary schools. The clear division between these two approaches was money. The rich upper classes sent their children to fee-paying public schools. The developing middle classes copied the ideas behind these schools to establish their own fee-paying public schools. The working classes had to wait until the late nineteenth century before free education for all children became available at elementary schools.

💡 Public school sports (1800–1870)

The English public school system was based on upper class boys, the sons of the landowners, being sent to rural boarding schools to be educated to be gentlemen and become the future politicians, doctors and lawyers by middle class teachers (they were called masters). Because of these class differences, and the freedom that the schools offered the boys, there was a disregard for authority, frequent riots and extensive bullying of the younger boys by the older boys. The boys had large amounts of leisure time when they were left on their own to entertain themselves. They would use this leisure time as they did at home – hunting, gambling, drinking and using younger boys as servants (they called it 'fagging'). In several schools the boys even managed to bring horses and hounds with them so they could continue hunting. So-called 'field' activities such as fishing or poaching were commonly pursued, causing tension between the school and the local community. The boys also played sports, mainly games, during their leisure time. Initially these were mob sports, the games that they played at their home villages and were brought to the school and adapted to be played within the grounds. These games were disapproved of by many headmasters and on occasions were banned, because they were unruly and violent. But gradually these games were seen as a way of allowing the boys to expend the excess energy that they had. The games kept them within the school rather than allowing them to roam free and it was a means of instilling discipline.

Activity

Watch the recent (2005) BBC production of *Tom Brown's Schooldays*, watch a copy of the original (1940) movie, or read the original book by Thomas Hughes that the films are based on.

Any of these will give you a clearer picture of what the public school system was like. Make a list of adjectives to describe the English public school system.

Fig. 12.1 *A village ball game in pre-industrial England*

Each school developed its own form of games to fit into the local environment. The games of the public schools became organised. They had rules with restrictions to the number of players and the boundaries of play. As the games became more popular so skills developed, as did playing positions. The first matches were between the various houses where the boys lived or boarded, with the captain of the house being given the job of organising his team. Leadership became an important aspect of these games, because for the most part, these early games were organised by the senior boys for the free afternoons that the boys had. This was a form of **social control**.

Schools began to play each other and as these games developed in stature, so the masters saw that the games had other values besides discipline. The masters began to promote games and encourage the boys by joining in themselves or bringing back former students (Old Boys) to coach and/or play. This improved playing standards, which was matched by technical developments in terms of playing facilities and equipment. Success on the playing fields became a good way of advertising the school

Key terms

Social control: mechanism where one group within society attempts to control another group. The sixth formers controlled the younger boys. The playing of games kept the boys under control.

to potential pupils. Fixtures and results started to appear in the press, and facilities, funding and teacher support continued to increase.

These games were played with a code of conduct that reflected the developments that were according within society in general. Governments at both national and local level were keen to civilise the working classes. Games were seen as a means of instilling certain virtues into the players. Moral qualities such as leadership, discipline, integrity, loyalty, bravery, decision making and 'correct' behaviour were seen as being valued and worthwhile aspects of playing games. Games were played not for the individual but for the team. Winning was not as important as taking part and trying your best. This concept is best described as **fair play**.

Key terms

Fair play: playing the activity fairly and obeying the rules – playing to the letter of the law.

Fig. 12.2 *Eton wall game*

Key terms

Athleticism: fanatical devotion to both the physical side of playing sport, but also the development of moral integrity.

Codification: formalising of the rules of a sport.

Activity

You may be asked to describe the characteristics of the public schools. Make sure you are able to reel off four or five words that would describe these schools.

This idea of developing both the physical side of your character as well as the moral side through the playing of team sports is known as **athleticism**. The desire for competition between various public schools and between former public school pupils when they were at university led to the need to establish an agreed set of rules for each game. Prior to this, rules were agreed between the teams before the match was played. Rules were even changed during a match. The modern idea of half time and all that that entails is derived from the simple notion of playing with one set of rules for a certain period and then changing to another set of rules for the remainder of the match. The public schools were where many of our major games developed. Football, rugby, athletics and rowing all developed into major sporting activities through the public school system.

When these boys went to university they wanted to continue playing their games and so had to agree sets of rules. This process of **codification** led to many groups being set up to arbitrate over areas of disagreement.

This level of expertise helped these groups become the original Governing Bodies of sport. Fixtures could now be arranged between groups. Clubs were formed and competitions organised.

Rational recreation (1850–1890)

During the same period as games were developing in the public schools, so society itself was developing. In the UK there was a change in working practices; from the largely rural farming communities to the city-based manufacturing industries. The main reason for this was the **industrial revolution** that permitted greater use of machinery and therefore increased production of goods. The working classes had to be prepared to work long, regulated hours, as the machines were never turned off. At the same time, and as a result of a move by the working classes to the cities, a process called **urbanisation** occurred. Urbanisation meant a change in work patterns for those who worked with the machinery. They had to live close enough to the workplace to be able to walk there, usually in cramped terraced housing built especially for the purpose of housing the workforce. Leisure time changed completely. Instead of leisure being governed by the need to work the land as farmers, leisure was governed by the hours that factory owners demanded. It became normal to work 12-hour days for six days a week. Sunday was their day off, but was the day of rest, and so leisure time was very restricted.

The working classes had little time for recreation, but the upper classes still had their former public school games. A major change in society, largely as a result of the industrial revolution, was the development of a growing middle class. These were the people who made money out of industrialization. They were the factory owners, the doctors who tended the sick, and the clergy. They wanted their sons (and daughters) to be educated and they founded many schools for that purpose. These schools followed the sporting pattern of the public schools and more and more ex-public schoolboys wished to carry on playing the games that they had played at school. These people also saw the value of sport in terms of its character-building, teamwork and sense of fair play. They invented new sports such as hockey, badminton and tennis to fill in their leisure time. They cycled and walked for recreation. The factory owners often provided the facilities for games to be played; churches also provided facilities. Between 1860 and 1890 most of today's modern sports were invented and formalised. This sudden boom in sport is part of what is called **rational recreation**. There were other reasons for the development of sports in a format that we would quickly recognise. The railways developed at the same time, making travel easier and cheaply available, so enabling fixtures and competitions to develop. Communications improved. More people could read and the media helped spread publicity about fixtures and events. The telegraph permitted the rapid spread of information, including results.

Initially there was a move by the middle and upper classes to keep their sports to themselves. They did not want the working classes involved. There were two main reasons for this. There was the social reason of not wishing to mix with the lower classes; the 'great unwashed'. There was also the practical reason that a man who worked 12 hours a day at a manual job was probably going to be fitter that a man who did no work; and a middle class man would not wish to be seen as not being as good as a working class man. The rules governing a sport were often made to exclude the working classes. Only the **gentleman amateur** was permitted to play.

AQA Examiner's tip

You may be asked to describe how the public schools helped the development of team games. Make sure that you can summarise the role of the public schools in the development of team games with four or five key words or phrases.

Key terms

Industrial revolution: period in history when the development of machines led to much greater production of materials, and the need to have a skilled workforce to run those machines.

Urbanisation: movement of the population to the cities from the countryside.

Rational recreation: the provision of activities for the lower classes whose work and leisure time had become strictly limited.

Gentleman amateur: played sport for pleasure; played to a strict moral code – fair play.

Fig. 12.3 *Football 1887 – Old Carthusians against Preston North End*

The separation of the classes through making sport exclusive did not extend to football. Many clubs were established by the ex-public school boys, and these formed most of the original teams who dominated the F.A. Cup. But in the industrial north and midlands, teams of working class players were beginning to emerge. One of the problems of urbanisation was a lack of suitable space to play sports. Often the only available land was that belonging to the local factory or church. Use of this land led to many factory- and church-based football teams. Linked into this was the reduction in the working week to permit a half-day on Saturdays. The workers would leave the factory and then watch their local football team play. Paying spectators gave the teams money, which they then used to bring in better players. This was the advent of professionalism in football.

Fig. 12.4 *Steeplechase event from an early athletics meeting*

Activities

- Research the history of the F.A. Cup on the internet and note the winners of the first ten competitions. Use this information and that provided in Figure 12.3 to suggest how changes in society were reflected in sport.

- Research dates for the professionalism of Tennis, Athletics, Rugby Union. Suggest why these sports only turned professional quite recently.

Social changes leading to rationalisation of sport

Pre-industrial	Post-industrial
Seasons dictated leisure time – recreation limited to occasional festivals	Factory hours dictated leisure time – 12-hour day, 6-day week
Limited transport and communications – local community-based activities	Improved transport and communications – travel to fixtures
Rural/farming lifestyle – very harsh, few amenities	Urbanised/industrial lifestyle – factory work, half-day closing
Two-class system – upper-class landowners and working classes	Emergence of a middle class
Limited technology – use of natural resources	Increasing technology – manufacturing of equipment and clothes
Uncivilised – drunkenness, gambling, riots common	Increased civilisation – policing, local government
Illiteracy common – word of mouth	Increasing literacy – advanced notice of fixtures, administration skills

Not all sports became professional at this time. For that you needed a regular income at club level, so that money can be paid to employ sports performers. Initially only football had that basis, but quickly some rugby teams followed suit, again in the north of England, and Rugby League was established. Many sports remained strictly amateur until quite recently. This was often a matter of choice: trying to maintain the established amateur ways, rather than succumbing to the wicked ways of professionalism.

🔎 State school education (1870–1940)

Schools for working class children were not established until 1870, and even then it took a number of years before all children were attending the schools. This was because the children had to stop working which meant there was less income coming into the family. The main aim of these first elementary schools was to provide a safe environment for the children away from the dangers of child labour.

The employers themselves wanted a much more disciplined workforce, with some degree of education in the basic skills of reading, writing and arithmetic. This was so the children would be of some value when they joined the workforces of the middle classes. They needed to be disciplined and obedient, willing to follow the orders of their employers. They did not need the leadership and decision-making skills of the public school boys.

State school education was based on lots of children of both sexes, in small schools, which was often a single large room. Conditions were cramped, with no recreational facilities. The essential philosophy at this time was discipline. What activities that did exist were designed to keep order. Pupils would learn their 'tables' and these were often recited while standing on chairs with accompanying movements. In simple terms the children were drilled into learning. Following the Boer War (1899–1902), it was decided that the working classes who had been recruited into the army were ill-disciplined and unfit. The model course (1904) was introduced. This meant that there was a change in emphasis in schools, with **military drill** exercises being introduced. These involved

AQA Examiner's tip

You may be provided with an image and asked to explain what differences can be seen in the image between historical events and modern-day versions.

Activity

From your own knowledge or through research on the internet/ newspapers, describe in a few words what you understand by terms such as 'sweat shops' or 'child labour' or 'workhouse conditions'. The very idea that such situations still occur in a modern world might be difficult for some people to understand, but your descriptions are just as valid for late nineteenth century UK as they are for modern developing countries.

Key terms

Military drill: mainly static exercises performed in unison, regimented, command style.

the children performing specific exercises, mainly free-standing through a regimented use of commands. Many schools employed former army non-commissioned officers (NCOs) to act as instructors. Pretend weapons in the form of staves were also used. This course was designed to instil discipline and obedience into the children through the use of tables of exercises that were delivered through command-style teaching of the children who stood in regimented ranks.

Fig. 12.5 *Early drill exercises*

The model course was replaced by a syllabus of physical training on several occasions, with 1919 being typical. This syllabus was introduced after the First World War that together with a major flu-epidemic had left the country in generally poor health. Recreative exercises had been beneficial for the recovery of injured soldiers and this idea was extended to schools. It was realised that physical activity could be enjoyable as well as improving fitness, and also have health benefits. The 1919 syllabus was therefore designed to have a **therapeutic** effect.

The 1919 syllabus still included some regimented free-standing exercises, but also introduced time for 'free-movement', dance and small games.

Key terms

Therapeutic: exercise having health as well as physical benefits.

Fig. 12.6 *Physical training*

The activities were becoming less formal. There were separate sections for the under and over 7s, with the focus on fun and play for the under 7s and on therapeutic exercises for the over 7s. There was more freedom for teachers to choose what to include, and less formality in how it was delivered.

During the 1930s there was a general lack of work available and the health of the nation, especially the working classes, was once again a cause for concern. The 1933 syllabus of physical training (PT) had different sections for the under and over 11s. Fitness and the therapeutic benefits of exercise remained objectives, but so did the idea of using your mind to decide what to do. Athletics, gymnastics and games were all included, and although much of the lessons were still formalised, there were opportunities for group work. Many schools had gymnasia built specifically for these lessons, but many lessons were held outside to benefit from the 'fresh air'. It was at this time that specialised 'kit' began to be worn for PT lessons.

The next big change in Physical Education followed the Second World War and the need to rebuild many schools. As part of this programme, apparatus was introduced into gymnasia, while playing fields were provided for all schools. There was a change in syllabus to make use of these changes and a move away from prescription and commands of Physical Training towards a more creative, child-centred, movement style of learning. The 1952 publication of moving and growing emphasised the need to develop children's physical, social and cognitive skills through agility exercises, dance, gymnastics, swimming and games. Physical Education lessons became child-centred involving teachers providing guidance rather than direction, problem-solving and discovery learning rather than command-style, using lots of apparatus.

National Curriculum Physical Education

The National Curriculum was established by the Government in the early 1990s to control what was being taught in schools. Physical Education is a core subject of the national curriculum and therefore compulsory.

The main aims of the National Curriculum for Physical Education (NCPE) are that children should be able to:

- achieve physical competence and confidence
- perform in a range of activities
- achieve physical skilfulness
- gain knowledge of the body in action
- become a '**critical performer**'
- learn competitiveness, creativity; face up to challenges
- learn how to plan, perform and evaluate
- discover their abilities, aptitudes and make choices for lifelong learning.

These aims are intended to make children more aware of the need to adopt a healthy lifestyle, and also enable them to choose suitable activities to undertake in adopting this healthy lifestyle. The children should also develop their imagination and creativity through devising their own solutions to problems put in place by the PE teacher. They should also experience a wide range of activities from which to select for their leisure time use. This often means that there is a need for more and better

Activity

Produce a table that highlights in a few words the major differences between the 1904 model course, the 1919 syllabus and the 1933 syllabus, under the headings of year, objectives, content and method of delivery.

Activity

Think back to the last few years. Make a list of what you did during core PE lessons (not GCSE PE). Compare your experiences to others in the class. What are the similarities or differences?

Key terms

Critical performer: understanding activities not just as a performer, but also as a coach, leader, official, choreographer or spectator.

facilities for schools and this may involve making use of community facilities where appropriate. The NCPE also wants children to understand that there are other ways to be involved in activities beyond performing, such as officiating, spectating, coaching and leadership roles.

Schools cannot offer every physical activity to all of its pupils all of the time. But neither should they limit the range to just one or two activities. The NCPE has six groups of activities:

▓ games (invasion, striking and fielding, net/wall)

▓ athletic activities

▓ swimming

▓ gymnastics

▓ dance

▓ outdoor and adventurous activities.

State schools are directed by the National Curriculum as to what types of physical activities are taught and when, by the pupil's educational life being divided into four stages. Each key stage has both a practical element (taking part in activities) and a theoretical part (understanding what's happening to their body during and after participation).

At key stage 1 – years 1 and 2 (infants) – pupils should experience dance, gymnastics and games; developing simple skills and eventually movement sequences, both individually and as a group. They should also understand and recognise the effects of exercise on their bodies.

At key stage 2 – years 3–6 (juniors) – pupils should follow six areas of activity: dance, gymnastics, games; and then two from athletics, swimming and adventure activities. The children's skill levels and coordination should develop, by being able to produce more complex movement patterns. They should also experience, understand and maintain sustained periods of exercise.

One of the problems with NCPE is that most primary schools do not have a PE teacher, and the classroom teacher is not a specialist. The Government has tried to cope with this problem by introducing the TOP programme and specialist Sports Colleges with their School Sport Co-Ordinators (SSCOs) to get expert help into primary school PE provision (see later).

At key stage 3 – years 7–9 (lower secondary school) – pupils should follow four of the six areas in key stage 2, one of which must be games and another either gymnastics or dance. Pupils should be refining their motor skills and developing the complexity of their movements. Children should be involved in smaller versions of adult activities and be learning rules and tactics of these activities as well as finding out about recovery from exercise.

At key stage 4 – years 10–11 (upper secondary school) – pupils should follow games and one other activity. Children should learn how to plan, prepare and evaluate a health-related exercise programme, and be able to understand the theoretical principles on which the programme is based.

During key stage 1 and 2 (primary school) the emphasis in PE is somewhat different to that in key stage 3 and 4 (secondary school). Learning is child-centred as opposed to competitive with an emphasis on participation rather than winning. This is as a result of teaching through play rather than games and being taught by non-specialist teachers.

AQA Examiner's tip

You may be asked about the six categories of NCPE activities – learn them.

Teachers have to write an assessment at each key stage to describe the level of attainment of each child. In order to do this there are expected levels of attainment for each key stage. Having these assessments provides clear goals and provides motivation for the children as well as recognising good quality teaching. However, not everyone is happy with the system as there appears to be too much time devoted to assessment rather than participating. Both teachers and pupils can become de-motivated due to comparisons to others, and all assessments involve pressure which takes away the fun element of Physical Education.

The NCPE provides a core curriculum for schools, but many children also benefit from 'extra-curricular' activities. These are usually offered voluntarily by teachers during lunchtimes and after school. They will include recreational activities as well as sports teams and competitive fixtures. This area is often called school sport and as such should be viewed as being distinctly different to Physical Education. One of the problems of extra-curricular sport is that teachers are not paid for this work, but it has become accepted as part of their role. In the 1980s there was a large drop in the amount of extra-curricular sport offered to children, mainly as a result of industrial action by teachers. More recently, the financial pressures of running fixtures, maintaining equipment and facilities and concerns over health and safety have also had an effect on the amount of extra-curricular sport on offer to many schools.

The NCPE provides schools with the broad framework of what can be taught. Parents may often judge the quality of the PE programme on the facilities available. Depending on the school, the pressure to be successful in specific sports may be reflected in the time allocation for that activity.

The extent to which individual schools are able to offer a fully rounded PE programme and whether the children at the school enjoy their PE experiences depends on many factors. Some schools simply have better and/or newer facilities than others. It is Government policy to make sure that all schools have sufficient facilities to provide a suitable PE curriculum, but there are financial, time and space considerations that have to be overcome before every school has the facilities it needs.

Schools may seek to overcome the problem of lack of facilities by sharing facilities with the local community. These **dual use** facilities provide the community with a sports hall or swimming pool and the school with extra income. In some cases public facilities have been built for all the local schools to use during school hours and the local community outside these times. Sharing a school facility with the public can however cause problems. The subsequent increase in usage can lead to overuse of the facility resulting in damage. This is compounded by a lack of maintenance. The poor management of the facility is most evident during holiday time when the lines of responsibility appear unclear. Security of the whole school is reduced. These problems can be overcome by thoughtful planning of the facility and effective management. The management is most effective when there is a single administrative body responsible for the smooth running of the facility.

Some problems appear unavoidable. Children find school facilities unattractive; school is always school. There is lack of flexibility. The demand of the school means there can be little provision for target groups such as house parents, unemployed or pre-school children. The advantages of operating a dual use facility are that the facility involves the whole community helping to create better links between the school and public.

Key terms

Dual use: where sporting facilities are provided that serve not only educational demands, but are also available for community use.

Activity

Write down a list of facilities that were available at your secondary school and the activities that were offered for core PE. Discuss within groups whether your experiences were limited by the range of facilities or activities offered to you.

Other factors that may affect a child's experiences of PE would include the teachers. Many schools have excellent PE teachers who have specific interests that they emphasise in their PE lessons. But this in turn may actually limit a child's experience to certain activities. In much the same way, a school may have a tradition in a certain area; they may be a 'rugby playing school'. In many schools the timetable is the problem. There may be a greater emphasis on academic achievement than the needs of the PE. department and so there may simply not be sufficient time allocated to PE. Some schools may simply not have the staffing to provide for all its needs. This is often the case in primary schools, where there are very few qualified PE teachers and the Government is well aware of the problem and has brought in a number of strategies to help (see later). Facilities and/or finance can also affect PE provision. For example, without a pool, a school may find it very expensive to provide swimming for its pupils. A similar restriction occurs with outdoor and adventurous activities, which are expensive to organise, especially when travel and accommodation become part of the cost. However it is not so much the curriculum PE that suffers, but the extra-curricular sport. Extra-curricular sport not only occurs during the child's lunch hour, but it's also the teacher's lunch hour and most sport in schools is undertaken by the teachers volunteering to run clubs, team and activities.

▌ Key terms

Social inclusion: the prevention of the limiting of people's and area's opportunities through not being in a similar status to the dominant social grouping in a society.

▌ Developing school–club links

The Government's policy on sport development and physical activity policy has **social inclusion** at its heart. Social exclusion is a term for what can happen when people or areas suffer from a combination of linked problems such as unemployment, poor skills, low incomes, poor housing, high crime, bad health and family breakdown. As part of this, the Government decided that sport could help prevent social exclusion by contributing to neighbourhood renewal by improving communities in terms of improving health, reducing crime, increasing employment and assisting education.

In 2000, the Government's sporting agency, Sport England (formerly the English Sports Council) produced a document called 'A Sporting Future for All', which eventually led to an action plan published in 2001 called 'The Government's Plan for Sport'. This document set out the Government's plans to develop sport in education, community and the modernisation of organisations involved in sport, and eventually produced 'Game Plan', a strategy for delivering the Government's sport and physical activity objectives.

Game Plan said that millions of people take part in sport and physical activity, both as a source of fun and to improve their health, without much involvement by the Government. However, it was felt that Government had a role to play in widening opportunities to participate, in developing talent, and in enabling our sportsmen and women to compete at the highest levels.

Game Plan said that Government should set itself two main objectives:

▨ a major increase in participation, mainly because of the significant health benefits and to reduce the growing costs of inactivity; and

▨ improved success in international competition, particularly in the sports which matter most to the public, primarily because of the 'feel good factor' associated with winning.

In order to achieve this, recommendations were made in four areas:

- **Grass roots participation**: a range of initiatives was needed, with a focus on economically disadvantaged groups, in particular young people, women and older people. These need to tackle all the barriers to participation (such as lack of time, cost, information or motivation), as well as failures in provision (poor coaches or facilities).

- **High performance sport**: there needed to be a better prioritisation of which sports are funded at the highest level, and better development of talented sportsmen and women to help them reach that level.

- **Mega sporting events**: there should be a more cautious approach to hosting these events. A set process for Government involvement, including a clear assessment of the benefits is needed.

- **Delivery**: organisational reform and determining exactly what works is needed before the Government considers further increases to its investment in sport. Public, private and voluntary sectors need to work together better towards a common goal.

It was decided that the Government needed to invest in sport and physical activity because they have a major part to play in promoting health, and as part of a group of measures can contribute to improved educational outcomes, reduced crime and greater social inclusion:

- The benefits of physical activity on health are clear, well evidenced and widely accepted. Thirty minutes of moderate activity five times a week can help to reduce the risk of cardiovascular diseases, some cancers, strokes and obesity. This inactivity is becoming an increasing problem, as the continuing rise in obesity and other inactivity-related health challenges demonstrates. As these increase, so will the costs of physical inactivity.

- Education plays a key role in affecting levels of participation. Equally, there is some evidence that sport and physical activity can benefit education. Evidence of benefits in crime reduction and social inclusion is less clear. Experience suggests that where such benefits exist they can be best achieved by using sport and physical activity as part of a wider package of measures.

- The role of sport in generating a 'feel good factor' through international sporting success also appears to be significant. The flip side of this is a 'feel bad' factor if there is poor performance. International success does not appear to stimulate sustained economic benefits (such as increased productivity or consumer confidence).

- The benefits of hosting mega sporting events, whether economic, social or cultural are difficult to measure and the available evidence is limited. If major new facilities are needed, the economic and regeneration benefits of hosting mega events must be carefully weighed against all costs, including opportunity costs.

The Government highlighted that many facilities in the voluntary sector (see Chapter 11 – Leisure provision, page 140) are not being used during the week. There is also the problem of the post-school gap (see Chapter 11) and the reduction in extra-curricular sport discussed earlier in this chapter. The Government is currently implementing several strategies to try and aim for 'high quality physical education and sport'.

Sports colleges

By 2007 there were nearly 350 designated **Sports Colleges** in England against a target of 400. They are helping deliver the Government's 'Plan for Sport' (1997). Schools apply to become Sports Colleges. As

Fig. 12.7 *Sports colleges logo*

Key terms

Sports College: a specialist Sports College is a maintained secondary school (in England) which receives additional funding from the Department for Education and Skills to raise standards in physical education and sport within its own school, in a local family of schools and in the wider community.

part of their bid they have to raise a considerable amount of money and provide evidence of a commitment to offer high-quality PE and sports provision. If they are successful they receive additional funding from the Government to improve their sports facilities and increase the number of PE teachers at the school. The school then has to use these extra resources to develop sporting excellence and widening participation in its community schools. What this means in practice is that the sports colleges offer outstanding facilities, opportunities and expertise to its own pupils, and wherever possible make the same offer to its local primary and secondary schools. The aim is to make sure that all pupils receive a minimum of two hours per week of high quality PE and school sport. There is a need for this programme to be organised, and this is the job of the School Sports Co-ordinator (SSCo).

The idea of Sports Colleges is that they will raise standards of achievement in physical education and sport for all their students across the ability range leading to whole school improvement. They will be focal points within the region for promoting excellence in physical education and community sport, extending links between families of schools, sports bodies and communities, sharing resources, developing and spreading good practice and helping to provide a structure through which young people can progress to careers in sport and physical education. Sports Colleges are supposed to increase participation in physical education and sport for all pre- and post-16 year olds and develop the potential of talented performers.

They will support the Government's aspiration for all young people to have two hours high quality PE per week within and outside the curriculum. They will take an appropriate role in the Physical Education, School Sport and Club Links Strategy (see below). Sports Colleges will help develop the skills and understanding of teachers and make imaginative use of new technologies as a means of raising the quality of teaching and learning in PE. They will extend provision and facilities to benefit all students of all sporting abilities, whilst also giving those with the greatest potential, opportunities to achieve the highest standards of which they are capable. They work with other schools and the wider community to develop and share good practice, facilities, human and other resources with a view to improving learning opportunities for all. They are involved in national initiatives (e.g. Step into Sport) and competitions that enrich provision in PE and sport for their own pupils and those in their partner schools.

💡 School Sports Co-ordinator (SSCo)

Sports Colleges are connected to their feeder primary schools and other secondary schools via the programme called 'school sports co-ordinators' (SSCos).

The School Sports Co-ordinator programme particularly has been developed (in scale at least) to have become a new tier in PE teacher provision having national conferences and, in effect, its own lead body in the form of the **Youth Sports Trust**.

The Local Education Authority (LEA) identifies an experienced teacher, normally within a Sports College, to support and manage the development of local school sports partnerships. The teacher is taken off the teaching timetable, usually for two days per week and is known as the Partnership Development Manager (PDM). Each PDM works with four to six partner secondary schools and within each of these an experienced

Key terms

Youth Sports Trust: charity set up in 1994 to support the education and development of all young people through physical education (PE) and sport.

teacher co-ordinates and drives the development of PE and sport within the school and an associated family of primary schools. The teacher is taken off teaching for two or three days per week and is known as the School Sport Co-ordinator (SSCo). Each SSCo works with up to five primary schools and within each of these schools an experienced teacher makes sure that the programmes are planned and delivered and that links are built with other schools and organisations across the partnership area. This teacher is taken off the teaching timetable for approximately 12 days per year and is known as a Primary Link Teacher (PLT).

The School Sports Co-ordinator initiative aims to develop the quality of delivery of physical education in schools and particularly the links between key stages 2 and 3 (the gap between primary and secondary provision) in addition to achieving the target of two hours of PE for every child per week The links made by Programme Development Managers (PDMs) and School Sports Co-ordinators with primary link teachers are designed to achieve these targets. This strategy appears to be instead of placing specialist PE teachers in every primary school.

In addition, Sports Colleges and School Sport Co-ordinator programmes have to develop 'community links'. These school/club/wider community links stem from an earlier idea that schools should be opening their doors to a wider population than just their own pupils and school partnerships. These wider community links have provided excellent recruitment material for the County Sports Partnerships and Local Authority Sport Development Units, who were previously almost excluded from the young sport talent that schools provided, other than in dual-use, joint-provision and the public school sports facilities and systems.

Recently (2007) the School Sport Co-ordinator programme was renamed as the School Sport Partnerships.

The Physical Education and School Sport Club Links (PESSCL) strategy

The PE, School Sport and Club Links (PESSCL) strategy is being delivered by the DfES and the Department for Culture, Media and Sport (DCMS) through eight work strands.

The eight strands are:
■ Sports Colleges
■ School Sport Partnerships
■ Gifted and Talented
■ Swimming
■ Step into Sport
■ School/club links
■ QCA PE and School Sport Investigation
■ Professional Development.

These two government departments are working with children, parents, schools, local authorities, National Governing Bodies and sports clubs, all of which have a role to play. In localised groups, these partners work together to ensure the effective delivery of these programmes to support schools and maximise the benefits for young people.

The overall objective of PESSCL strategy is to improve the take up of sporting opportunities for 5–16 year olds, by increasing the percentage of children in England who spend a minimum of two hours each week on

> **Activity**
>
> Draw an organisational chart that shows the relationship between PDMs, SSCos and PLTs.

high quality PE and school sport within and beyond the curriculum to 75 per cent. Currently (2007), about a quarter of schools provide this at key stage 1 and a third of schools at key stages 2, 3 and 4. The intention is to improve the quality of teaching, coaching and learning in PE and school sport and increase the proportion of children guided into clubs from School Sport Partnerships. The strategy has the following targets:

- 400 (at least) Specialist Sports Colleges (subject to sufficient high quality applications)
- 400 School Sport Partnerships
- 3,200 School Sport Co-ordinators in secondary schools
- 18,000 Primary or Special School Link Teachers.

School Sport Partnerships

School Sport Partnerships (SSPs) are part of the national infrastructure for PE and school sports. Sports Colleges are at the centre of SSPs. They are given funding to employ a full-time Partnership Development Manager (PDM), who is responsible for the strategic development of the partnership and liaison with other agencies.

Around each Sports College there should be a number of secondary schools, each having a School Sport Co-ordinator, who is responsible for the co-ordination and development of school sport in their own school and family of primary/special schools.

Each secondary school is linked to a number of primary or special schools. Each of these will have a Primary Link Teacher (PLT). Funding is provided to enable the schools to release these teachers to undertake the Co-ordinator and PLT roles. In the case of the secondary schools, the partnership can use the funding to employ full-time Specialist Link Teachers (SLT) to provide the cover for the SSP release time. This enables the schools to enhance their PE provision by recruiting SLTs with specific skills, for example in dance, gymnastics or inclusion.

The Youth Sport Trust is contracted by DfES to provide support to partnerships.

All specialist Sports Colleges are expected to play an appropriate role in implementing the PESSCL strategy. They should do this through their school and community plans as well as by hosting a School Sport Co-ordinator Partnership and building on links with other bodies associated with strategic developments in sport.

One of the great anomalies of sport in the UK is that various groups seem to operate in isolation. For example we have thousands of children involved in sport at their schools, but then these same schools close for weekends and holidays. At the same time we have thousands of adults involved in sport through their clubs at weekends and evenings, but these clubs then close when the adults are at work. One of the many concerns for the Government is that many children who take part in physical activities do not go on to participate as adults.

PESSCL tries to strengthen the links between school sport and the voluntary club sector. It is part of the SSCo partnership to provide opportunities for children to take part in sport through their school, but using the facilities of local clubs. This not only makes use of facilities that are normally closed to them, but it also makes the children aware of the location of their local clubs. This should be seen as another attempt to reduce the 'post-school gap'. In practical terms what this usually means is that the SSCos organise events or competitions that take place at the local clubs. This will also involve the local National Governing Bodies, who themselves normally employ a Sports Development Officer to encourage such attempts at increasing participation.

▉ Active Sports

The aim of the Active Sports programme is:

> to help young people with the ability and desire to improve their sporting skills through a co-ordinated programme across England that will provide access to organised sports'. The Active Sports programme is a Sport England initiative aimed at encouraging an increase in participation through liaison between local providers such as schools, clubs, local authorities and community groups. This programme is designed to link with the Sport England pyramid model of differing levels of participation.

Active Sports provides a link between the three separate programmes of Active Schools, Active Communities and the World Class programmes. It provides young sports people with the support they need to continue their involvement in sport at a level which best suits their abilities and motivations. For a young person taking part in sport the idea is that they will eventually be involved in one of the following:

- continuing involvement in club sport
- continuing involvement in a sports governing body performance programme
- fast-tracking into the World Class Programme.

Fig. 12.8 *Active sports*

The Active Schools programme is designed to increase opportunities for children to take part in a range of activities at foundation level, while the Active Sports programme is trying to increase the range of activities offered to children in schools and complements the participation level of the pyramid. Active Communities looks at reducing the post-school gap and increasing participation by breaking down barriers, especially those linked to issues of equality.

Active Sports aims to identify and support different ways to ensure the programme is equally available to all young people with the ability and desire to progress in sport. It also aims to improve local coaching and competitive opportunities for young people, and to create and support local development squads in specific sports. Active Sports is trying to improve the number and quality of sports clubs available for juniors and to increase both the number and quality of coaches, officials and volunteer helpers working with young people at different levels. It also wants to provide a range of partnership services for young people, parents, coaches and officials and volunteers to support the development of active sports.

The Active Sports programme encourages local authorities, the education and sports organisations to work together on selected sports for the benefit of young people in their area. Financial help is available from Sport England to support the preparation and delivery of Sports Specific Action Plans if they are approved by the national Governing Bodies of Sport. A series of special measures are being developed, including the targeted use of Lottery Sports Funding, to encourage and support positive action for talented young sports people from disadvantaged communities/ groups.

■ Sports Leaders UK

The Government's Step into Sport initiative is part of its policy to increase participation. But if more people take part in sport, it means that there is also need to find more people to take control of the courses and programmes that will provide these opportunities to take part in sporting activities. There is therefore a need for more instructors or leaders in sport. Sports Leaders UK (formerly British Sports Trust) provides opportunities for young people to gain experience and qualifications to become volunteer leaders in the community. Sports Leaders UK are working with the Youth Sports Trust and Sport England to create a vast army of volunteers, mainly aged 14–19. A Sports Leaders UK qualification has the core value of developing leadership skills such as how to organise activities, how to motivate and communicate with people. As well as this the Sports Leader courses can encourage volunteering in communities, reduce youth crime by engaging young people in positive activities and a suitable qualification may be used as a stepping stone to employment.

Sports Leaders UK offers a range of four suitable qualifications:

- ▓ The Junior Sports Leaders Award (JSLA) is for 14–16 year olds. This award is commonly taught as part of the NCPE core PE programme.
- ▓ The Community Sports Leaders Award (CSLA) is for those aged 16 and above and is often taught in colleges and schools, but courses are also offered in young offenders' institutions, youth clubs and leisure centres.
- ▓ The High Sports Leaders Award (HSLA) develops the broad range of skills provided by the CSLA to enable people to lead specific groups such as disabled, older people and primary children. This award also has units in first aid, event management, sports development and leads on to sport-specific coaching awards.
- ▓ The Basic Expedition Leader Award (BELA) is especially for those who wish to develop their skills at leading outdoor activities safely and organising overnight camps.

■ TOP programme

The TOP programme is largely organised by the Youth Sports Trust (YST), which is a charity whose mission is to implement and develop high quality PE and sport programmes in schools and within communities for all children aged 18 months to 18 years. In order to do this the YST works with national agencies such as Sport England as well as private companies. The YST manages the TOP programme. It also supports schools that have applied for or received sports college status. It also extends its role to assisting SSCos in their work. The TOP programme aims to provide opportunities for children to experience a greater range of physical activities through providing sport-specific equipment that is designed to be used by the age of the child targeted. In other words, TOP provides suitable equipment that may not necessarily be normally available, such as cricket for inner city schools. The TOPs programme also provides illustrated resource cards to introduce sporting skills and provides training and ongoing support for teachers to help them deliver the programmes.

The TOP programmes are divided and named according to the age groups involved:

- Top Tots helps children aged 18 months to 3 years to learn and understand about simple activities and games.
- Top Start encourages 3–5 year olds to experience various types of physical activity.
- Top Play helps 4–9 year olds develop their core skills.
- Top Sport is for 7–11 year olds.
- Top Skill is for 11–14 year olds.
- Top Link is for 14–19 year olds.
- Top Sportsability is for disabled people.

National Governing Bodies and Whole Sport Plans

National Governing Bodies (NGBs) are responsible for organising their own sport in the UK. Several NGBs are powerful and self-regulatory, for example the FA and the RFU, while many others are much smaller and rely on financial support from Sport England.

In 2003 Sport England identified 30 priority sports, based on their capability to contribute to Sport England's vision of an active and successful sporting nation. Sport England is now working with the national governing bodies of these sports to assist the development and implementation of their Whole Sport Plan (WSP).

Whole Sport Plans are plans that have to be produced by each NGB for the whole of a sport from grass roots right through to the elite level that identifies how the NGB will achieve its vision for the next five years and how it will contribute to Sport England's start, stay and succeed objectives. Sport England uses WSPs as a way of providing funding and resources to NGBs. The plans identify the help and resources NGBs need to deliver their whole sport plans, for example, partners such as county sports partnerships and programmes such as PE School and Sport Clubs Links (PESSCL) and the Community Club Development Partnership (CCDP). WSPs provide Sport England with the opportunity to measure how the NGBs are delivering their sports.

WSPs make sure that NGBs follow the Sport England aims of start, stay and succeed. They allow Sport England to justify what funding to give to NGBs against the funding they have requested they need to promote their sport. They provide measurable results which will give Sport England an indication of how well NGBs are performing and whether Sport England is getting value for money from their investment. In simple terms, an NGB produces a WSP that says what it will do to promote start, stay and succeed in their particular sport, and requests funding for these ideas. Each year, the NGBs performance is judged against its plans. If they have achieved their aims the NGB gets its funding for the following year. If it fails to meet its aims, then its funding is reduced.

Sport England

Sport England evolved out of the Sports Council which was set up in 1972 to promote sport and physical activity. Following the launch of the National Lottery in 1994, and the identification of sport as a good cause, the Sports Council became responsible for distributing lottery money to sport in England. In 1997, the Sports Council was reorganised into four national councils – one each for England, Scotland, Wales and Northern Ireland. In addition, UK Sport was established to oversee those areas where a UK-wide policy is needed, such as doping control, sports science, sports medicine and elite sports where performers compete as the United Kingdom, rather than England, Scotland, Wales or Northern Ireland. The English Sports Council, which had responsibility for community sport and those sports where we compete as England, was re-branded as Sport England in March 1999. Further reorganisation in 2006 led to responsibility for elite sport being transferred to UK Sport. Sport England now focuses exclusively on sport in the community; working closely with local, national and regional partners to create an active nation through sport. Sport England is the Government agency responsible for advising, investing in and promoting community sport. Its intention is to create a more active nation, with two million people more active in sport by 2012. It also needs to make sure that participation is sustained.

Sport England's aim is to increase and sustain participation in community sport. This includes informal activities such as aerobics and pilates; newer activities, such as skateboarding; and more traditional team sports such as football and netball. Sport England does this by promoting, investing in and advising on the development and maintenance of high quality sporting pathways which release potential through:

- community sports activities
- sports clubs
- coaches and officials
- player pathways
- volunteering
- sports facilities.

Sport England is also working with a number of partners to help ensure the London 2012 Olympic and Paralympic Games deliver a lasting sporting legacy across England, including:

- The Government
- London Organising Committee of the Olympic Games
- Youth Sports Trust
- UK Sport
- Greater London Authority.

Sport England is concerned about all those people who play sport – or those who might play given the right encouragement, environment or opportunities. In order to make opportunities available, Sport England is now much more regionalised in its workings. The majority of its workers are based at its nine regional offices. They use the phrase Sport England's Supply Chain – the Delivery System for Sport – the idea being that only local people know what's required at the local level.

This Delivery System connects those involved with sport at national, regional, sub-regional and local levels. It brings together NGBs, regional sports boards (RSBs), county sports partnerships (CSPs), community sports networks (CSNs) and the coaches, clubs and volunteers across England.

Sport England is one of the three national agencies involved in the delivery of sport in England. The others are the Youth Sports Trust which is mainly concerned with sport in schools, and UK Sport which is concerned with elite sport. These three agencies therefore each work at different levels of the participation pyramid.

Youth Sports Trust	Sport England	World Class Programme
School-aged children	Communities	Elite performers

Fig. 12.9 *Levels of operation of the three sports agencies*

In order to make the transition from school sport to community sport, Sport England needs to reach down into the Youth Sports Trust's area to run alongside them ahead of the handover at 16. By ensuring that the sporting environment is attractive and supportive of young people it will help ensure they stay in sport once they leave compulsory schooling.

In turn, Sport England needs to reach up and link with UK Sport. It does this by investing in NGBs to help them develop effective pathways that take talented athletes from club to UK Sport's World Class Performance Programmes.

Since 1994 Sport England has invested more than £550m exchequer or government funding and £2.2 billion National Lottery funding into sport and physical activity.

At a national level money is channelled through national partners, such as the Women's Sport Foundation or the English Cricket Board; and some major projects, for example, Wembley Stadium or the 2012 Olympic Aquatics Centre.

At a regional level, there is a Community Investment Fund, which is distributed via Sport England's nine regional sports boards. These RSBs meet several times a year to assess CIF grant applications against criteria laid down in each region's regional sports plan. The nine Sport England regions are responsible for providing regional advice and making regional investment decisions.

Youth Sports Trust

The Youth Sports Trust was established in 1994. In the early years it concentrated on providing equipment and resources to help teachers deliver high quality PE and sport in primary schools. This has now been extended to programmes to create a sporting pathway for all young people aged 18 months to 18 years.

The Youth Sports Trust (YST) works essentially with children of school age to help promote participation in sport. It is involved in a number of approaches to grass roots sport such as the TOP programme. The YST has helped develop environments and opportunities for young people to enjoy a quality introduction to PE and sport suited to their own level of development.

The TOP programmes play a major role in making sure that all children are able to access quality PE and sport at every stage of their development. Core features of the programmes are the provision of quality resources, simple, cheap but effective equipment, and quality training. The YST not only provides the resources but they also help coach the teachers who are using the resources by providing appropriate courses.

The YST works in partnership with a number of other agencies making sure that young people benefit from competitive activities, including:

- national governing bodies of sport (NGBs)
- national school sport associations
- The National Council of School Sport
- Sport England.

The YST is committed to increasing young people's involvement in PE and school sport in the belief that by becoming more active it can make a major contribution to the health of the nation. It also wants to provide a structured pathway of sporting opportunities, by increasing provision for young people to take part in sporting opportunities during extra-curricular time and to enhance school–club links.

 You should now be able to:

- describe the historical, social and cultural factors that led to the development of the current provision of Physical Education

- describe how the range of physical activities within state elementary schools has changed and the reasons for these changes

- describe the characteristics of each of the key stages of the National Curriculum for Physical Education and the relevance of each in relation to increasing opportunity for participation

- identify possible factors that influence provision of PE in schools and the impact this has on pupils' experiences

- explain why there is a policy to increase school–club links

- describe the role of Physical Education School Sport and Club Link Strategy (PESSCLS), School Sports Co-ordinators, Sports Colleges, Active Sports, Sports Leaders UK, TOP's programme and Whole Sport Plans that encourage the development of school–club links and explain the potential benefits to the Government, individuals and community

- describe the role of national governing bodies, Sport England and Youth Sports Trust in increasing participation.

1   In today's schools pupils are prepared to use their leisure time effectively.

   (a)   How do schools achieve this objective through physical education and
          extra-curricular sport?   *(4 marks)*

   (b)   What roles, other than 'performer', does the National Curriculum for
          Physical Education encourage children to develop?   *(2 marks)*

2   The development of a number of sports was greatly influenced by public schools
     during the late nineteenth century.

   (a)   State three changes made to sports by the public schools.   *(3 marks)*

   (b)   How did the ex-pupils of public schools open up sport to the wider
          community?   *(3 marks)*

3   During the late 1800s, modern sports replaced traditional mob games. What
     social and economic changes accounted for this development?   *(6 marks)*

4   There have been many developments in state school PE since 1900. Identify the
     similarities and differences in terms of objectives and delivery between the early
     state school (1904–1918) Physical Training syllabuses and the current National
     Curriculum for Physical Education.   *(6 marks)*

Equal opportunities

In this chapter you will:

- understand and accurately identify examples of discrimination, stereotyping and prejudice in sport

- understand what is meant by inclusiveness and equal opportunity

- identify the specific barriers to participation that occur as a result of gender discrimination; discrimination towards those from different socio-economic classes, ethnic groups or towards those who have a disability

- understand the current policies and strategies designed to overcome discrimination and raise the participation levels of those who suffer from discrimination in sport and physical recreation.

AQA Examiner's tip

One of the important objectives of the specification is to challenge misconceptions and preconceptions. You will be required to examine your own assumptions and views, and you must be prepared to examine evidence in an open-minded manner.

If you have already worked through Chapters 10, 11 and 12 you will understand the great value and benefit that individuals receive from participation in physical recreation, active leisure and sport. You will have an appreciation of the breadth of opportunity that exists for any individual, to experience a wide range of activities or to be able to develop one's skills and capabilities to perform at the highest level. You will also have understood that in the UK, national and local government have developed policies and strategies for the provision of physical recreation and sport, and that a significant proportion of national and local tax revenues are devoted to providing facilities and supporting those who have the skill, physical attributes and determination to become an elite performer. Finally you will have understood the impact that all those who are active in the voluntary sector have upon providing opportunities for others.

Given the level of national support, the benefit that participating in physical recreation and sport brings to communities and individuals, and the opportunities available though the voluntary, private and public sectors surely it is safe to assume that in the United Kingdom we would have a high level of participation and that all those that do wish to participate in a particular activity are able to do so?

Well it is not safe to assume that this is true. Despite national policies on participation, clear health messages given by schools and doctors and the efforts of the millions of people involved in the voluntary sector, there are high levels of variation in participation by different social groups. In this chapter we shall examine the levels of participation of different groups within society, why these vary so much and what we are doing to address this situation.

To be able to answer questions on this topic in an examination you need to be able to debate an issue, challenge misconceptions and to critically evaluate the range of policies and strategies that have been deployed to overcome what has become known as 'the barriers to participation'.

Participation – a level playing field?

It has been government policy for the last 40 years, since the early days of 'Sport for All', to ensure that every individual in the country has the opportunity to participate in sport and other forms of active leisure. We have seen the building of sports centres, the provision of outdoor recreation and sports facilities, the opening up of the countryside, the establishment and use of lottery funding and an on-going information campaign within school physical education programmes. All of these efforts have been focused on getting more people involved in active leisure and sport – has it worked?

Sport England and the Department of Culture, Media and Sport (DCMS) have regularly researched the levels of participation across the country, and a number of independent researchers have looked at specific groups and their participation. What does the research tell us? The most recent research is contained within two reports – the 'Taking Part Survey' commissioned by the DCMS and the 'Active People Survey' undertaken by Sport England.

The Taking Part Survey uses data from the General Household survey. The 2006 report found that:

- 69 per cent of people participated in active sport.
- Rural inhabitants are more likely to participate in sport than urban dwellers.
- The South East was the most sporty region.
- Swimming is the most popular sport – beating going to the gym, jogging and playing football.

The Active People Survey showed some similarities but also some differences:

- 21 per cent of the adult population take part regularly in sport and active recreation –a hugely different figure to the DCMS survey!
- The South East was the most active region (23 per cent participating regularly) with the West Midlands having the lowest level (19 per cent).
- There can even be a difference between neighbouring local authorities in the same region – in Berkshire the borough of Windsor and Maidenhead is in the top 25 per cent of all local authorities and the next door borough of Slough is in the bottom 25 per cent.
- Disability – 8.8 per cent of people with a longstanding illness or disability participate regularly in sport compared to 23.3 per cent who do not have such a condition.
- Ethnicity – 18.6 per cent of adults from black and other ethnic minority groups participate compared to 18.6 per cent of white origin – 21.2 per cent.
- Socio-economic class – 16.3 per cent from the lowest socio-economic groups participate compared to 25.1 per cent from the highest.
- Male participation is 23.7 per cent; and female participation is 18.3 per cent.
- Wide differences in participation by age (See Table 13.1).

Table 13.1 *Participation by age*

Age	16–24	35–44	55–64	75–84
Percentage that regularly participate	32.7	24.7	16	6

Participation by age group

http://www.sportengland.org/active_people.htm

The most popular recreational activities were:

- Walking – 8 million adults (20%) did a recreational walk in the last month.
- Swimming – 5.6 million people (13.8%) swim at least once a month.
- Fitness – 4.2 million people (10.5%) go to the gym once a month.
- 10.2 million of the adult population (25%) participate within a sport club.

However even within the broad groups of gender, ethnicity and social class there are wide variations. For example the Women's Sport Foundation, in their report 'Muslim Women in Sport – a minority within a minority' found that Muslim women participate less than other women generally and less than their male counterparts, an already low figure.

AQA Examiner's tip

In this part of the specification and in this topic particularly you will be asked for opinions. It is important that any views you give are supported by evidence and show evidence of critical analysis.

AQA Examiner's tip

Whenever you compare research evidence from several different research exercises be careful to look at how the research has been conducted and the criteria that are used when placing individuals in groups. All too often they are very different.

Activity

Research the levels of participation in the sport you are offering for practical assessment. As a group present the data from different sports in a table. If available, analyse the participation for different sub-groups – women, young people, ethnic minorities, etc.

■ Key terms

Quantitative research: data is collected that allows for a numerical or statistical analysis.

Qualitative research: conclusions are drawn from the basis of discussions or descriptions from individuals.

Barrier to participation: an obstacle or a perceived obstacle that prevents an individual from participating in an activity, excluding their own capabilities.

Equality of opportunity: an equal chance to participate regardless of gender, sexual preference, age, race and social class.

■ Activity

Using the data in Table 13.1 draw some conclusions about the participation of people in different age groups. Imagine that your group had surveyed people in your local area and arrived at different conclusions to the Sport England data – why might that have been the case?

So although there is a general picture of variations in participation amongst different groups within society it is not a simple picture nor does the data seem to be consistent. For example there are even differences between Sport England's data and the government data on general levels of participation – why should this be?

■ Surveys and research will often use different criteria for 'participation'. For some surveys it is regular participation – every week, or so many times a month, for other surveys the criteria is defined as 'having participated in the last 12 months'.

■ Not all surveys categorise groups in the same way.

■ Not all surveys are **quantitative** – some are based upon **qualitative** research where a smaller number of people are surveyed but they discuss or describe their experiences in sport.

Therefore when looking at research data and the conclusions that are drawn it is important to see how the data has been collected and interpreted.

We have enough information however for us to recognise there are wide differences in participation in sport and active leisure and we need to examine the reasons why.

Variations in levels of participation occur due to **barriers to participation** – things that prevent individuals or groups of people from participating.

There are five general barriers to participation in sport and physical recreation:

■ lack of opportunity
■ lack of personal resources
■ discrimination
■ self-discrimination
■ group or peer pressure.

These are considered in more detail later in the chapter.

It should already be clear to you that the variations in levels of participation are not a simplistic issue. Rarely is there one cause, it is more often multi-causal with certain individuals facing significant and varied obstacles to them becoming engaged in sport or active recreation. In the next section we shall look at the nature of these and how they have arisen.

■ What is meant by inclusiveness and equal opportunity?

Equality of opportunity means that all individuals have the same chance to participate and that they are not denied an opportunity on unreasonable grounds. Equality of opportunity can be denied in a number of ways:

■ a lack of facilities
■ inadequate recreational or sporting infrastructure
■ lack of sufficient personal resources
■ discriminatory actions against individuals denying them access to facilities, clubs, teams or access to elite performer support.

The government, through Sport England, local authorities and the voluntary sector are all attempting to ensure that there is equality of opportunity in terms of facilities and the infrastructure of sport and recreation (clubs, teams, groups and competitive structure).

Does 'equality of opportunity' mean that all individuals should be able to access and participate in all forms of sporting and physical recreation? For example, should everybody have the opportunity to participate in skiing, regardless of their personal circumstances and the cost? You might think that we should offer individuals the chance to experience the challenge and adventure that skiing brings – but it does not need to be skiing – it could be climbing, canoeing, walking, caving, which could be provided at low cost through schools, youth clubs or voluntary organisations such as the scouts or guides.

Public and voluntary sector provision can therefore go a long way to achieving equality of opportunity by providing facilities and support, at low or little cost to those of more limited means. Having said that we can never ensure equality of opportunity, we can only seek to achieve the following:

- access to a reasonable range of physical recreation and sport opportunities for all within a community
- provide the opportunity to receive the benefits of participation, but without attempting to provide access to all activities
- a level of provision that enables talented individuals to fulfil their potential.

A term that is often linked to equality of opportunity is **inclusiveness**. Inclusiveness means that individuals are not excluded on unreasonable or irrelevant grounds, or made to feel that they are not wanted. For example a local authority leisure centre, in an ethnically and religiously diverse local community, may state that it provides recreational opportunities for all members of the local community. Is this true if they do not provide women-only sessions, including only female instructors and to allow flexibility of dress to meet dress codes? If they don't they may be excluding some individuals of the Muslim faith.

What are the barriers to participation?

A **barrier to participation** is an obstacle that prevents any group or individual within society from participating in sport or physical recreation. A range of barriers to participation have been identified:

- lack of facilities or sporting infrastructure – a lack of opportunity
- lack of personal resources in terms of time or money
- discrimination as a result of prejudice
- the fear or belief that you will suffer discrimination and therefore not attempt to participate in an activity
- self- or group-imposed limits on participation based upon sport having a low status within a social group
- pressure to undertake certain activities based upon stereotypical views of the strengths and weaknesses of any particular group.

Lack of opportunity

Even with public sector and voluntary support there is a variation in the level of provision and this reflects the economic conditions within a local area or community. Despite increased central government funding to areas of lower economic wealth there are still large differences between communities in different parts of the country. Public sector provision is

Key terms

Inclusiveness: including people of all kinds within an activity or group.

Barrier to participation: an obstacle placed in an individual's way by others, themselves or members of their community or family that is a deterrent to participation or personal development in a sport or physical activity.

Activity

For each of the barriers reflect on each one and consider whether it is something you or somebody you know may have suffered from.

Fig. 13.1 *Eight million adults did a recreational walk last month*

focused on providing a level of opportunity that is deemed to be sufficient to meet minimum needs. It is likely that as exchequer and Lottery funding continues to be focused on less wealthy areas this disparity in provision will reduce but not disappear.

Personal resources

As a result of our family circumstances, personal income, family or work commitments we all have different levels of disposable time or income – time or money that we can devote to things other than providing for our basic needs or meeting our commitments to others. These differences inevitably affect our opportunity to participate.

Discrimination in sport

It is not inherently wrong to discriminate – in one sense the term means to choose between, to make a selection based upon criteria. It is the grounds on which the discrimination is made and whether those grounds

■ Link

Look back at Chapter 10 – Concepts and definitions (page 123) to see how this concept relates to a definition of leisure.

are relevant or accurate, and apply to the individual. For example a tennis club may restrict membership to those who have a certain ranking; a fitness club may restrict numbers on a first-come first-served basis so that members get easy access to equipment, etc. These would be quite reasonable criteria on which to discriminate between individuals so long as the criteria are fairly and consistently applied.

However research shows that individuals suffer from unfair **discrimination** which impacts upon their participation. Discrimination results in an individual being excluded or prevented from participating, usually because of **prejudice** about race, ethnicity, age, religion, or gender, or whether they have a disability. This discrimination is often based upon a stereotypical view of that individual.

Discrimination, as expressed above, is illegal in the United Kingdom where we have laws that are designed to prevent somebody being excluded or treated differently on the basis of race, gender, disability or age.

Many discriminatory views are based upon beliefs about the qualities and characteristics of that person – a **stereotype**. Often these views are incorrect or based upon poor knowledge or half truths. You might have heard the following stereotypical comments today or in the past – 'women are not physically capable of standing the rigours of a marathon', 'black people are genetically good sprinters', 'a person with a disability can never compete on equal terms with those who do not have a disability', 'once you are over 50 you should avoid contact sports'.

Discrimination may also be caused by prejudice – an irrational view of somebody or group of people. Those who hold prejudicial views consider that a particular group of people are inferior and therefore unable to participate in a particular activity, or are in some way not worthy of being part of the group, club or team. They then discriminate against that person by preventing them from participating.

Fear of discrimination

The fear of being abused, or being made to feel unwelcome is likely to lead people to avoid such treatment by not trying to join. It may also lead to groups setting up their own organisations or teams solely to avoid any possibility of discrimination or to provide the security of being with others like themselves. Such actions which may increase participation may also lead to a greater sense of isolation and does not address the central issue of discrimination.

Table 13.2 *Those reporting suffering discrimination in sport*

	Black Caribbean	Black African	Black – other	Indian	Pakistani	Bangladeshi	Chinese	Other
Men	11	6	21	8	7	10	2	7
Women	6	2	14	1	3	9	0	3
Total	8	4	17	5	5	9	1	4

Stereotypical views – the push factor

Discrimination is often only thought of in terms of preventing somebody from joining or participating but discrimination can also occur through assumptions about what an individual may be good at due to stereotypical views of their strengths and weaknesses. Boys from UK Caribbean or African background are encouraged to engage in

Key terms

Discrimination: treating people differently through prejudice: unfair treatment of one person or a group often based upon a stereotypical view of that group or person.

Prejudice: holding a preformed judgement or opinion of someone based upon irrational, incomplete or inaccurate stereotypical views.

Stereotype: an oversimplified view of someone, a standardised image. May include attributes that are incorrect or only partially true.

Activity

As an individual spend 5 minutes making a list of sports that you believe to be suitable for either men or women. Present your list to the group and be prepared to justify your decisions. Collate lists – are there similarities or differences between your list and the lists of others?

explosive sports, or positions where speed and strength are an advantage due to erroneous beliefs about genetic advantages. Women are encouraged to take up 'female appropriate' activities based upon a female stereotype.

The status of sport

Research has shown that for some groups within society sport is of low social and economic value and young people within those groups are actively discouraged from devoting time and resources to developing their talents and abilities. This can lead to a lack of fulfilment and cause tensions within families and communities as well as diminishing the number of elite performers coming through from the grass roots.

Who suffers from the barriers to participation?

Research has identified that these barriers have an effect on specific groups within our society. They have been identified by Sport England as under-represented groups and are the subject of specific national policies to improve their levels of participation. Those groups are:

- women
- those from different **ethnic** backgrounds
- those with a **disability**
- those from disadvantaged **socio-economic groups.**

Within those main under-represented groups specific sub-groups have been identified, or it has been recognised that if you fall into two or more of those categories than you face considerably more difficult barriers.

Women

Prior to discussing the barriers that women may face we need to understand the terms **sex** and **gender**. Sex is whether an individual is biologically male or female. Gender refers to the culturally determined roles that men and women play in a particular society. Women's participation is affected by issues of **sexism**. Sexism occurs where women (or less frequently men) are discriminated against as a result of stereotypical views of the strengths and qualities of women in a sport and physical recreation context and the gender role that women are expected to undertake within our society.

Despite the growth in sport and physical recreation that has occurred over the last 100 years women's participation has been adversely affected by a range of stereotypical views – some of which you may now find quite bizarre:

- Women do not have the physical strength or endurance to undertake the same range of sport or physical recreation activities as men.
- It is not considered to be feminine for women to compete aggressively.
- Women may damage their ability to bear children if they engage in excessive physical activity.
- Women who train hard to develop musculature to enable them to compete more effectively become more 'male' and have their sexual orientation questioned.
- A woman's role is to be the care giver, the mother, the manager of the home and this is not compatible with a role in highly competitive sport.

Key terms

Ethnic group: people who share a common and identifiable religious, racial, national or linguistic background.

Disability: a disability is any restriction or lack (resulting from impairment) of ability to perform an activity in the manner or within the range considered normal for a human being (WHO 1980).

Socio-economic group: a classification that groups together people with similar social and economic status.

Sex: a biological term for male or female.

Gender: the role of male or female as determined by society or cultures.

Sexism: discrimination based upon one's sex or gender.

Table 13.3 *Participation levels of women compared to men (%)*

Women – Frequency of Participation in Previous 4 weeks (excl. walking)			
Group	At least once	4 times or more	12 times or more
Male	50	37	19
Female	37	26	11

It is true of course that these views have been challenged and are still being challenged. Sport does not exist in a cultural or social vacuum, and feminist politics has had an impact in sport as well as in wider society. As a result of those stereotypical views other barriers have been erected which deter women from participating, or from participating in as wide a range of sports as men.

▮ Sport is a male-dominated activity.

▮ Women elite sport performers receive less media coverage than men.

▮ Women receive less support from peers and family.

▮ Facilities and the sporting infrastructure for women have lagged behind that developed for male performers.

▮ Media coverage of elite women performers is likely to include details that are not relevant to their performance – looks, attractiveness, whether they are a mother, etc.

More detailed research has identified that specific groups of women are affected by these issues more than others:

▮ Teenage girls (15–19) participate less.

▮ Muslim women participate less than women from other social or cultural groups.

Research undertaken by Sport England, published in 2006, found that the major reasons for the decline in participation by teenage girls centred on the perceived lack of interest in physical activity from their friends and family, concerns over their weight and appearance, a lack of self-confidence and a lack of information as to how they could stay involved.

According to a report published by the Women's Sport Foundation in 2006, Muslim women have a number of barriers to overcome in addition to those traditionally faced by women from all social groups. However the barriers that Muslim women face are more cultural than religious. As a religion Islam promotes good health and fitness, but has restrictions on men and women participating in mixed gender sports and must follow a strict dress code. The report identified the specific barriers to participation facing Muslim women:

▮ negative experiences of PE in schools

▮ mixed groups – lack of opportunity to participate in single sex groups (also linked to PE experiences)

▮ problems with dress code – some sport facility and school PE dress codes make it difficult for Muslim women to participate

▮ lack of positive role models.

It can be seen that the three groups we have identified face some similar barriers and some that are unique to their specific group. This means that any plan or policy designed to improve levels of participation must deal with the specific barriers as well as the general ones.

▮ **Activity**

In groups discuss which of the stereotypical views you think have now been discredited and are no longer held. Secondly which of the barriers to participation are no longer relevant?

Ethnic groups

An ethnic group is defined as a group of people who share common origins – be they cultural, religious, racial, or linguistic. As you have already seen within the UK we have a range of what are described as minority ethnic groups that reflect the range of people from different racial, religious and national groups who at some stage in the past have emigrated to this country and to one degree or another are now integrated within our diverse multi-cultural society. In the UK we have a range of identified ethnic minority groups and a range of terms that are used when referring to those groups. These groups are principally identifiable on grounds of nationality, race or religion. It is important to use appropriate terminology, both for purposes of accuracy and to avoid causing offence.

These terms are those used by the government's General Household Survey.

- UK Caribbean – people whose origins are from the Caribbean. Forming 1 per cent of the population.
- UK African – people whose indigenous origins are from the African sub-continent. Forming 1 per cent of the population.
- UK Asian – people originating from the Asian sub-continent. Forming 4.5 per cent of the population further divided into Indian, Pakistani and Bangladeshi depending upon country of origin. Religiously speaking – principally Muslim, Hindu and Sikh.
- UK Chinese – 0.5 per cent of the population.
- Other non-white – comprising mixed race and other groups – 0.5 per cent of the population.

A more detailed look at participation rates, as reported within Sport England's report 'Sports Participation and Ethnicity in England', showed that there is a significant variation between ethnic groups and between males and female within those groups. From Table 2 we can see that there is a difference in levels of participation between various minority ethnic groups and we must look at the barriers that may account for those differences.

Table 13.4 *Sport participation by ethnic group*

Ethnic group	Average level	Black Caribbean	Indian	Pakistani	Bangladeshi	Black African	'Black other'
Participation level % (Men)	54	39	47	42	46	60	80
Participation level % (Women)	39	34	31	24	19	34	45

What could account for these differing levels of participation?

- There is evidence that people from ethnic minorities suffer from discrimination as a result of prejudice and may find it harder to access opportunities, or may voluntarily avoid situations where discrimination and prejudice are anticipated.
- A higher than average percentage of people from ethnic minority communities are in economically deprived areas and have lower levels of disposable income.

- There is some evidence to suggest that although personal health and exercise may be culturally valued in themselves, devoting time and other resources to reach an elite level may be discouraged.

- Women and young girls may find participating in sport and physical recreation more difficult due to the traditional views of the role of women within the family and difficulties over mixed-sex groups and dress codes.

We have been focusing on general levels of participation but there is also an unevenness of representation at elite levels of sport. For example:

The GB athletics team at the 2007 World Championships comprised 30 per cent of team members from the Black Caribbean or Black African ethnic minority communities.

In the England football squad 30 per cent of players are also from those communities. Why?

The response that is often given to this question is that people from Black Caribbean and African groups have the correct physiological or anatomical attributes due to their genetic make up – i.e. they have a genetic advantage. Athletics and football often require speed, power and strength and claims are made that those ethnic groups have a higher proportion of fast twitch muscle fibre, have a longer Achilles tendon allowing for greater power transfer or have a higher ratio of muscle to other body tissues.

At the time of publication there is no research evidence to substantiate these claims. No valid or peer-reviewed piece of research has been able to show that people from the UK Caribbean or UK African ethnic groups have a genetically derived physiological and anatomical characteristic that predisposes them towards sports that require power, speed and strength. There are of course many other sports that require these physiological characteristics – for example tennis and rugby union, yet we do not see the same 'over' representation there.

It is true of course that to be an elite athlete (in the explosive or speed events) or an elite footballer you are very likely to have a higher proportion of fast twitch muscle fibre – indeed for sprinters it is the most important single factor. So all elite sprinters have a high percentage of fast twitch fibres – a genetically endowed factor that is then honed by training. It has not been shown that one ethnic or racial group has a higher incidence of those than any other.

So what factors may account for this higher than average representation?

- The role model effect – the existence of high-profile members of these communities as elite sport performers encourages others to take up those activities with more therefore coming through at the elite level. This is further enhanced by a lack of role models in other sports or walks of life. Certain sports may seem to offer opportunities for social and economic advancement and will encourage those with the ability to choose that path.

- Young people from this ethnic group may be encouraged or pressured to undertake certain activities based upon the mistaken 'genetic advantage' belief that we discounted earlier.

- Athletic achievement is based upon objective, factually based outcomes – times, distance, height and a clear rank order based solely upon performance. There is less likelihood that talented performers can be overlooked or ignored – there is much less room for selection to be based upon prejudiced or discriminatory views.

The socio-economic groups from which the largest proportion of elite footballers and athletes come have a higher than average percentage of members of the UK Black African and Caribbean communities within them. Conversely we have no member of our elite tennis squads from those socio-economic or ethnic minority groups.

Sport, physical recreation and those with a disability

There is a clear definition as to which members of our society are described as having a disability. A person with a disability has some form of impairment which affects their ability to engage in an activity.

An **impairment** is a loss or deficiency of the body or mind that affects the functioning of the body.

Within that broad definition of disability there are a range of **disability types**. These are often grouped together into four categories:

- mobility impairments, which take into account the skeletal and disfiguring impairments
- sensory impairments, which take into account impairments of hearing and sight
- mental impairments, which take into account those with a learning difficulty and other psychological impairments
- other impairments such as language, cognitive or perceptual impairments.

To enable people with a disability to compete against each other within specific sports a **profile system** has been developed which has a complex system of scoring which gives each performer a profile score based upon their level of impairment. Competitors with different profiles may then be grouped together, dependent on the nature of the sport. Javelin throwing may have different groupings of profiles as compared to rifle shooting. Each sport has its own groupings of competitors to allow for fair competition within that sport.

Five broad categories are usually used:

- Amputees – includes athletes who have at least one major joint in a limb missing, for example the elbow, wrist, knee or ankle.
- Cerebral palsy – a disorder of movement and posture due to damage to areas of the brain that control and coordinate muscle tone, reflexes, posture and movement.
- Wheelchair – athletes compete in this category if they have at least 10 per cent loss of function in their lower limbs. Commonly this would include paraplegia and quadriplegia, spinabifida, polio, amputees, cerebral palsy and all non-ambulant les autres athletes.
- Vision impaired – performers who have any condition which interferes with 'normal' vision. This incorporates the entire range of vision difficulties from correctable conditions through to total blindness.
- Les autres – a French term for 'the others', used to describe athletes with a range of conditions, such as dwarfism, that don't fit into the traditional classification systems of the established groups.

It can be seen that there are a wide range of conditions that fall under the umbrella term 'disability' and it is easy to make assumptions and talk generally of those with a disability without paying attention to their specific requirements. It is very easy to stereotype members of this group and this can easily lead to discrimination. Many people with a disability will consider themselves to be 'differently abled' rather than 'disabled'.

Key terms

Impairment: any loss or abnormality of psychological, physiological or anatomical structure or function (WHO 1980).

Disability types: a group of people with a specific and recognised impairment.

Profile system: a method of grouping people with different disability types, or with degrees of the same impairment, together so that they may compete against each other.

AQA Examiner's tip

Do not fall into the trap of only considering wheelchair performers when answering questions relating to disability. Be prepared to use and quote examples from the full range of impairments and disabled sport categories.

Evidence from the Active People Survey 2006 shows that only approximately 9% of people with a longstanding illness or disability participate regularly in sport compared to 23 per cent who do not have such a condition. A Sport England survey in 2001 concluded that people with a disability are 39 per cent less likely to participate in sport and active leisure.

Why should this be the case?

- There are some people whose disability is so severe that it precludes any participation in physical activity or sport. This is only a small percentage of this group.
- Although all new buildings must be designed to have ease of access for those with mobility or other disabilities many physical recreation or sport facilities are not easily used by those with a disability.
- The stereotyping of people with a disability, making inaccurate assumptions of their difficulties, and giving insufficient thought as to how appropriate support and opportunities can be provided.
- Despite government legislation such as the Disability Discrimination Act 2004 people with a disability are often an 'invisible' minority whose needs are ignored or seen to be less high profile.
- There can be a lack of consensus over the best way to provide opportunities for those with a disability – whether to participate with non-disabled people or develop adaptive sports such as wheelchair basketball specifically for disabled people. This issue is discussed later in the chapter.
- A lack of status and public recognition given to our elite level disabled performers, who in global terms are more successful than our non-disabled performers. Great Britain has been in second place in the medal table for the last two Paralympic Games.

Social class issues

Social class is determined by your socio-economic group. Since 2001 an individual's occupation has been the major factor when classifying them into a group. The groups that are currently used can be seen in Figure 13.2.

The National Statistics Socio-economic Classification	
1	Higher managerial and professional occupations
2	Lower managerial and professional occupations
3	Intermediate occupations
4	Small employers and own account workers
5	Lower supervisory and technical occupations
6	Semi-routine occupations
7	Routine occupations
8	Never worked and long-term unemployed

Fig. 13.2 *Socio-economic classes*

In the United Kingdom the way in which people have been subdivided in to social classes or socio-economic groups has changed a great deal particularly over the last 30 years. You will have heard the terms upper, middle or lower classes, working classes, professional classes and so on. These sub-divisions or classes are based upon many common characteristics, which usually include income, education, occupation and social status or prestige. This change in the way society is classified causes problems when trying to analyse whether or not people from different socio-economic groups or social classes participate more than another, particularly if we are trying to assess these levels of participation over time.

The report 'Participation in Sport in Great Britain 1987–2002', based upon the General Household Survey, did not even mention socio-economic groups. The 'Active People Survey' showed that individuals from a lower socio-economic group are likely to participate less in sport or active recreation. Sport England's Sport Equity report of 2002 had a more detailed breakdown of participation by social class and is shown in Figure 13.3.

The National Statistics Socio-economic Classification	
1	Higher managerial and professional occupations
2	Lower managerial and professional occupations
3	Intermediate occupations
4	Small employers and own account workers
5	Lower supervisory and technical occupations
6	Semi-routine occupations
7	Routine occupations
8	Never worked and long-term unemployed

Fig. 13.3 *Participation by social class*

The reasons for this lower level of participation by certain socio-economic groups are as follows:

▨ Most sports and active recreation activities require some expenditure – individuals in lower socio-economic groups have less **disposable income** and therefore have less money to spend on sport or recreation. They have less opportunity due to personal resources.

▨ Some physical recreation activities are associated with specific social classes. For example golf or yachting are seen to be middle class activities and individuals from other socio-economic groups may feel that they will be rejected or discriminated against if they attempt to engage in that activity.

▨ Individuals from different socio-economic groups from the dominant one within the activity may suffer actual discrimination and be prevented from participating in the activity. For example a club may have membership application processes that are open to discriminatory practices.

▨ Individuals from lower socio-economic groups (3–7) may have less leisure time available to spend on physical recreation and therefore their participation levels are lower.

These factors will result in individuals not having the full range of physical activities available to them. This may also mean that talented individuals will have less opportunity to exploit and develop their talent and the country has fewer elite performers. For example there are concerns that tennis does not draw from a large enough pool of talent and this severely limits the development of internationally ranked players.

▨ **Key terms**

Disposable income: money left over after the essentials for living have been taken out.

▨ **Activities**

1 Research the costs of entry to a range of local sport facilities or clubs. Express those as a multiple of the hourly minimum wage of £5.35.

2 Make a list of sports that you think are associated with upper, middle or low socio-economic groups or classes. What is it about the activity that makes you associate it with one social class or another?

What is being done to overcome the barriers to participation?

A range of national and local organisations are tasked with the responsibility of overcoming the barriers to participation, from the Department of Culture, Media and Sport to your local tennis club.

Which groups are involved in providing equality of opportunity?

The major player in this role is Sport England. They are charged by government and by law to address the problem of uneven levels of participation in sport and physical recreation and since 2007 this has become their major focus. Sport England has two general targets:

- To increase the general level of participation across the country.

  In 2007 their target was to get two million people more active in sport by 2012. Sport England has developed the National Framework for Sport which aims to increase participation by 1 per cent each year for 20 years. This is an ambitious target and will only be achieved by involving those groups that have relatively low participation levels and the organisations that support them. For young people the PE, School Sport and Club Links (PESSCL) strategy involves investing money to increase the take up of sporting opportunities by 5 to 16 year olds so that by 2008 85 per cent of them will experience a minimum of two hours high quality PE and school sport each week.

- To address the uneven level of participation by identifying who the under-represented groups are and then developing specific policies for each group. Sport England has produced an Equality Scheme and an Action Plan both based on its 'No Limits' policy, and involves the setting up of the Sports Equity Alliance.

The Sports Equity Alliance brings together a range of partners – Women's Sport Foundation, Sporting Equals and English Federation for Disabled Sport, along with the national governing bodies of sport to promote equality of opportunity for women and girls, disabled people, people from ethnic minorities and those from lower socio-economic groups.

National governing bodies of sport have to achieve a required level of the Equality Standard as a condition of funding. Each NGB must therefore have policies designed to improve the participation of the under-represented groups within each of their sports.

AQA Examiner's tip

You must understand that there can also be self-imposed barriers by groups or individuals that limit participation.

Exam questions will demand knowledge of barriers, their effect and how they may be overcome.

Link

You will find more information on Sport England in Chapter 11 – Leisure provision (page 146).

Disability Sport Events

English Federation of Disability Sport

Fig. 13.4 *Sport England's equality partners*

Activity

Research the national governing body targets for participation and the policies for improving the participation of the under-represented groups for the sport you are offering for practical assessment.

Women

The Women's Sports Foundation (WSF) is the UK organisation dedicated to improving and promoting opportunities for women and girls in sport and physical activity. In 2007 the Gender Equality Duty (GED) came into force and placed a statutory obligation on all local authorities and sports bodies to promote equality of opportunity between men and women and eliminate discrimination and harassment.

The WSF tries to achieve its goal of improving women's opportunities by:

- providing advice and information to sport and recreation providers using up-to-date research
- helping sport and recreation providers with their policy and strategy development and to find sources of funding to improve women's level of participation
- influencing national government, local government and sports council strategies and policies to ensure that they seek to provide equality of opportunity for women
- collecting, developing and sharing examples of best practice in terms of encouraging women to participate
- celebrating women's sporting success by working closely with the media.

Two examples of the way in which the WSF operates are its 'Women into Coaching' programme which aims to get more women to take up and become coaches and its website 'What works for women' which gives advice and information on how women are discriminated against in sport and how sports bodies and local authorities can overcome this discrimination.

Ethnic minorities

Using the 'Active People Survey' Sport England monitors participation rates amongst all sections of society including that of black and minority ethnic groups.

To help overcome the problem of under-representation of many ethnic minorities Sport England, together with the Commission for Racial Equality, funds Sporting Equals, a national initiative with a specific remit to promote racial equality in sport.

As well as being concerned about under-representation in terms of participation Sporting Equals believes that the success of ethnic minority elite sportsmen and women in sport is not reflected in the role they play in terms of coaching, sports administration and sports management.

Sporting Equals states that its mission is 'to eradicate racial discrimination in sport'. In order to achieve its mission it has three core objectives:

- Raise awareness and understanding and therefore change attitudes in sport.
- Help individuals and communities play a part in this change and achieve their full potential through sport.
- Challenge and support sports leaders to achieve change within their own organisations.

The key factor used by Sporting Equals to measure the effectiveness of its policies is an increase in numbers from ethnic minority communities who participate, volunteer and are employed in sport – although it has not set a specific number or percentage increase as its target.

Those with a disability

Using the Active People survey Sport England monitors participation rates including detailed data regarding people with disabilities. To fulfil its role and meet its obligations under the Disability Act Sport England included an action plan for those with a disability within the Equality Scheme.

There are a number of bodies with whom Sport England works to help improve the levels of participation of those with a disability. The three main ones are English Federation of Disability Sport, National Disability Sports Organizations and Disability Sport England.

English Federation of Disability Sport

This is the national body responsible for developing sport for disabled people in England. Sport England has a contractual relationship with the English Federation of Disability Sport to ensure that the needs of disabled people are taken into account. This includes consultation on regional and local issues.

National Disability Sports Organizations

This represents the interests of the major categories of people who are assessed as having a disability:

- British Amputees and Les Autres Sports Association
- British Blind Sport
- WheelPower – British Wheelchair Sport
- Mencap Sport/Cerebral Palsy Sport (CP Sport)
- UK Deaf Sport
- English Sports Association for People with Learning Disability (ESAPLD).

Disability Sport England (DSE)

This is responsible for coordinating and delivering a network of national events in a range of sports such as swimming and athletics.

The EFDS is the major organisation and has produced a 4 Year Plan – 'Count Me In' (2004–2008) which has had the effect of helping local councils increase community opportunities for disabled adults, where physical activity is often more important than sport. For example the 'Inclusive Fitness Initiative' has brought new accessible fitness equipment into local authority gyms and helped train staff to recognise the needs of their disabled customers and to promote new opportunities to disabled people.

Within education EFDS have developed an after-school club programme with DfES funding – 'One Small Step'. They have also devised a course 'Including Disabled Pupils in PE' which gives teachers the skills to work with disabled pupils.

For the more potentially able performer a strategy 'Identifying and supporting talented young disabled people' is an initiative intended to support gifted and talented young disabled pupils via the PESSCL project. Sport England, UK Sport, the British Paralympic Association (BPA) and Youth Sports Trust (YST) launched a strategy known as 'Playground to Podium' and commissioned the development of a framework for athletes with a disability to achieve their full potential.

The EFDS also works with NGBs and a number of sports have appointed staff to specifically support the development of disabled athletes. In

Fig. 13.5 *Paralympic shot putter*

football a project called 'Ability Counts' trained coaches to work with disabled footballers in clubs in the Premiership and Football League.

The EFDS is also trying to encourage and empower disabled people to take a full and active role within any aspect of the sport and physical activity industry. Part of this process is to get the media to report the success in sport achieved by disabled people and thereby raise the profile of sport, physical education and healthy activities for disabled people.

Together or separated?

Are disabled people better served by a policy of integration within the mainstream or by having competitions and other sports opportunities that are specifically for them? Those who argue for sports integration point out that by separating people with a disability you increase the possibilities of them being discriminated against, that people who do not have a disability acquire a stereotypical view and this simply increases the hurdles or raises more barriers.

Those who argue for separate opportunities believe that some separation better serves the needs of people with a disability, allowing for a greater range of opportunities as programmes and activities can be designed specifically to meet their needs. In general the argument for integration rather than separateness is winning the day within the UK and therefore PE and sport will continue to seek ways of integrating sport and physical recreation opportunities for those with a disability within mainstream activities.

Adapted sports or designed sports?

One way that people with a disability are enabled to participate in sport is by either adapting a mainstream version of the sport or by designing a new sport.

Adapting the mainstream version of the sport is known as an **adapted sport**. An example of an adapted sport would be wheelchair basketball or the various forms of adapted athletics. Adapting a sport means that people with a disability can participate in mainstream sports and at times be able to compete with people who do not have a disability.

Sports designed to enable people with a disability often come under the umbrella heading of 'sportsability games'. These are games that have been specifically designed to be accessible to people with a disability, and to support inclusion. The games were designed by the Youth Sports Trust. The sportsability games include the following:

- boccia – a bowls-type game, played at the Paralympics and suitable for players of all abilities
- poybat – table-top bat and ball game aimed at young people with higher support needs
- table cricket – all the possibilities of cricket on a table-top aimed at children with physical impairment for whom ambulant cricket may not be an option
- table hockey – suitable for young people who have physical or visual impairments, or learning disabilities
- goalball – active court game for visually impaired or sighted players.

Socio-economically disadvantaged groups

The Government, through the use of exchequer and Lottery funding, has as one of its major objectives the provision of equality of opportunity for

■ Key terms

Adapted sport: where a sport has its rules or playing conditions altered so that people with a disability may take part.

■ Activity

For your own sport research whether or not there is an adapted version. If so how has the sport been adapted and what rule changes have been undertaken?

those people from socially excluded and poor backgrounds. Specifically the Government via Sport England has introduced a number of initiatives to help redress social inequalities.

The Community Club Development Programme is a collaboration between the Department for Culture, Media and Sport, Sport England and 16 national governing bodies of sport. Funding for the programme is £60 million and is intended to allow for a total of around 250–300 projects supporting the development of local community sport clubs. One of the criteria is to support clubs that are in areas of greatest social deprivation.

Secondly Sport Action Zones were initiated in 2000 and were designed to bring the benefits of sport to deprived communities. They do this by developing a wide network of schools, sports clubs, and other voluntary groups working together to provide more opportunities.
The Sport Action Zone aims are to:

- Work to help those that excel succeed in their chosen sport.
- Work with young people involved in anti-social behaviour.
- Work with community health services to support people in poor health.
- Provide education, training and support for community sports workers.
- Set up local sports clubs where none exist.
- Make sports centres more accessible.

Thirdly the Respect Athlete Mentoring Programme (RAMP) supported by Sport England and the Youth Sports Trust is a mentoring programme for local schools and community groups, using inspirational elite sports people as mentors, aiming to improve the lives of disadvantaged and disaffected young people in targeted neighbourhoods. Through mentoring it aims to improve confidence and self-esteem, raise aspirations and give disaffected young people the sort of positive and challenging experiences that will inspire and motivate them.

How effectively are we overcoming the barriers and achieving equality of opportunity in sport?

It is extremely difficult to assess the impact of the many policies that have been developed to overcome the barriers to participation. This is due to a number of reasons:

- a lack of longitudinal research that can show trends
- changes in the criteria for measuring participation
- changes in the criteria for the socio-demographic groups that are being surveyed
- simple lack of research for groups such as those with a disability.

However some research has been carried out for the period 1987–2002:

- Young people in Sport 1994–2002
- Participation in Sport in Great Britain: – Trends 1987 to 2002.

Both of those reports showed a small but general decline in levels of participation, both generally and for the specific groups we have been focusing on.

AQA Examiner's tip

Exam questions will require the use of examples of national or group-specific policies designed to overcome barriers.

Activity

Prepare mind maps on the policies of the following bodies – Sport England, English Federation of Disability Sport, local authorities, WSF, and one NGB.

Activity

Prepare pie charts comparing the proportion of ethnic minority performers in a range of elite teams – football, netball, hockey, athletics, swimming and cricket – to that of group representation in the population generally.

Table 13.5 *Comparison of adult participation 1996–2002*

Rank	Group	Index (2002)	Index (1996)
1	16–19	169	172
2	20–24	143	152
3	25–29	141	139
4	30–34	126	126
5	NSSEC 1 & 2	125	(117)
6	Male	117	118
7	Without a disability	113	113
8	White	102	101
Norm	All Adults	100	100
9	45–49	92	88
10	Female	86	85
11	BEM	79	89
12	NSSEC 6, 7 & 8	69	(73)
13	60–69	65	65
14	With a disability	61	64
15	70 or over	34	27

Table 13.6 *Participation levels for ethnic minority communities 1996–2002*

	Year*	Ethnicity						
		White	All Ethnic Minority Groups	Indian	Pakistani and Bangladeshi	Black (Caribbean, African, Other)	Other (Chinese, none of the above)	Total
At least one activity	1990	63.0	55.5	51.0	38.7	55.4	68.3	63.4
	2002	59.4	45.5	48.3	25.0	43.7	50.5	58.3
At least one activity (exc. walking)	1990	40.1	40.4	30.7	25.8	40.2	53.3	45.9
	2002	44.1	34.0	30.4	21.7	33.2	45.1	43.4
Base	1990	12,701	695	168	124	164	199	13,401
	2002	11,482	1,326	202	160	418	546	12,841

For example Table 13.5 shows the comparison of casual participation by various groups, benchmarked against an average (represented by a score of 100) comparing 1996 with 2002.

Women's and ethnic minority groups participation showed a similar trend as shown in Table 13.5 and Table 13.6.

Given that Sport England is now committed to researching levels of participation and the impact of its own policies and strategies there is likely to be more consistent data available in the future.

One example of Sport England's recent research is that carried out to assess the impact of the Sport Action Zones (2006) which showed a 5–10 per cent increase in participation. Among socio-economically deprived (5–7) groups it increased by a staggering 10 per cent (43% to 53%). This is encouraging as this was the very purpose for which the Sport Action Zones were set up.

 You should now be able to:

- know which groups suffer from the barriers to participation and why those barriers exist

- understand the impact that discrimination has upon levels of participation both for individuals and groups

- use statistical data and qualitative research from accounts of personal experiences to understand the impact of discrimination

- describe the various policies and strategies that attempt to overcome the barriers to participation

- know how these strategies are implemented at grass roots level

- debate the appropriateness of policies of positive discrimination, separate development and selection quotas.

Activity

The South African Rugby Union has introduced quotas for different racial groups within its regional teams. It has done this to improve equality of opportunity. Do you think the use of positive discrimination/quotas is the correct way to provide equality of opportunity? Prepare bullet points for both sides of the argument and discuss with your group. Be prepared to use your arguments in a debate.

1   Disability Sport England has a responsibility to promote participation in
    sport for people with all forms of disability.

    (a) Physical disability is one major category; state one other category
    of disability. *(1 mark)*

    (b) What benefits can participation in sporting activities have for people
    with disabilities? *(3 marks)*

    (c) Apart from adapted sports, in what other ways can the participation
    of people with disabilities be increased? *(2 marks)*

2   Participation in sporting activities is often dependent upon the opportunities
    available to individuals within society.

    (a) Explain the term 'discrimination'. *(1 mark)*

    (b) What is the effect of stereotyping on ethnic minority groups in the
    UK in relation to their participation in sporting activities? *(2 marks)*

    (c) Other than stereotyping, how else might social groups such as women,
    those with a disability or low socio-economic status be discriminated
    against in sport? *(3 marks)*

3   Research shows that some individuals and groups in the UK participate less
    than others.

    (a) Give three reasons for the lower participation rates among some
    ethnic minority groups. *(3 marks)*

    (b) How does the Government promote sport within socially and
    economically deprived areas? *(3 marks)*

4   Women have historically participated less in sport and physical activities than men.

    (a) How might women experience discrimination in recreational and
    sporting activities? *(3 marks)*

UNIT 2

Practical aspects of physical education

Introduction

Chapters in this section:

The next section of the book – Chapters 14, 15 and 16 – will help you develop your knowledge and understanding for the work you will encounter in Unit 2. Unit 2 accounts for 40 per cent of the marks available within the AS specification.

Chapter 14 is the practical component and marks are accredited to you according to how well you demonstrate the ability to develop and improve performance in two sport-related roles. There are three roles to choose from:

▓ performer
▓ coach
▓ official.

You are assessed on how you perform your chosen roles in a physical activity selected from a list of forty different activities. Most students will undertake both of the roles within one physical activity but it is possible to select two physical activities and develop a role in each. You are marked, firstly, on your performance in the two roles, and then on your ability to improve performance. You demonstrate your ability to improve performance by observing and analysing the performance of yourself and others, and then by putting into practice the methods of improving performance that are covered in Chapters 15 and 16.

You are assessed on how well you can demonstrate the core skills that are identified in the specification, both in isolation and in what are called 'modified conditions or conditioned practices'. This means that you will be performing in a modified version of the activity – for example, a 3 on 3 situation in basketball, with varying levels of opposition and competition. You will not be asked to perform in the full version of the activity, although you will be assessed whilst engaged in a normal competitive situation.

Chapter 14 has been written to give you advice and support in developing your own performance in your chosen two roles.

Chapters 15 and 16 are the theoretical component of Unit 2 which is assessed both by how you apply the knowledge, skills and understanding to developing your practical performance and also by a twelve-mark question on Section B of the Unit 1 exam paper.

The specification requires you to show an understanding of how to improve performance in two ways:

▓ improvements in physical fitness
▓ improvements in skill.

To improve physical fitness you gain an understanding of the principles of fitness training, how to decide the correct workload for yourself and other performers, how to test physical fitness levels, the correct methods of warming up and cooling down, and the range of training methods that can be used. Chapter 15 will help you acquire and apply the theory.

To improve skills you are taken through how to plan and execute skill development sessions – from deciding which teaching style is appropriate, how to structure the time available, the best way of presenting the skill to be learnt or improved and how best to guide the performer and give them feedback. Chapter 16 will help you in acquiring the required knowledge and show your understanding through both the practical and examination routes.

This theoretical knowledge is used to improve practical performance and therefore gain marks within the coursework elements of the specification, but is also assessed in section B of the Unit 1 exam paper.

In addition you will find many opportunities to apply the knowledge and understanding you gained in Unit 1, of both exercise physiology and the psychology of skill acquisition.

For the overwhelming majority of AS level Physical Education students their enjoyment of sport and physical activity is the reason they chose the subject to study at AS level (and on to the full A level). The coursework component in Unit 2 gives a great opportunity to turn that enthusiasm and enjoyment into a valuable AS Level grade, as well as getting better in your chosen sport or activity.

Good luck!

14 Practical coursework

In this chapter we shall be looking at how you can gain the best marks from the practical elements of the course. You are required to show proficiency in two out of three roles as a performer, as a coach or leader, or as an official. To enable you to have the best possible chance of gaining marks in either your practical performance or in the examinations it would be beneficial if you were to gain experience in all three roles as they inter-relate very strongly. In addition you may find that you have a hidden talent as either an official or as a coach – you never know so try it.

You will have noticed throughout all the chapters of the book that the learning activities frequently ask you to refer to your practical activity. In this chapter however we shall be reversing that process and referring you back to the theoretical elements that we have already covered. Indeed to be an effective performer, able to analyse your own performance, or to function effectively as a coach or an official you will need to have a secure knowledge of the physiological, psychological and socio-cultural factors that affect all physical activity performance.

In this chapter you will be shown how you can prepare yourself for assessment in any of the three roles, and what to do when you find yourself in an assessment situation. In this part of the course you will find that you will have to be more proactive, and take more responsibility for your own progression than in any other element. Within most school or college timetables there is insufficient time available to spend on individually helping each student. Your progression as an official, coach or performer is very much in your own hands. This chapter will give you general advice that will be relevant to your chosen activity but as there are 40 different activities within the specification, the actual skills and knowledge for your chosen activity must be sourced by yourself, although we will guide you towards where you find the necessary information

You should view your development as a coach, performer or official as a continuous process, beginning on day one of the course, running right up to the final assessment date set by your school or college. In addition

Fig. 14.1 *PE students and staff working together*

Fig. 14.2 *A student in the role of 'performer'*

Activity

Using a printed copy of the specification or the AQA website list the core skills or techniques that you can expect to be assessed in.

a continuous focus on the practical will help you put the theoretical concepts into context and give you a wealth of examples you can use when answering examination questions.

Finally the practical elements are no doubt the reasons you decided to do the course – you enjoy being a performer, coach or an official – so enjoy them!

This chapter is divided into three sections – firstly an explanation of how the marks are applied within the specification, secondly how best to prepare yourself for assessment and finally how to get the best marks when you are actually being assessed.

 See accompanying online video resources to help you understand what makes a practical coursework perormance in the role of performer, coach/leader or official.

How the marks in Unit 2 (Practical Coursework) are awarded

How the marks are awarded, what skills and knowledge you have to acquire is given in the specification. Every student should have a copy of the AQA specification – it is available for download from the AQA website. However the criteria can seem to be complex to the uninitiated and this section will act as a simple and clear guide to the assessment criteria.

Firstly you are assessed in two out of three roles:

- performer
- coach or leader
- official.

You can choose to undertake the roles in two different activities – but be careful as not all activities allow you to be an official.

For each of those three roles you will need to:

- Demonstrate a range of skills and techniques, relevant to the role both as a demonstration and in modified (not in a full game or fully competitive situation) competitive situations.
- Observe, analyse and evaluate how others perform in the role.
- Be able to analyse your own performance in the role.
- Apply the theoretical knowledge from Unit 1 (anatomy and physiology, skill acquisition and information processing, the social context of sport and physical activity) to each of the roles, so that you can improve your performance and the performance of others.

How you do this is slightly different for each of the roles and we shall take each role in turn.

At AS level 40 per cent of your final grade is determined by the marks you gain in this section. There are 100 marks available, 50 marks for each of the roles you undertake.

How the performance marks are allocated

At AS Level there are 50 marks available for the role of performer. Performance marks are awarded in a range of ways:

Demonstrating the specified skills (see the specification for the actual skills relevant to your activity) against a recognised skill model. You will be asked to demonstrate each skill or technique on its own and in a modified competitive situation. This is most usually done using a modified version of the activity, for example in basketball using a 3 on 3 situation.

You will have to show your assessor that you can use these skills consistently – a fluke one-off performance will not be enough.

Showing that you can use the skills or techniques within the rules or laws of the activity and an understanding of any safety considerations.

Be able to analyse your own performance to identify strengths and weaknesses so that you can perform better in the future.

Show your skill and techniques in a variety of situations, principally in attack and defence where this is appropriate (you are not expected to attack a mountain but see the specific requirements for your own activity!).

You will have seen from the specification that there are three groups of activities:

▨ Activity Category 1 – a range of team, invasion, racket and net games.

▨ Activity Category 2 – individual activities such as swimming and athletics.

▨ Activity Category 3 – activities where the outcome is determined on a more subjective judgement against criteria, such as dance and trampolining.

Each of the categories makes slightly different demands on you as a performer and you are advised to read the specification closely and discuss with whoever is going to assess you the exact criteria you have to meet. Broadly half of the 50 marks are given for the demonstration in isolation and half given for performing in the modified competitive situation.

How the marks for acting as a coach or leader are awarded

There are 50 marks available for how well you perform in this role.

Marks are broadly given for:

▨ How well you are able to analyse, change and improve skills/techniques as shown by performers (in isolation and in a modified competitive situation).

▨ How well you can plan, coordinate and lead sessions for performers who are showing these skills.

▨ Your understanding of the coach/leader role – in terms of how you keep the performer safe and ensuring that they develop recognised techniques (you need to know the approved skill models as well as in the performer role).

▨ Your ability to use strategies and tactics that help performers to perform well in a session, and if necessary change those tactics or strategies so that the performer is more successful.

Of the 50 marks available approximately 25 are given for your work with a performer when they are showing skills in isolation and half when they are working in their modified competitive situation. Again this varies slightly, depending upon which category of activity you are coaching or leading.

You will be asked to show the abilities listed above by actually coaching or leading groups and being assessed as you do so.

How the marks for acting as an official are awarded

As for the other two roles 50 marks are available for your performance in this role. Before discussing how these marks are given here is a brief

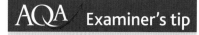
AQA Examiner's tip

Good candidates are able to explain strengths and weaknesses in relation to the theory they have covered in Unit 1 – making use of applied physiology, skill acqusion and improving by using methods of training and practice from Unit 2.

 Activity

Using the AQA specification for your activity, prepare a check sheet for the skills in isolation and the semi- or modified competitive situation.

Fig. 14.3 *Be a coach – a great way to gain marks!*

discussion of what is meant by the role of official. As you might expect it certainly includes the role of umpire, referee and judge but must also include the roles of scoring, timekeeping, line judging, assistant referee, linemen, etc. (as appropriate to your chosen activity).

Marks are given for the officiating role for showing the following skills.

▓ Being able to officiate performers showing the core skills in isolation and in the modified competitive situation – for example in badminton during a restricted stroke rally, or being able to judge gymnastics skills in isolation and as part of a sequence.

▓ Knowing what to do before, during and after the activity to keep the performers safe.

▓ Applying the rules and etiquette of the activity accurately and consistently to maintain fair play and safety.

▓ Knowing how to prepare and equip yourself to undertake the role of official. (This would include being up-to-date with rules/laws, being physically fit enough and mental preparation).

▓ You must show a clear understanding of the scoring system and apply it within the modified competitive situation.

The marks will be awarded by your assessor when you carry out the 'official' role. They will be judging you on:

▓ Knowledge and explanation of rules or judging criteria in relation to the core skills or techniques.

▓ Consistent application of the rules or judging criteria.

▓ How well you communicate with the performers through voice or by correct signals.

▓ The safety checks you make before and during the session.

▓ Your rapport with the performers and the atmosphere you create within the performance situation.

▓ How well you undertake the subsidiary roles – timekeeper, line judge, scorer, etc.

▓ Your personal analysis and evaluation of how well you have officiated, and the justifications you make for the decisions you made.

These judgements will be made on how well you actually do these things – it is not a theoretical activity – **you actually have to officiate**.

Having looked at the how the specification awards marks (and therefore grades!) we should now look at how you can develop and improve your performance in the two roles you have chosen.

▓ Practical coursework – preparing for assessment

As was said in the introduction you must have a very proactive approach in terms of your own personal development in these roles. It is highly unlikely that within your school or college staff will be able to constantly give you individual help and support for each of these roles. Nor will there be curriculum time to be spent given the very wide number of activities. At best you will get sound support on the general areas for improvement and advice on how you can plan a personal improvement programme.

As in the previous section we shall take each of the roles in turn and give you advice and support on how you can improve.

Fig. 14.4 *The role of the official*

Improving yourself as a performer

To improve as a performer you need to know:

- The core skills or techniques for your activity – they can be found in the specification.
- The approved perfect skill model – these can be found from national governing body publications or sometimes on their websites.
- The required fitness components for your activity (check back to Chapter 1 – Improving fitness and health, page 2).
- The form that the modified competitive activity will take for assessment – again this can be found in the specification but you *must* also discuss this with your assessors.

Having established what you have to achieve you need to know where you are now. Any improvement plan must begin from a base level – a start point. To get your start point you need to know how well you perform against the criteria – how can you do this?

Setting a baseline:

- Ask your assessor at your school or college to carry out an assessment of you and give you feedback.
- Ask your team or club coach to assess **using the AQA criteria**. (You do belong to a team or club don't you?) Remember that you have to be proactive and independent in improving yourself.
- Get a friend or fellow student to video you performing the required skills in a competitive situation (you will need to provide video evidence for moderation purposes as part of final assessment). Use this video to assess yourself (it also helps develop those all-important self-evaluation skills and the ability to evaluate others if you are in the coach role as well.
- It would also be a good idea to carry out the fitness tests found in Chapter 15 to help you set the baseline.

Having now got an estimate of your current level of performance, how do you improve?

Useful improvement strategies:

1 Identify major weaknesses – these are likely to be either related to insufficient levels of fitness or insufficiently developed skills. Remember to push yourself when demonstrating or showing the skills, it is no good being able to do a skill just in isolation without any opposition or just as a one off.
- Plan a fitness or skill development programme (or both). In terms of fitness the programme must be:
  - specific to the fitness demands in relation to the required fitness components (see Chapter 1)
  - specific to your identified fitness weaknesses.
- An appropriate training system or method, clearly linked to your fitness needs (see Chapter 15).

2 In relation to skill development:
- Devise appropriate practices in relation to the type of skill you are trying to improve (see Chapter 16).
- An evaluation of your mental preparedness if the skill is breaking down in the modified competitive situation (see Chapter 9).

Activities

1 Using coaching manuals, coaching websites or national governing body websites research the approved or perfect skill models for the core skills and techniques for your activity.

2 Analyse the video of yourself with a partner and then vice versa. This will give you another useful insight into your level of skill and help you develop the coaching eye.

- Join a club or team! This is by far the best way to get regular opportunities to train and put your improved skills and fitness to the test.
- Make sure you practise <u>all</u> core skills – we have a tendency to practise the ones we are best at rather than the reverse.
- Develop an appropriate warm up and cool down regime relevant to your activity. (See Chapter 15).
- Show your development plan to one of your school or college assessors.
- Keep a training diary or log and include any data from repeated fitness tests.

Improving yourself as a coach

Like any other skill or process coaching can be improved by practice. You will have had experience of being coached in the past or currently. Reflect upon that coaching – how successful was it? Did it reflect the good practice that you intend to develop? You may already have undertaken some coaching yourself – younger teams at club or school/college. You may have taken awards such as the Level 1 Award in Sports Leadership, or the Community Sports Leader Award.

It is by actually doing some coaching that you can acquire and improve those coaching skills that are required in the specification. Remember that you need to know how to:

- analyse, change and improve the skills/techniques of other performers
- plan, coordinate and lead practice sessions
- keep the performer safe during practices
- make sure they develop recognised techniques
- use strategies and tactics that help performers to perform well in a session, changing them if necessary.

There are several ways in which you can gain the knowledge of the skills and tactics of your sport and how to coach them:

- Take the introductory coaching awards as provided by your sport's national governing body – almost all now have a coaching pathway from the most basic qualifications to national coach. Many of the basic or community coaching awards are also linked to things such as the Community Sports Leaders Award. Check out your sport's national governing body website for more information.
- Take the Level 1 or Community Sports Leaders Award at school or college. It is very straightforward for a school or a college with qualified PE staff to register to run these courses.
- For more information go to the Sports Leaders website www.sportsleaders.org.
- Look at the sports coach UK website for a host of useful tips on how to coach, mostly in the Resources section of the site.

If you are unable to take formal coaching or leadership qualifications there are still various practical ways in which you can develop coaching skills. If you are taking a coaching or leadership qualification then these

Activity

For your chosen activity research the coaching qualification structure by using their website or by getting a copy of their coach development programme. Is there a base line qualification suitable for you?

activities will help you put your knowledge into practice and help develop your confidence.

▨ Offer to help your PE department during younger year groups lessons. You might get the opportunity to work with small groups during the lesson, run the warm up or cool down, or even deliver a small part of the lesson.

▨ Help coach younger teams at school or college.

▨ Help coach younger teams at your club.

One of the most important skills a coach requires is the ability to observe and to analyse the skills in action and again there are a number of ways you can practise this skill.

Observe other teams or performers, using a checklist of the core skills as in the specification. On your checklist have a column for strengths and a column for weaknesses in those skills. The specification also gives guidance on how a skill should be analysed.

For example a netball pass should be analysed by looking at the:

▨ feet and hand placements

▨ early preparation/feet/hand/head

▨ skill action

▨ follow through/recovery

▨ result/overall effectiveness/accuracy.

Look at the specification for the guidance for your sport or activity.

At the end of the session take your check sheet away, look at the weaknesses and try and think of ways in which you could help the performer improve. Think of actual individual skill or group skill practices you could use.

▨ Watch sport on television – but with the sound down, and your core skill checklist, try and see how elite performers use those core skills. Think how you would change the way the team is playing if you were coaching – **write down those ideas**.

▨ Using a video camera (your PE or Media department will probably have one), video school/college/club matches. Then using the slow motion feature and your core skill checklist analyse the strengths and weaknesses. You should also be doing this for yourself as a performer. If it is a team or racket game also consider the way the tactics and strategies are being used – would you change them?

▨ Discuss with your school or club coach the strategies they use and why they use them. Be prepared to offer comments during your own or your team's practice sessions.

There is no substitute for doing all this for real though. As part of the assessment or moderation process you will be asked to observe, analyse and offer suggestions for improvement **on the spot**. If that is the first time you have actually done it you will not know what to look for, be disorganised in your analysis and miss vital points and be tongue tied when asked to suggest ways in which you could help others improve.

 Activity

Prepare a coaching check sheet for each of the core skills using the skill analysis marks given in the text and in the AQA specification.

Remember when coaching live:

- observe
- analyse
- give strengths
- give weaknesses
- suggest ways to improve
- be clear, but use technical language
- be calm.

There is only one way to become confident in the skills of observation and analysis, to be able to plan a practice session, to deliver a practice session, and to be able to coach a team in the heat of the match – **get out there and actually do it!**

Improving yourself as an official

The advice for improving yourself as an official – and remember this needs to be in a range of 'official' roles – is very similar for that for being a coach. As you will know from watching or playing sport we all know that we are the best referee in the world and why can't the ref see what you see?

As an official you will need to:

- Have a clear understanding of the rules or judging criteria.
- Be able to apply and use these rules or criteria fairly and consistently, in a range of roles.
- Manage a performance situation by clear communication with participants, and by establishing a good atmosphere in the game.
- Be able to evaluate and improve your own performance as an official.

How can you acquire the skills and knowledge to be an effective referee, umpire or judge?

- Get hold of a copy of the national governing body's rule or law book, plus any officiating guides they may have. For example, England Hockey produce a book entitled 'A guide to umpiring hockey', and 'A Fitness Guide for Hockey Umpires' as well as being able to download the rules from their website. Read and learn the rules for your sport or activity.
- Watch officials on television – try watching with the sound down and see what decisions you would have made.
- Offer to referee or umpire during PE lessons or younger team practices.
- All national governing bodies have qualification routes for becoming an official. These will often start at a very basic level so that younger people, often from the age of 13 or so, can start to acquire the necessary skills and knowledge. Try and do at least the base level qualification.
- When you are performing or playing, get to the venue early and carry out your own pre-match safety checks.
- If you become very confident, offer to referee, umpire or judge in school or club fixtures, or be prepared to be a linesmen or judge.
- When you are acting as an official get somebody else to video your performance – then you can look at:

Activity

From the NGB website research the officiating qualifications for your activity. Check the syllabus and requirements and see if there is one suitable for you.

- how well you use the official signals
- how well you communicated with the performers
- how well you analysed the situation and used the laws or rules to maintain fair and safe competition.

When you first start to act as an official it can feel strange, and sometimes isolated. Being able to blow your whistle confidently, give the correct decision in a clear and simple manner and then get the game going again takes practice and hard work. Good officiating goes a long way to ensuring an enjoyable performance situation.

Health and safety for all

Ensuring that players are able to perform in a safe environment, in the context of the activity (some activities by their nature carry a higher level of risk than others) is the responsibility of coaches and officials and of course you as a performer. Although each activity within the specification has its own specific safety requirements there are some general points that can be made.

- Players should perform within the rules of the activity. Any deliberate attempt to injure another performer should be dealt with firmly and effectively by officials, and should not be tolerated by coaches. As a performer you need to think carefully how you react to a teammate who falls below this standard.
- Playing areas should be checked for sound footing, objects on the pitch or court, and whether or not the surface is safe to play on (frozen pitches, etc.).
- Any equipment used must be in good repair and meet the NGB specifications.
- Player equipment must be inspected (especially studded boots, etc.) to ensure that it falls within NGB rules or laws.
- Performers should know how to warm up and warm down.
- Performers should have an appropriate level of skill for the competitive or performance situation. For example gymnasts should not attempt high tariff skills if they have not trained at that level, or rugby players must have experience of scrummaging techniques.
- Referee and umpires should always have their authority respected. To not do so can place performers at risk.

Having prepared yourself as a performer, official or coach you now need to ensure that you can give of your best whilst actually being assessed.

Practical assessment – being the best you can be

Some general points on how you can gain the best marks possible from the assessment situation, be it for coach, official or performer.

- Find out well in advance, preferably at the beginning of the year, as to when you are likely to be assessed – dates, times, formats.
- Will you be assessed on the basis of on-going continuous assessment? If so ask your teacher or assessor for an update on the marks you have achieved and work on the weaker, less highly marked areas.
- Check if it is all right for your club coach to assess you. This will normally be fine but *they have to use the assessment criteria as in the specification*.

Well in advance of the assessment opportunity ensure that you find out the format for the session – what will the format of the session be, what practices will be used for you to demonstrate your expertise.

Ensure that on the day you are well turned out for the role you are undertaking.

Make sure you have had yourself videoed performing the role – this will help you if you become injured and are unable to attend or perform in an assessment situation.

Finally here is some advice for each of the roles.

As a performer

Make sure you warm up properly – you do not want to be injured prior to the assessment!

Remember that it is an assessment situation – you may be asked to perform in an adapted competitive situation but it is not a top of the table league match. Show that you can perform under the pressure of competition but it is a demonstration.

In group situations help each other to show the skills and techniques as well as possible.

As a coach

When asked to analyse an individual performance remember to analyse the skill by referring to:

- feet/hand placements (for each skill)
- early preparation/feet/hand/head
- skill action
- follow through/recovery
- result/overall effectiveness/accuracy.

When giving feedback and analysis do not be rushed. Take some time to absorb what you have just been watching and marshal your thoughts before speaking. Listen carefully to any questions asked by the assessor.

Make notes when you are watching, particularly if you are going to give feedback to players during a competitive situation – time out or half time.

Do not be frightened to change the tactics if things are not going well.

If you have been asked to plan and deliver a coaching or practice situation, make sure you plan thoroughly. Remember you need to think about:

- session objectives
- how many performers
- what equipment is needed
- how long are you going to spend on each part of the session
- can you demonstrate the skills or techniques you are using in the session
- what will you do if a performer is injured during a session – remember you are in charge.

Remember – look, think . . . pause . . . speak.

Use the technical, specialist language that you have learnt in the theoretical areas of the specification. Try not to use layman's terms – you should have learnt plenty of specialised language from anatomy, physiology and sport psychology so use it.

As an official

▧ Before the assessment session check you have all the necessary equipment – whistle, cards, rule book, notepad, pen/pencil, coin (if needed) and any specialist equipment used by officials in your activity.

▧ Arrive early – make it obvious to your assessor that you are checking the venue or performance space for any health and safety issues. If this is not possible make sure they know what you would have done.

▧ Be smartly turned out – it does not need to be official officiating kit but you need to look the part. Your shirt/top needs to be a distinguishing colour, and the rest of your clothing needs to be clean, tidy and appropriate for the activity.

▧ Make any decision with an air of confidence and authority (even though you may not feel it).

▧ Explain to the performers what you have called and why, what is going to happen next and how the game will be restarted.

▧ Use appropriate technical language and specialist terms, either when speaking to performers, teacher, assessor or moderator.

▧ Try and show to your assessor your knowledge of the rules but also of the ethics of the activity you are involved in.

▧ Remember you are there to enable the performers to have an enjoyable, competitive and safe experience – you are not there to show how many times you can blow your whistle, or how many minor infringements of the laws or rules you can spot and call – remember many activities have an advantage rule.

▧ Concentrate all the time – things happen quickly.

What happens if you perform badly during an assessment session?

Well, this need not be a disaster. Firstly the board asks teachers to give a mark that reflects a level that you **consistently** achieve, and this should not be unduly affected by a poor one-off performance (equally you cannot expect a fantastic, one-off, out of your skull performance to have the opposite effect).

Secondly you should try and give your teachers as much evidence of your usual level of achievement (in both of the roles) as you can.

▧ Get references from team coaches about the standard you have reached, competitions performed in, etc.

▧ Have plenty of video evidence of your best performances.

▧ Get references from team managers or other club officials about the contributions you may have made in terms of coaching or officiating.

▧ Take every opportunity to undertake any of your roles at school or college. Good performances outside of assessment sessions build up your teacher's view of you.

To ensure that all teachers in all examination centres are interpreting and applying the assessment criteria accurately the board sends out moderators to check the standard of marking. It will be useful for you to know something about the moderation process.

Moderation

It is likely that you will be asked to participate in a moderation session. This is when a moderator from the AQA attends a session where you

 Activity

Using your national governing body, find out the recommended equipment for officials in your activity.

AQA Examiner's tip

As far as you can try and ensure that your assessment is continuous, or give your teacher/assessor plenty of evidence, plenty of opportunities to see you perform in any of the roles.

and others from your centre and possibly other centres are asked to perform one or more of your roles. This often causes feelings of mass panic amongst students but it need not. Here are a few points about moderation.

- It is not an assessment of you. It is an assessment of how accurately your centre has assessed you, how well the staff have applied the criteria. Your teachers are on trial not you.

- Naturally you will want to perform at your best – so find out from your teachers how the session will be conducted, what practices and modified competitive situations they intend to use.

- Treat it as another opportunity to be assessed – be well turned out and focus on your own performance. Most of the time you will not know if the moderator is actually watching you warm up, perform, coach, officiate or warm down.

- During the moderation session you may get an opportunity to undertake both of your chosen roles. The moderator will ask the teachers who are present to mark some of the performances they are watching – and this could be of students taking on any of the three roles. The moderator also marks what they see and then compares notes with each teacher.

- The moderator will expect to see all performers show a range of skills from the easy to the more difficult; they will want to see how well you can perform. There is no point you just being asked to show low level skills or very easy competitive situations.

- The important thing is how close the teacher assessor and the moderator's marks are in relation to the performance they see in front of them. If the moderator believes that the teacher assessor consistently over- or under-marks, and it falls outside what is known as the 'zone of tolerance' then it is possible that all the marks from the students in a centre have to be adjusted.

Finally you must be clear that the moderation session **is not a practical exam**. It is not a one-off test of you as a performer, coach or official but there is no harm in performing well. Moderators are happy to advise a centre to improve your marks (teacher assessors can be miserly with marks in an attempt not to over-mark). It may be that you are on the boundary of the next grade up and a good performance from you may just push you over, so you should try and produce one of your best on the day.

It is worth it!

Remember that 40 per cent of your final AS grade is achieved by how well you do in the practical. It is worthwhile spending time on understanding what you need to show, and how you can improve and prepare for your assessment opportunities.

✔️ *You should now be able to:*

- know the skill models and techniques you have to show as a performer, coach or official in your activity

- show those skills and techniques in demonstration and semi-competitive situations

- observe and analyse the performance of yourself and others in the role of performer or coach

- use the correct technical language when reporting your analysis of a performance
- compare skill performances against the recognised model
- show skilful responses in challenging performance situations
- use the theoretical knowledge in Unit 1 and Unit 2 to help improve performance of yourself and others
- evaluate your own performance as a coach, official or performer.

15 Practical exercise physiology

Activity

Go for a run or go to the gym to exercise. When you have finished, make a list of the immediate effects of exercise on the body. Why is each of these responses occurring?

In Chapter 1 – Improving fitness and health (page 2) we looked at health and fitness and the components of fitness. As AS Level Physical Education students you are going to need a certain level of physical fitness in order to make best use of your talents when it comes to the practical assessment. If you wish to improve your performance you will need to improve both your physical fitness and your skill levels. But it's no good just going out for an occasional run, or popping down to the local gym for a quick weights session whenever the mood takes you. Improving fitness and/or skills needs to be planned and organised, with a long-term aim or goal. The occasional fitness burst has no physiological value whatsoever. Improving fitness and skill is a long-term commitment that needs to follow well-established principles that make sure that the time you are devoting to training is having the maximum benefit.

You will be well aware of the body's short-term responses to exercise; these happen to everybody who undertakes exercise. When we exercise we need to provide oxygen to our muscles so that they can provide the energy required for muscle contraction. At the same time there is a need to remove the carbon dioxide that is produced by the exercising muscles as a waste product. The oxygen is delivered by the blood (see Chapter 4 – Blood transport system, page 41). Carbon dioxide is also removed by the blood. In order to get more blood delivering more oxygen to the muscles our heart rate increases (see Chapter 5 – Heart function, page 51). Therefore one of the immediate effects of exercise is an increase in heart rate that increases the delivery of oxygen to muscles. In a similar way the increase in heart rate delivers more carbon dioxide to the lungs so that it can be removed. Hence heart rate increases from its resting levels of 60–80 beats per minute to cope with the need to supply nutrients, especially oxygen to the working muscles. The extent of the increase in heart rate is dependent on the intensity of the exercise, but can approach 180–200 beats per minute. As you learnt in Chapter 5 – Heart function (page 51), this response is immediate, and may even occur before the commencement of exercise due to anticipation and the release of adrenaline.

At the same time there is a need to maintain the oxygen content of the blood. If oxygen is continuously removed by the exercising muscles it needs to be replaced so that the haemoglobin is as saturated as possible with oxygen. Oxygen is taken into the body through the lungs (see Chapter 3 – Lung function, page 29). In order to do this we increase both our rate and depth of breathing. This is the second immediate effect of exercise. Breathing rate increases in response to exercise, and the need to oxygenate the blood, from its resting level of about 12–15 breaths per minute, to levels approaching 30 breaths per minute. The increase in breathing rate is less dramatic than that for heart rate, as there is a mechanical limit to how fast we can breathe. The increased depth of breathing is because as we exercise, the tidal volume increases from its resting levels of 500 cm^3 to levels that approach 1000 cm^3.

Another effect of exercise is an increase in body temperature. Normally our body operates at a temperature of 37° C. During exercise, as muscles contract, they generate waste heat while producing energy. This may cause an increase in muscle temperatures to levels approaching 40° C.

Because the body operates at a constant temperature, this excess heat must be lost. This occurs in two main ways. Just below the surface of the skin, the blood vessels supplying tiny blood capillaries open (**vasodilation**), which means there is more blood flowing near the skin's surface which produces a reddening of the skin. This blood is relatively warm and some of this heat is lost from the body by radiation. Similarly, there is increase in sweat production. The sweat forms a layer on the surface of the skin which evaporates. This process means that some additional heat may be lost by evaporation.

Depending on how hard the exercise is there may also be some tiredness in the muscles. This is more accurately described as localised muscular fatigue. The beginning of relatively strenuous exercise may produce a waste product called lactate (lactic acid) that may produce fatigue in the exercising muscle if it accumulates.

The long-term effects of exercise, more accurately called training, are much more widespread and depend on what type of training is being undertaken, for how long and how hard. This is why training needs to be planned, because the effects of training can be so different that there is a need to know what is required as a result of training. Because there is such a range of different effects, training has a set of rules that need to be followed to make sure the training programme is effective. These are the **training principles**.

Principles of training

Training is undertaken by some individuals to improve performance through skill development, and/or physical fitness. Other individuals take part in training as an activity in itself, often within a health-related fitness programme.

Training must be seen as a long-term commitment. The changes that are associated with training, whether physiological or psychological, take time to develop. The human body responds to training through adapting to the stresses placed upon it, but this **adaptation response** is not immediate; it takes place over periods of months rather than days or weeks. The main principles of training are specificity, overload, progression, overtraining, reversibility and tedium.

Specificity

The effects of training are very **specific** to the system being used for that training. As a simplistic example, in order to improve your swimming ability you need to swim; jogging will have little benefit. Similarly, in order to improve sprinting ability you need to sprint; long distance running will have little benefit because the main energy system used, the type of skill involved and the main muscle fibre type used, are not being stressed in an appropriate way.

In order to make sure that training is specific to the activity concerned, the relevance and the choice of training exercise needs to be considered by asking yourself the following questions:

■ Does the training exercise stress the appropriate energy system – the same one as is used in the activity being trained for? Is the type of muscle fibre being stressed during training the same type as is used during the chosen activity?

In many games for example, there are both aerobic and anaerobic activities, and therefore energy systems are involved to differing extents, and each needs to be stressed to some degree during training.

■ **Key terms**

Vasodilation: opening of arteriole supplying a capillary bed.

Training principles: a set of rules that need to be followed to make training effective.

Adaptation response: the changes that occur in the body as a result of training.

Specificity: making training specific to the demands of the activity.

■ **Link**

See Chapter 4 – Blood transport system (page 41) on redistribution of blood.

AQA Examiner's tip

You may be required to provide reasons for using a certain training method. Always use the principle of specificity.

In a similar way, the type of energy being used is reflected in the main type of muscle-fibre being used and some activities involve using different types of muscle fibre.

▒ Are the skills being practiced relevant to the chosen activity? Because learning theory (Chapter 9 – Learning and performance, page 102) tells us that the development of a stronger bond between the stimulus and the response (muscles) will occur through practice, and similarly there will be the development of a more efficient use of the muscles in a sequence (motor programme) required by the stimulus.

In many activities, training involves a conflict between skill and fitness, since fatigue caused by training is known to have a negative effect on skilled performance. Hence there is a tendency to separate skills training from fitness training, but taking the idea of specificity to its extreme, then if an activity involves performing skills when fatigued, they should be practised when fatigued!

In order for a training programme to be successful, it must develop the specific physiological capabilities required to perform a given sports skill or activity. One of the more important physiological capabilities related to sports skills and to exercise in general, is the supplying of energy to the working muscles.

If you followed a course in GCSE PE you might have learned about anaerobic and aerobic exercises. The energy for these exercises may be supplied anaerobically or aerobically. For any given exercise, the predominant energy source used will depend on the total amount of energy required, and its rate of demand. For example, when sprinting 100 metres, because of the high intensity and short duration, this is an **anaerobic** activity. To improve the performance of a 100-metre sprinter, a training programme that leads to greater energy output through the anaerobic energy systems would clearly be needed.

On the other hand, in exercises of lower intensity and longer duration, the predominant energy system will be **aerobic**, for example, a marathon. In this case the development of the aerobic energy systems of the performer should be the main objective of the training programme.

In many activities, both energy systems are used, although a specific system may predominate at differing times during an event. For example, in a 1500-metre race, the anaerobic system provides the majority of energy during the sprint at both the start and finish of the race, with the aerobic system predominating during the middle, or 'steady-pace' period of the run.

In order to improve performance in this type of activity, a training programme that increases both the anaerobic and aerobic capacities must be selected. A training programme should however take regard of other types of specificity as well as the predominant energy demand. For example, although cycling may improve the aerobic power for cycling, it will have a lesser effect on the aerobic energy systems when the trainee runs.

Similarly, swimming training programmes have been found to have effects that are specific only to swimming. For maximal training benefits therefore, the mode of exercise used during the training sessions should be consistent with that used during the performance of the skill in question. Runners should run, cyclists should cycle and skiers should ski.

Another type of specificity relates to the muscle groups used during the training programme. In simple terms, if the performance demands leg

Key terms

Anaerobic: without using oxygen.

Aerobic: using oxygen.

AQA Examiner's tip

Anaerobic and aerobic describe both the type of exercise being done, but also, and more importantly at A Level, the way that the energy needed for muscle contraction is being produced – with or without the use of oxygen.

power, then the training should be designed to increase leg power, and not arm power. The effects of training are specific not just to the muscle groups, but to the movement patterns of these muscle groups as well. In other words, training appears to be motor-skill specific.

Accordingly, training programmes should contain, whenever feasible, exercise activities related as closely as possible to those actually performed during the execution of the sports skill in question. Basketball players need to perform the movements that occur during basketball as part of their training programme.

The body has the ability to react and adapt to the stresses placed upon it, which in turn will cause the cardiovascular and respiratory systems to adapt, thus allowing the person to handle the stresses. If minimal stress is applied, only minimal adaptations can be expected; similarly, if too much stress is applied, there is little or no permanent adaptation. The level of stress applied through training must therefore be above the athlete's threshold level for improvement. In simple terms this means that in order to get fitter the performer must exercise at a level that will produce adaptations; the threshold level depends on the performer's level of fitness.

- Too little stress – little or no adaptation.
- Too much stress – little or no adaptation.

The level of adaptation is dependent on the following factors:

- The performer's base level of fitness, e.g. a sedentary person can be trained further than an elite athlete, hence sedentary people have greater possible levels of adaptation.
- The performer's health or injury status.
- The performer's previous experience with stress, e.g. a person who has been previously trained will be mentally prepared to meet the demands of training.
- The environment within which the training occurs. If the training is performed at altitude or at high temperatures, the adaptations will be different to normal, as secondary stresses are being applied simultaneously.

Exhaustion and stresses are common reactions to training programmes which are too intense or poorly structured. If the stress applied through training is too great, it leads to a system breakdown caused by intolerance. An analogy would be a car being driven too far, too fast, until something goes wrong.

Overload

The basic idea underlying athletic training is that to produce performance improvements, athletes must **overload** the energy system, or systems, required to perform certain movements. In this context, overloading refers to the fact that the workload, or resistance against which the athlete is working, is greater than is normal.

Overloading is perhaps the fundamental principle of fitness. It is basically an increase in demand to force bodily adaptation. A training load is the work or exercise that an athlete performs in a training session. Loading is the process of applying training loads – training programmes.

 Key terms

Overload: improvements in fitness result from exercising harder than normal.

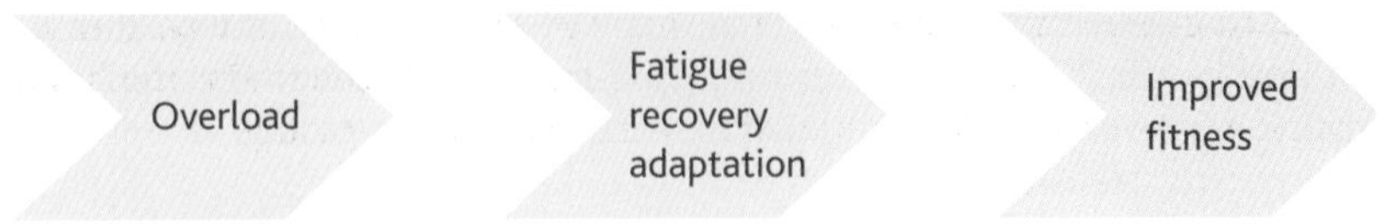

Fig. 15.1 *Essential idea of training*

When an athlete's fitness is challenged by a new training load there is a response from the body. The initial response is fatigue. When the loading stops there is a process of recovery. Recovery and adaptation take the athlete to a higher level of fitness from where they started.

The safest way to overload the body is by altering one of the three factors below. The load is changed in a slow, systematic manner to allow gradual adaptation of the body. Overload is achieved by increasing the frequency, intensity or duration of training. These terms are often referred to as the **FITT principles**.

Key terms

FITT principles: overloading by varying frequency, intensity, type and time of training.

The FITT principles of training

The FITT principles are like a set of rules that must be used in order to benefit from a fitness training programme. These four principles of fitness training are applicable to individuals exercising at low to moderate training levels and may be used to establish guidelines for both cardiorespiratory and resistance training.

Frequency

Following any form of fitness training, the body goes through a process of rebuild and repair to replenish its energy reserves consumed by the exercise. The frequency of exercise is a fine balance between providing just enough stress for the body to adapt to and allowing enough time for healing and adaptation to occur.

Frequency means how often. For most aerobic-based activities it is recommended that training should take place 4–5 times per week. For anaerobic-based activities, the recommendation is three times per week; to allow full recovery, because the adaptations take longer to achieve. Exceptions would include the explosive sports, where 5–6 sessions a week are better, with alternating hard and easy sessions.

Activity

Work in small groups and produce a presentation or poster that explains why anaerobic-based activities need more time to recover than aerobic-based activities.

Intensity

The second rule in the FITT principle relates to intensity. It defines the amount of effort that should be invested in a training programme or any one session. Like the first FITT principle – frequency – there must be a balance between finding enough intensity to overload the body (so it can adapt) but not so much that it causes overtraining.

Intensity means how hard. Measuring intensity is much more difficult than you first think. Most of the time we rely on how our body feels, or our own opinion to estimate how hard we are working. Opinions vary between people. What one person considers quite hard, another may describe as fairly easy. One way of measuring intensity is to use opinions, but we need to make those opinions standard. For this we use the Borg scale. Many performers involved in aerobic activities use their heart rate as a means of measuring performance. The intensity of a strength training programme may also be measured by the amount of weight being lifted.

Overload can be adjusted by varying the intensity at which the performer works. There are many ways of varying intensity, but the major methods involve increasing or decreasing one or more of the following:

- load
- repetitions
- range of movement
- duration of effect
- sets
- recovery
- frequency of sessions
- speed.

Activity

Work in small groups and using press-ups as the exercise; identify how each of the above parameters may be used to adjust the intensity of press-up exercises. Produce your ideas as a poster or presentation.

Type

The third component in the FITT principle dictates what type or kind of exercise you should choose to achieve the appropriate training response. There are many ways of training, but most can be grouped into the following:

- continuous
- intermittent
- circuit
- weights
- plyometrics
- mobility (see later).

Time

The final component in the FITT principle of training is time – or how long you should be exercising for. The time involved depends largely on the type of training.

For the largely aerobic training methods such as continuous, circuits and mobility, those individuals with lower fitness levels should aim to maintain their exercise programme for a minimum of 20–30 minutes. This can increase to as much as 45–60 minutes as fitness levels increase. Beyond the 45–60 minute mark there are diminished returns. For all that extra effort, the associated benefits are minimal. This also applies to many elite athletes. Beyond a certain point they run the risk of overtraining and injury. There are exceptions however – typically the ultra-long distance endurance athletes. In terms of the duration of the programme as a whole, research suggests a minimum of 6 weeks is required to see noticeable improvement and as much as a year or more before a peak in fitness is reached.

For those involved in anaerobic methods of training such as intermittent, weights and plyometrics, the common consensus for the duration of a resistance training session is no longer than 45–60 minutes. Again, intensity has a say and particularly gruelling strength sessions may last as little as 20–30 minutes.

Measuring intensity

Borg scale

The Borg scale is a simple rating of how hard the performer thinks their body is working, or Rating of Perceived Exertion (RPE). It is used by many coaches to assess an athlete's level of intensity during training or testing sessions. It is based on the physical sensations a person experiences during physical activity, including increased heart rate, increased respiration or breathing rate, increased sweating, and muscle fatigue. Although this is a subjective measure, a person's exertion rating may provide a fairly good estimate of the actual heart rate during physical activity.

Most coaches tend to agree that perceived exertion ratings between 12 to 14 on the Borg scale suggests that physical activity is being performed at a moderate level of intensity. During activity, you can use the Borg scale to assign numbers to how you feel. Such self-monitoring can help you adjust the intensity of the activity by speeding up or slowing down your movements.

Through experience of monitoring how your body feels, it becomes easier to know when to adjust your intensity. For example, a performer who wants to engage in moderate-intensity activity would aim for a Borg scale level of 'somewhat hard' (12–14). If he describes his muscle fatigue and breathing as 'very light' (9 on the Borg scale) he would want to increase his intensity. On the other hand, if he felt his exertion was 'extremely hard' (19 on the Borg scale) he would need to slow down his movements to achieve the moderate-intensity range.

Research has shown a high correlation between a person's perceived exertion rating times 10 and the actual heart rate during physical activity. So a person's exertion rating may provide a fairly good estimate of the actual heart rate during activity. For example, if a person's rating of perceived exertion (RPE) is 12, then $12 \times 10 = 120$; so the heart rate should be approximately 120 beats per minute. Note that this calculation is only an approximation of heart rate, and the actual heart rate can vary quite a bit depending on age and physical condition.

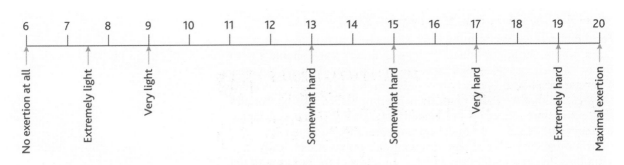

9   corresponds to 'very light' exercise. For a healthy person, this would be the equivalent of walking slowly at his or her own pace for some minutes:

13 on the scale is 'somewhat hard' exercise, this would correspond to working hard but it still feels OK to continue.

17 'very hard' is very strenuous. A healthy person can still go on, but he or she really has to push him- or herself. It feels very heavy, and the person is very tired.

19 on the scale is an extremely strenuous exercise level. For most people this is the most strenuous exercise they have ever experienced.

Fig. 15.2 *Borg scale*

Heart rate

One way of monitoring physical activity intensity is to determine whether a person's pulse or heart rate is within their target zone during physical activity. It is based on knowing your maximum heart rate and then being advised or shown a heart rate training zone, in which to keep your heart rate while you are exercising.

The simplest but least accurate way of calculating your maximum heart rate is using the formula:

$$\text{Max. heart rate} = 220 - \text{age}$$

For example, for a 16-year-old person, the estimated maximum age-related heart rate would be calculated as 220 – 16 years = 204 beats per minute (bpm).

For moderate-intensity physical activity, a person's target heart rate should be 50 to 70 per cent of his or her maximum heart rate. For the above example 50 per cent and 70 per cent levels would be:

- 50% level: 204 × 0.50 = 102 bpm, and
- 70% level: 204 × 0.70 = 143 bpm.

Thus, moderate-intensity physical activity for a 16-year-old person will require that the heart rate remains between 102 and 143 bpm during physical activity.

For vigorous-intensity physical activity, a person's target heart rate should be 70 to 85 per cent of his or her maximum heart rate. To calculate this range, follow the same formula as used above, except change '50 and 70%' to '70 and 85%'. Thus for a 16-year-old person, the 70 per cent and 85 per cent levels would be:

- 70% level: 204 × 0.70 = 143 bpm
- 85% level: 185 × 0.85 = 173 bpm.

Thus, vigorous-intensity physical activity for a 16-year-old person will require that the heart rate remains between 143 and 173 bpm during physical activity. Most performers who use this method tend to wear a heart rate monitor which is more convenient and accurate than taking your own pulse rate. Target heart rate training zones are available where most calculations have been done for you – see Figure 15.3.

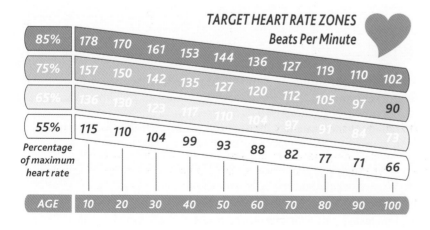

Fig. 15.3 *Target heart rate*

Another method for calculating target heart rate zones is the Karvonen method. This method uses your heart rate range, which is your maximum heart rate minus your resting heart rate. So for our 16-year-old who has a resting heart rate of 74 and a maximum heart rate of 204; their heart rate range is 204 – 74 = 130. This value is then used in the following formula to find the appropriate heart rate for any intensity level. The formula is:

(Heart rate range × Intensity %) + (resting heart rate).

So if the 16-year-old were required to work at 50% intensity they would need to get their heart rate up to: (130 × 50%) + 74 = 139 bpm.

To work at 70% intensity would need to get their heart rate up to: (130 × 70%) + 74 = 165 bpm.

To keep things simple, many coaches use five zones or training intensities:

1 Easy/Recovery = 60–70%
2 Moderate endurance = 71–80%
3 Hill work = 81–85%
4 Race pace for endurance athletes = 86–90%
5 Speed/racing (short distances) = 91–100%.

So now you have all the information to calculate the lower and upper heart rate limits for each zone. The following table summarises the calculations.

Table 15.1 *Table summarising calculations of heart rate training zones using Karvonen method*

Zone	Formula	Calculated HRs
1	Lower limit = HRR × 0.6 + RHR Upper limit = HRR × 0.7 + RHR	Lower = _____ bpm Upper = _____ bpm
2	Lower limit = HRR × 0.71 + RHR Upper limit = HRR × 0.8 + RHR	Lower = _____ bpm Upper = _____ bpm
3	Lower limit = HRR × 0.81 + RHR Upper limit = HRR × 0.85 + RHR	Lower = _____ bpm Upper = _____ bpm
4	Lower limit = HRR × 0.86 + RHR Upper limit = HRR × 0.9 + RHR	Lower = _____ bpm Upper = _____ bpm
5	Lower limit = HRR × 0.91 + RHR Upper limit = HRR × 1.0 + RHR	Lower = _____ bpm Upper = _____ bpm

HR – heart rate   HRR – heart rate reserve   RHR – resting heart rate   bpm – beats per minute

Some words of caution need to be said when talking about heart rates and heart rate training zones. Firstly the idea that your maximum heart rate is 220 minus is a generalisation, in much the same way as saying that everybody is the same height. Secondly, there are many factors that affect both your resting heart rate and training heart rate:

▨ Stress (work, emotional, etc.) will increase your heart rate.

▨ What you eat and especially hydration levels will also greatly influence your heart rate. Dehydration will rocket your heart rate.

▨ Increasing temperatures due to changes in the weather will also increase heart rate until your body adapts to it; usually 7 to 12 days.

Altitude will affect your heart rate as well. You will have a higher heart rate for the same level of intensity at higher elevations so give your body three weeks or so to adapt.

One rep max

In weight training and some circuit training programmes we are able to measure intensity as some proportion of a performer's one repetition maximum or one rep max.

Workload can have three components:

- the amount of weight lifted during an exercise
- the number of repetitions completed for a particular exercise
- the length of time to complete all exercises in a set or total training session.

So, you can increase workload by lifting heavier weights. Or you could increase the number of repetitions with the same weight. Finally, you could lift the same weight for the same number of repetitions but decrease the rest time between sets. However, you should only increase the intensity using **one** of the above parameters. Be aware however that determining a one rep max can be dangerous, especially if using free weights.

Progression

The principle of **progression** is the idea that if you overload, you will gain the adaptations that we call improved fitness and therefore because you are fitter, you will need to overload more as time goes on to make your training harder than 'normal'. It also implies that there is an optimal level of overload that should be achieved, and an optimal timeframe for this overload to occur. Overload should not be increased too slowly or improvement is unlikely. Overload that is increased too rapidly will result in injury or muscle damage. Exercising above the target zone is counterproductive and can be dangerous. For example, the weekend athlete who exercises vigorously only on weekends does not exercise often enough, and so violates the principle of progression.

The principle of progression also makes us realise the need for proper rest and recovery. Continual stress on the body and constant overload will result in exhaustion and injury. You should not (and cannot) train hard all the time. Doing so will lead to overtraining and a great deal of physical and psychological damage will result.

Overtraining

It is important to not overtrain or overload the body so much that it experiences complete exhaustion and cannot adapt properly because there is too much damage. Rest is no longer adequate for recovery. Decline in performance caused by incomplete adaptation is one of the most obvious signs of **overtraining**.

Additional common signs of overtraining include the following:

- irritability and moodiness
- altered sleep patterns
- loss of appetite
- loss of motivation or competitive drive
- persistent muscle soreness that does not go away

Key terms

Progression: gradually increasing the level of workload in training as the body adapts and fitness improves.

Key terms

Overtraining: training too hard and not allowing sufficient time for the body to adapt to the training loads.

- fatigue not relieved by rest
- increased incidence of minor illness or injury.

Reversibility

You know the saying, 'if you do not use it, you lose it'. If athletes are not training regularly, there is no need for their bodies to adapt. Maintaining or even increasing training frequency will not only help performers improve their performances, but their fitness levels will improve as a direct result of increased training. However, when training ceases the training effect will also stop. Fitness gradually reduces at approximately one-third of the rate of speed that it was gained.

Research has shown the effects of a long period of inactivity on physical fitness. A UK Olympic rower took more than 20 weeks to fully recover his fitness after an eight-week lay-off. He needed 12 weeks to return to most of his pre-break fitness levels.

Tedium

Training is a long-term process and overloading in exactly the same way all the time introduces **tedium**. Even recovery can become boring. Variety needs to be introduced into any athlete's training programme. Training similar muscle groups in similar ways, sometimes called cross-training, is beneficial. Elite rowers will spend time rowing on water, rowing on machines, but also cycling, climbing, doing weights and doing circuits because these all use the same muscles in much the same way. Variation is an alternative way of producing stress and is a necessary part of an athlete's progression. A weekly and monthly schedule should contain alternating periods of hard and easy work. Work should alternate with periods of rest to allow the body to adapt to the changes that have occurred.

Fitness testing

Before anybody begins a training programme they need to have some idea of what level to set the programme at. You need to have some idea of your starting level of fitness. For this we use fitness tests.

Reasons for testing

Fitness tests not only provide a starting point for any training programme, but they also establish the strengths and weaknesses of the athlete. This is done by comparing test results to other athletes in the same training group, the same sport, or a similar population group. Previous test results of large groups are often published as normative tables or norms. Then by comparing results to successful athletes in your sport, you can see the areas which need improvement, and the training programme can be modified accordingly. This way valuable training time can be used more efficiently. However, beware that some athletes perform well in their sport despite their physical or physiological attributes, and it may not be advantageous to be like them.

Once standards of fitness have been measured and the performer has an idea of where their fitness levels are at the start of a programme, then by repeating tests at regular intervals, you can get an idea of the effectiveness of the training programme. How frequently you repeat tests will depend on the availability of time or costs involved, or the phase of training the athlete is in. Depending on these factors, the period between tests may

Key terms

Reversibility: is the idea that you lose fitness faster than you gain it.

Tedium: training the same way all the time is boring; everybody needs variation in their training.

range from two weeks to six months. It usually takes a minimum of 2–6 weeks to see a demonstrable change in any aspect of fitness.

Fitness testing also helps motivate performers by providing the incentive to improve enough to reach the 'goal' of a certain test score. By knowing that they will be tested again at a later date, the athlete can aim to improve in that area.

Fitness testing also provides an indication of whether the training programme is being successful. If the programme is designed to improve specific aspects of fitness, then testing to see whether those aspects have improved will give the coach some idea of how well the programme is working. It may also provide the coach with some knowledge of the performer's future performance.

In addition, fitness tests break up, and add variety to, the training programme. They can be used to satisfy the athlete's competitive urge out of season. Since they demand maximum effort of the athlete, they are useful at times as a training unit in their own right.

In order to be useful, fitness tests must fulfil certain criteria. If they don't they can produce misleading information with undesirable consequences. In order to generate meaningful information, fitness tests must be:

- applicable to the sport
- valid
- reliable
- accurate
- sufficiently sensitive to detect changes in fitness.

There can be problems with fitness testing, and the ethics of testing need consideration. Whenever a test is conducted thought needs to be given to the effect of the test or the results of the test on the subject. For example taking part in a fitness test may hinder a performer's preparation for an activity, or interfere with their training. Undertaking some tests may cause fatigue to a performer, making them unable to train or compete. For example the most specific test for an endurance athlete would be a test that replicates their actual event, but the level of exhaustion involved in completing something like a marathon as a fitness test would make it very unethical to complete. Specific tests may also make the performer susceptible to injury with the resulting loss of training and unavailability to competition. Knowledge of the result of a test may cause psychological harm to a performer. If the results are not as good as they might be expecting, the performer's confidence may be dented and this will affect their performances.

Making the test specific to the sport

To be relevant to a sport a fitness test must mimic one or a combination of the fitness demands of that sport. For example, if a sport requires the participants to run, then the tests should involve running rather than cycling. If players have to sprint and repeatedly change direction then a test should be designed to assess this, with each sprint being run over the kind of distances experienced in the sport. In some sports such as badminton, tests may be designed to include running backwards and sideways. Sport specificity may also extend to requiring the participant to perform the test in full kit. For example, it may be appropriate for a cricket batsman to wear a helmet, pads and carry a bat when being tested for speed between the wickets.

Making the test valid

To be valid, a test must assess what it is intending to. For example, an assessment of maximal strength must indeed measure maximal strength, not muscular endurance. So whilst completing as many press-ups as possible may be a good measure of endurance for those muscles, it is not a valid measure of maximal strength. Similarly, if a test lacks sport specificity it is unlikely to be a valid test for that particular sport. Problems of validity can also arise if other factors have the potential to mask what is being assessed. For example, if assessing sprinting speed in hockey, it would be inappropriate to require the player to dribble a ball, as this would be an assessment of dribbling speed not sprinting speed. Validity is a major problem with fitness tests, because the tests available to most A level PE centres are generalised tests, not really sport-specific, and therefore not overly valid.

Making the test reliable

Reliability refers to how repeatable a test is, or how consistent the results are. In an ideal situation if a performer was to repeat a test under exactly the same conditions, with no change in their fitness they should produce identical results. This is essential for fitness tests, because if a test is reliable, then any differences in scores are due to changes in the performer's fitness, rather than inaccuracies in the test. Of course in reality achieving exactly the same results is most unlikely due to differences in the performer from one day to the next. Coaches and performers simply need to be aware that a relatively small change in the test scores may not mean a change in fitness. For example, if a coach knows that test results can vary by about 5 per cent due to variations from one day to the next, then a test result within this margin suggests no real change in fitness. If however a test result is substantially different from the previous result by more than 10 per cent then this implies a real difference.

Ensuring accuracy

Testing accuracy is part of the test validity and reliability. It covers such aspects as the accuracy to which measurements can be recorded, such as the stopwatch timing of a sprint. A highly skilled coach may be able to hand-time with an accuracy of + or – 0.1 of a second, but would not be able to accurately record to + or – 0.01 of a second. This needs to be borne in mind when using any instrumentation and the results recorded accordingly.

Maximal and sub-maximal tests

These concepts are mainly concerned with tests of stamina. Remember from Chapter 2 – Nutrition (page 16) that stamina is the ability to delay fatigue. A maximal test is one where the performer works at maximum effort or is tested to exhaustion, for example the Multi-Stage Fitness Test. Maximal tests are more accurate as they do work the performer to exhaustion and so measure the limits of fatigue. But they also have disadvantages. These include the difficulty in ensuring the subject is exerting maximum effort; the health and injury dangers of over exertion and injury; and the fact that performance is largely dependent on the athlete's level of motivation.

Sub-maximal tests involve the performer working, but not to exhaustion. In sub-maximal tests, your results are compared to tables that estimate a

▨ **Key terms**

Reliability: the test would give the same result if the test was repeated.

maximal score. An example of a sub-maximal test is the Queen's College step test or the Rockport Walking test. Sub-maximal tests remove the disadvantages of exhaustion and motivation that limit maximal tests, but they have limited accuracy as they are only estimating stamina.

Standardising the test protocol

A test protocol is the way a test is run or conducted. Unless a test protocol is closely standardised it will not generate meaningful data that can be compared. For example, there are a number of variations of the sit-up, including the subject having their feet free or held by a partner; having their knees and hips flexed at different angles; having their hands positioned on their thighs, across their chest, or behind their ears. Each of these variations affects the difficulty of the exercise and consequently the number of repetitions they are likely to achieve. Therefore, the preferred version needs to be selected, carefully administered and the details recorded for future test comparisons.

In tests where the number of repetitions completed within a set time limit is being recorded the quality of the movement must be standardised and must not be sacrificed in the desire for speed. In an attempt to overcome problems of standardisation sports coach UK (formerly the National Coaching Foundation) developed an abdominal curl conditioning test which requires the participants to perform standardised sit-ups in time to a pre-recorded cassette, on which the speed of performing the sit-ups increases every minute until exhaustion. Although primarily designed as an abdominal test it could be used with many other exercises such as press-ups.

If conducting a test of speed or agility which requires the use of markers or cones, it is vital that the position of these is recorded precisely.

💡 Health-related fitness tests

The following fitness tests are fairly standard and are easily performed in a school or college environment. They are all chosen because they are reliable, but most suffer from limits in validity.

Multi-Stage Fitness Test – a test for stamina

Resources

To undertake this test you will require:

- a flat, non-slippery surface at least 20 metres in length
- 30 metre tape measure
- marking cones
- pre-recorded audio tape
- tape recorder
- recording sheets
- assistant.

Procedure

The test is made up of 23 levels where each level lasts approximately one minute. Each level comprises of a series of 20 m shuttles where the starting speed is slow but gradually increases at each level. On the tape a single beep indicates the end of a shuttle and three beeps indicates the start of the next level. The test is conducted as follows:

■ Measure out a 20 metre section and mark each end with a marker cone.

■ The athlete carries out a warm-up programme of jogging and stretching exercises.

■ The athlete must place one foot on or beyond the 20 m marker at the end of each shuttle.

■ If the athlete arrives at the end of a shuttle before the beep, the athlete must wait for the beep and then resume running.

■ The athlete keeps running for as long as possible until he/she can no longer keep up with the speed set by the tape at which point they should voluntarily withdraw.

■ If the athlete fails to reach the end of the shuttle before the beep they should be allowed two or three further shuttles to attempt to regain the required pace before being withdrawn.

■ Record the level and number of shuttles completed at that level by the athlete.

■ At the end of the test the athletes conduct a warm down programme, including stretching exercises.

Table 15.2 *Multi-Stage Fitness Test ratings*

Ratings (level)		
Males	Females	Rating
>13	>11	Excellent
11–12	9–10	Good
9–10	7–8	Average
7–8	5–6	Fair
<7	<5	Poor

Sit-ups test – a test for muscular endurance

Resources

To undertake this test you will require:

■ flat surface

■ mat

■ a partner to hold the feet.

Procedure

The Sit-ups test is conducted as follows:

■ Lie on the mat with the knees bent, feet flat on the floor and the arms folded across the chest.

■ Start each sit-up with back on the floor.

■ Raise yourself to the 90 degree position and then return to the floor.

■ The feet can be held by a partner.

■ Record the number of sit-ups completed in 30 seconds.

Table 15.3 *Sit-up test ratings*

Ratings (number in 30 seconds)		
Males	Females	Rating
>30	>25	Excellent
26–30	21–25	Good
20–25	15–20	Average
17–19	9–14	Fair
<17	<9	Poor

An alternative test could be the number of press-ups preformed in a given time.

Leg/back dynamometer – a test for strength

Resources
- Back and leg or handgrip dynamometer.

Procedure
A dynamometer measures the amount of force that particular muscle groups can exert with very little movement. Every dynamometer needs to be set up correctly for the size and physical dimensions of the person being tested.

Back/leg dynamometer:

- Stand on platform with knees slightly bent (chain is adjustable).
- Pull up on handlebars with maximum effort.
- Repeat three times.
- Record the best effort.

Handgrip dynamometer:

- Adjust grip to suitable size.
- Squeeze with maximum effort using preferred hand.
- Repeat three times.
- Record best effort.

Table 15.4 *Back and Leg Dynamometer test ratings*

Ratings for back and leg dynamometer (kg)		
Males	Females	Rating
>180	>105	Excellent
145–180	90–105	Good
130–145	75–90	Average
105–130	60–75	Fair
<105	<60	Poor

Table 15.5 *Handgrip Dynamometer test ratings*

Ratings for handgrip dynamometer (kg)		
Males	Females	Rating
>70	>41	Excellent
62-69	38-40	Good
48-61	28-37	Average
41-47	22-27	Fair
<41	<22	Poor

Sit and reach test – a test for flexibility

Resources

To undertake this test you will require:

- sit and reach box
- marking slider.

Procedure

- The starting position is sitting on the floor with shoes removed, feet flat against the table, and legs straight.
- The slider should be set with the edge level with the 'toe line' (at 14 cm).
- Reach forward and push the slider along the table as far as possible.
- The distance from the toe line that the slider reaches represents the score for that person.
- It is important to have several warm-up attempts first, and to record the best score.

Table 15.6 *Sit and reach test ratings*

	Ratings (cm)				
Gender	Excellent	Above average	Average	Below average	Poor
Male	>24	21– 24	17–20	14–16	<14
Female	>25	22–25	17– 21	14–16	<14

Bioelectric impedance – a test for body composition (percentage body fat)

Resources

- Bioelectric impedance analyser.

Procedure

- The subject enters the required information into the machine.
- The subject stands up with hands holding machine straight out in front of their body at arm's length.
- After several seconds the machine produces a read-out of percentage body fat.

Table 15.7 *Biometric impedance test ratings*

		Lean	Acceptable	Moderately Overweight	Overweight
General population	Males	< 12	12 – 21	21 - 26	> 26
	Females	< 17	17 - 28	28 - 33	> 33
Athletes	Males	< 7	7 - 15		> 15
	Females	< 12	12 - 25		> 25

Skill-related fitness tests

Sergeant jump test – a test for power

Resources

To undertake this test you will require:

- a wall
- 2 metre measure
- a chair
- an assistant.

Procedure

The athlete:

- chalks/licks his/her fingertips
- stands side onto the wall, keeping both feet remaining on the ground, reaches up as high as possible with one hand and pushes the sliding green scale up the wall with the tips of the fingers (M1)
- from a static position jumps as high as possible and marks the wall with the chalk on his finger tips (M2)
- An assistant then reads off the distance from M1 to M2.
- The test can be performed as many times as the athlete wishes.

Table 15.8 *Sergeant jump test ratings*

Ratings (cm)		
Males	Females	Rating
>65	>58	Excellent
50-65	47-58	Good
40-49	36-46	Average
30-39	26-35	Fair
<30	<26	Poor

20 metre sprint test – a test for speed

Resources

- 20 m tape measure
- stopwatch.

Procedure

- Mark out 20 metres accurately on a flat, non-slip surface.
- Using a standing start, run from the start line as quickly as possible to the finish line.
- Have someone start the run and time it to the 100th/sec.

Table 15.9 *20 metre sprint test ratings*

	Ratings (sec)	
Males	**Females**	**Rating**
>2.80	>3.30	Excellent
2.81-3.10	3.31-3.60	Good
3.11-3.40	3.61-3.90	Average
3.41-3.80	3.91-4.20	Fair
<3.81	<4.21	Poor

Illinois agility run test – a test for agility

Resources

To undertake this test you will require:

- flat surface – a 400m track
- eight cones
- stopwatch
- assistant.

Procedure

The Illinois agility run test is conducted as follows:

- The athlete lies face down on the floor at the start point.
- On the assistant's command the athlete jumps to his/her feet and negotiates the course around the cones to the finish.
- The assistant records the total time taken from his command to the athlete completing the course.

Table 15.10 *Illinois agility run test ratings*

	Ratings (sec)	
Males	**Females**	**Rating**
>15.2	>17.0	Excellent
16.1–15.2	17.9–17.0	Good
17.1–16.2	21.7–18.0	Average
16.3–18.2	23.0–21.8	Fair
<18.3	<23.0	Poor

The Ruler drop test – a test for reaction time

Resources

To undertake this test you will require:

- Metre ruler.

Procedure

▨ A partner holds a metre ruler at the zero end.

▨ The subject places their thumb and index finger either side of the 50 cm mark, without touching the ruler.

▨ Without warning, the person holding the ruler lets go.

▨ The subject must catch the ruler between their thumb and index finger as quickly as possible.

▨ The score is the number just above the index finger (to nearest 0.1 cm).

▨ Record the average distance that the ruler drops (subtract the score achieved from 50cm) out of three attempts using your dominant hand.

Table 15.11 *Ruler drop test ratings*

	Ratings			
Excellent	Above Average	Average	Below Average	Poor
<7.5cm	7.5 - 15.9cm	15.9 - 20.4cm	20.4 - 28cm	>28cm

Stork stand test – a test for balance

Resources

To undertake this test you will require:

▨ warm dry location – gym

▨ stopwatch

▨ an assistant.

Procedure

▨ Stand comfortably on both feet.

▨ Place your hands on your hip.

▨ Lift one leg and place the toes of that foot against the knee of the other leg.

On command from the coach:

▨ Raise the heel and stand on your toes.

▨ Coach starts the stopwatch.

▨ Balance for as long as possible without letting either the heel touch the ground or the other foot move away from the knee.

▨ Coach records the time you were able to maintain the balance.

▨ Repeat the test as many times as the athlete wishes.

Table 15.12 *Stork stand test ratings*

	Ratings			
Excellent	Good	Average	Below average	Poor
>50 secs	40–49 secs	26–39 secs	11–25 secs	< 11 secs

Anderson ball-catch test – a test for hand–eye coordination

Resources

You will need:

- a ball
- a stopwatch
- a flat wall
- an official (who also acts as timekeeper)
- a subject.

Procedure

- You start with a tennis ball in one hand.
- Stand 2 metres from the wall, with both feet together.
- The official shouts 'go!' and starts timing 30 seconds.
- Throw the ball against the wall and catch it in your opposite hand.
- Keep repeating the action.
- After 30 seconds ask your official to shout 'stop!'
- Record the number of catches you completed in the 30 seconds – you are allowed two attempts.

Table 15.13 *Anderson ball-catch test ratings*

Ratings				
Excellent	Good	Average	Below average	Poor
>35	30 - 35	20 - 29	15 - 19	< 15

The warm-up

Warming up can improve performance and reduce injury. Understanding the benefits of the warm-up and using appropriate procedures help you to maximise your performance. Warming up increases the temperature of the body, and more specifically the muscles. This results in:

- better oxygen delivery to muscle tissues
- better chemical reactions that improve energy production and reduce fatigue
- improved muscle blood flow and relaxation
- increased sensitivity of nerve receptors and speed of nerve conduction.

Warming up also allows for:

- rehearsal of movement
- improved psychological preparation
- reduces incidence and likelihood of musculoskeletal injuries
- supplies adequate blood flow to heart so increasing its efficiency.

Effective warming up allows you to gradually prepare for maximum effort and should include:

- general warm-up
- stretching
- specific warm-up
- psychological preparation.

General warm-up

A warm-up should start with general activities such as jogging, easy exercises or stationary bicycling to produce sweating without fatigue. This will increase body temperature, which reduces muscle viscosity, enhances enzymatic activity to improve muscle contraction and neurologically relaxes muscles.

Stretching

Incorporate a range of stretching exercises that work on those parts of the body that will be used during the exercise. Many performers have a set series of exercises, often starting at the head and working down the body. This usually involves moving into the stretching position. Then gradually increase the force of the stretch to continue to produce a stretching sensation without pain. That position should be held for 30 to 60 seconds. Then relax for 5 seconds. Repeat this process three to five times for each stretch. Stretching improves flexibility, increases relaxation of the muscles and improves the muscle's ability to withstand the forces involved in intense exercise.

Specific warm-up

Practise those skills that you will be performing in your sport. Gradually increasing the intensity of an exercise that duplicates the movement involved with your sport adds to the benefits of the general warm-up. This also provides a 'rehearsal' of the skills involved in your sport.

Psychological preparation

The pre-event time can be anxiety producing. Excessive anxiety can be detrimental to performance. The warm-up can be an effective procedure to control anxiety of competition and provide optimal psychological preparation for an event.

A warm-up should be specific to the physical capabilities of the athlete and the intensity of the activity. A brief warm-up of 10 minutes of jogging and stretching would adequately prepare the 'weekend athlete' for a run. Conversely, an elite athlete's preparation for a run might include 10 to 15 minutes of jogging, 5 to 10 minutes of stretching, 5 to 10 minutes of running with gradual increase to race pace and 5 to 10 minutes of jogging, during which time they may have covered 2 or 3 miles.

A specific warm-up should be included for each activity you participate in. Experiment with various warm-ups to determine the amount, intensity and duration that will provide maximal preparation without fatigue.

Types of stretching

There are different types of stretching. Stretches are either dynamic (meaning they involve movement) or static (meaning they involve no movement). The different types of stretching you need to know are:

- active stretching
- passive (or relaxed) stretching
- static stretching
- ballistic stretching.

Active stretching is where you assume a position and then hold it there with no assistance other than using the strength of your agonist muscles.

Key terms

Active stretching: holding a stretched position by contraction of your own agonistic muscles.

For example, bringing your leg up high and then holding it there without anything (other than your leg muscles themselves) to keep the leg in that extended position. The tension of the agonists in an active stretch helps to relax the muscles being stretched (the antagonists).

Active stretching increases active flexibility and strengthens the agonistic muscles. Active stretches are usually quite difficult to hold and maintain for more than 10 seconds and rarely need to be held any longer than 15 seconds. Many of the movements (or stretches) found in various forms of yoga are active stretches.

Passive stretching is where you assume a position and hold it with some other part of your body, or with the assistance of a partner or some other apparatus. For example, bringing your leg up high and then a partner holds it there with their hand. The splits is an example of a passive stretch (in this case the floor is the 'apparatus' that you use to maintain your extended position).

Slow, passive stretching is useful in relieving spasms in muscles that are healing after an injury. Obviously, you should check with your doctor first to see if it is okay to attempt to stretch the injured muscles. Passive stretching is a technique in which you are relaxed and make no contribution to the range of motion. Instead, an external force is created by an outside agent, either manually or mechanically. Passive stretching is also very good for 'cooling down' after a workout and helps reduce post-workout muscle soreness.

Static stretching involves holding a position. That is, you stretch to the farthest point and hold the stretch. Static stretching involves the resistance of muscle groups through isometric contractions of the stretched muscles. The use of static stretching is one of the fastest ways to develop increased flexibility and is much more effective than either passive stretching or active stretching alone. Static stretches also help to develop strength in the 'tensed' muscles, and seem to decrease the amount of pain usually associated with stretching.

The most common ways to provide the needed resistance for a static stretch are to apply resistance manually to one's own limbs, or to have a partner or use apparatus such as a wall to apply the resistance. An example of manual resistance would be holding onto the ball of your foot to keep it from flexing while you are using the muscles of your calf to try and straighten your instep so that the toes are pointed. An example of using a partner to provide resistance would be having a partner hold your leg up high (and keep it there) while you attempt to force your leg back down to the ground. An example of using the wall to provide resistance would be the well-known 'push-the-wall' calf-stretch where you are actively attempting to move the wall (even though you know you can't).

Ballistic stretching uses the momentum of a moving body or a limb in an attempt to force it beyond its normal range of motion. This is stretching by bouncing into (or out of) a stretched position, using the stretched muscles as a spring which pulls you out of the stretched position (e.g. bouncing down repeatedly to touch your toes). This type of stretching is not considered useful and can often lead to injury. It does not allow your muscles to adjust to, and relax in, the stretched position. It may instead cause them to tighten up by repeatedly activating the stretch reflex.

Principles of safe practice

Maintaining sufficient flexibility for activities must be kept sport-specific. You should concentrate on the range of motions and the muscle groups

Key terms

Passive stretching: a stretch position being held by something other than the agonistic muscles.

Static stretching: stretch to limit of range and then isometrically contract the stretched muscles.

Ballistic stretching: using movement to 'bounce' in and out of a stretched position. Can cause injury.

which you use in your activity. You should begin stretching slowly and gently. Stretches should be held because it takes time to lengthen muscle tissue safely. Hold your stretches for at least 30 seconds and even up to a minute with a particularly tight muscle or problem area.

Make sure you only stretch 'warm' muscles. Stretching a cold muscle can strain the muscle fibres. Warm up first. Many people suggest that it's more beneficial to stretch after you exercise, when the muscle is heated by blood flow and is more likely to be flexible.

Never hold a painful stretch. You should ease off just to where it's not painful, and hold for the duration of the stretch. Remember that stretching lengthens muscle tissue, making it less liable to tears. Stretching should be a relaxing part of your exercise session.

Don't bounce. Bouncing causes minute tears in the muscle, which must heal itself with scar tissue. The scar tissue tightens the muscle, making you less flexible and more prone to pain. Bouncing sets up a vicious circle.

Balance and equalize your stretching. Work on both agonists and antagonists. A tight hamstring can cause a knee injury that side.

Cooling down

Cooling down should consist of the following:

- Stop exercising and walk around to allow your heart rate to decrease.
- 5 to 10 minutes jogging/walking, which will decrease body temperature and remove waste products from the working muscles.
- 5 to 10 minutes of static stretching exercises, which will decrease body temperature, remove waste products from the working muscles and help to increase range of movement.

Static stretches are more appropriate to the cool-down as they help muscles to relax and increase their range of movement.

Benefits of a cool-down

An appropriate cool-down will:

- aid in the dissipation of waste products – including lactic acid
- reduce the potential for the delayed muscle soreness (DOMS) that often accompanies strenuous workouts
- reduce the chances of dizziness or fainting caused by the pooling of venous blood at the extremities
- reduce the level of adrenaline in the blood
- allow the heart rate to return to its resting rate.

Training methods

There are several different types of training that can be used to improve fitness.

Continuous training regimes

Continuous running, swimming, rowing or cycling will help train the aerobic system and help develop stamina. Continuous or 'steady state' effort can be maintained for a considerable period provided that the intensity does not go above a certain level. If training is required to develop stamina or endurance, then training needs to be hard, but not too hard. An easy way to estimate whether training is at a suitable level is to exercise at an intensity that just makes conversation difficult. Researchers have shown that such exercise is of an intensity that is sufficient to raise heart rate to about 130–140 beats per min. and this provides for aerobic endurance improvement.

Measuring intensity has been discussed previously in this chapter, and the Borg scale and exercising heart rate can both be used. A Borg scale rating of 13–15 or a heart rate of 70 per cent of maximum should produce benefits to the non-serious performer. A level of intensity above 15 on the Borg scale or above 70 per cent of maximum heart rate will be required as fitness improves. Remember the idea of progressive overload.

Intermittent training regimes

This type of training programme involves alternating periods of effort and recovery so that the body may be exposed to a greater total workload than it could manage during a continuous period of training. By adjusting the duration, intensity and type of activity undertaken, such training permits an almost infinite variety of possible sessions.

Interval training is the name given to intermittent training that is characterised by having periods of intense exercise followed by periods with only a low level of energy expenditure (rest). Interval training is thus predominantly an anaerobic conditioning programme, and as such does require a good base of aerobic fitness before commencement.

Interval training bases the training prescription on:

■ intensity of exercise
■ duration of the exercise
■ length of recovery
■ number of repetitions of the exercise-recovery interval.

A greater number of intense exercises can be achieved by dividing the session up into blocks of work called sets of work and rest, which in turn have longer rest intervals between them.

Circuit training

This involves a circuit of exercises being performed one after the other. Each exercise is said to exist at a 'station'. Circuits are almost infinitely variable, such that they can be established to cover every aspect of fitness, or be designed to concentrate on one specific aspect of fitness, such as strength, anaerobic power, aerobic capacity, local muscular endurance, etc.

The number and variety of work stations, the number of repetitions required, and the length of the rest interval can all be adjusted to suit the performers involved.

Usually, circuits are designed to last 20–30 minutes, with consecutive stations designed to stress different muscle groups and/or different aspects of fitness, so as to spread the fatigue. Normally, performers undertake 2–4 laps of the circuit, with whatever rest interval is decided between laps and/or stations.

Weight training

Weight training can be used by everyone, and when paired with regular aerobic exercise, weight training increases your strength and muscle endurance as well as your overall feeling of fitness in ways that no other single exercise can. Bicycling develops one set of muscles, basketball another, but weight training works out a whole range of muscles in a very short amount of time.

Specific weight-training routines can be used to help you develop particular muscle groups that will improve your performance in your chosen sport. True enough, nothing improves your tennis game as much as playing tennis: specificity is the iron rule of modern sports training. Nonetheless, upper-body training will give you an extra edge in tennis, and developing your leg muscles will improve your swimming kick. The basic principle of any sort of muscle development is that of overload: contracting a muscle group against added resistance. Machines can isolate muscle groups very efficiently by maintaining your body in a particular position and by making you move a weight along a predetermined path. A typical workout with weights includes a warm-up of five to ten minutes followed by an exercise routine that leaves the muscles thoroughly exhausted. Your exact exercise routine should be designed to use those muscles that are involved in your activity.

Plyometric training

Plyometrics is a form of power training that involves powerful muscular contractions in response to a rapid stretching of the muscles. This stretching of the muscles, prior to the explosive contraction that follows, is often called 'loading'. The faster and greater the load, the more powerful the subsequent contraction. A good example of this is watching any basketball player jump. They jump higher when they can take a few steps before the jump. The steps are used to create a bigger and faster 'load' on the leg prior to jumping. The response to this greater load is a greater contraction by the legs and a higher jump height. The same phenomenon exists with all explosive actions. The physiology behind plyometrics is that the loading activates the stretch reflex which produces a more forceful contraction than a 'normal' concentric contraction.

A jump onto a 24-inch box is a power exercise, but not a plyometric exercise. To make it a plyometric exercise one can jump off a 6–12-inch box, hit the ground and immediately jump onto the 24-inch box. The landing from the smaller box loads the legs quickly enough to create the stretch reflex needed in plyometric training. This is very demanding – don't try it without consulting a professional!

Plyometric exercises are very intense and must be treated as a very strenuous form of training. Care must be taken when devising a plyometrics programme that the overload is not too excessive as injuries can easily result. However the benefits of plyometric exercises can be large in terms of power gains.

Mobility training

What you do just before your workout begins can have a big impact on what you are able to do during your workout. Many athletes prepare for a training session by carrying out some routine stretching exercises, but it's important to remember that stretching helps to improve your static (non-moving) flexibility and may not do such a good job at preparing your body to move quickly and efficiently.

Dynamic mobility exercises during your pre-workout warm-up period prepare your body completely for the vigorous movements that make up the main part of most training programmes. Mobility exercises and drills stimulate your nervous system, muscles, tendons and joints in a very dynamic manner. Static stretching exercises, in which you're not moving around at all but are simply stretching a particular muscle or group of muscles, have a place in any training programme, but their value and proper usage are often misunderstood.

■ **Key terms**

Plyometrics: form of power training involving the stretching of a muscle followed by an immediate contraction. Think of jumping and bounding exercises.

It's probably best to place static stretches at the end of your workout as part of the cool-down, not at the beginning of a training session. Static exercises help bring your body back toward a state of rest and recovery and allow you to focus on relaxing and lengthening the muscles that you have put under stress during your workout. Placing static stretches at the beginning of a training session, on the other hand, tends to interrupt the natural flow of an optimal warm-up and fails to prepare you fully for the dynamic movements that will follow.

Dynamic mobility exercises should be performed as smoothly as possible, and progress gradually from small to large ranges of motion over the course of the repetitions. Begin exercises by keeping all swings and bends at a slow and safe speed of movement. As mobility increases, gradually increase the speed to make them more dynamic. Stay within your own normal range of motion, but work to increase the amplitude (range of motion) and speed of movement in small amounts from week to week. Don't go beyond your limit (in speed or amplitude) and injure yourself. The key point about mobility training is to train – not strain.

✔️ *You should now be able to:*

- describe the principles of training – specificity, progression, overtraining, overload, reversibility, tedium and the FITT principles of intensity
- calculate and suggest optimal workload intensities through use of heart rate, Borg scale and one repetition maximum tests
- describe the reasons for fitness testing and the principles of maximal and sub-maximal tests
- discuss the limitations of testing such as validity and reliability
- describe specific suitable testing protocols
- describe the physiological and psychological value of a warm-up and a cool-down
- describe the different types of stretching exercises – active and passive; static and ballistic; and the principles of safe practice
- describe the principles, advantages and disadvantages and provide specific examples of the following training methods – continuous, intermittent, circuit, weights, plyometric and mobility.

1   Explain how you would use the principles of training when developing a
    training programme to improve the fitness of A Level Physical Education
    students.   *(6 marks)*

2   Explain how a heart rate monitor may be used to measure the intensity of a
    training programme.   *(6 marks)*

3   Training only produces improvements if there is overload.
    (a) What do you understand by the term 'overload'?   *(1 mark)*
    (b) Explain the FITT principle of overload.   *(5 marks)*

4   (a) Why should fitness testing be an important aspect of any training
         programme?   *(3 marks)*
    (b) What ethical problems are associated with fitness testing?   *(3 marks)*

5   (a) Describe the static method of stretching.   *(3 marks)*
    (b)   What safety precautions should be taken when taking part in a
         stretching programme?   *(3 marks)*

6   What are the main benefits of:
    (a) warming up;   *(3 marks)*
    (b) cooling down?   *(3 marks)*

16 Practical skill acquisition

A performer can either improve their performance by getting fitter or by improving their skill. This chapter is concerned with the latter – how you can improve your own skill or the skill of another.

In Chapter 7 – Skills (page 78) we learnt about the different types of skill and how we first acquire them. We learnt that there are different types of skill, and that learning may be undertaken in a number of different ways. In Chapter 8 – Information processing (page 87) we learnt how we receive and use information to help us make a decision about which skill to use and when to use it. However it should be clear to you from what you learnt in those two chapters and from your observation of others that there is a huge difference between a beginner and an expert performer in terms of how well they perform a skill. In Chapter 9 – Learning and performance (page 102) we learnt about the stages of learning – from cognitive to autonomous – and it is clear that practice can help move from one phase to the next, from the beginner to the expert.

How well we practise, how well we help others construct their practice sessions has a fundamental effect upon how quickly a skill can be developed, and whether or not we reach our full potential.

As a practical performer you will almost certainly have personally experienced many of the methods and techniques covered in this chapter. You will have received instruction from a teacher or a coach and received feedback from them about how well you performed. You will have engaged in practice time when you have been required to keep repeating a skill, striving to match it to some model you have been given, or been helped to move a limb in a particular way. You may have been struggling to acquire the skill and had it broken down into its component parts.

As a coach you can help another person improve more quickly if you understand when it is the right time to intervene, or how long to ask a performer to carry on practising, or give them advice on improving their technique. This chapter is designed to give you as a performer and as a coach an insight into making the most effective use of practice time. The work you undertake in this section will help you in the practical coursework in Unit 2, and also in answering the question in Section B of the exam paper.

Teaching or coaching?

When helping a performer to improve their skill are we teaching or coaching? A dictionary definition of coaching implies that it is about instructing or training, whereas that for teaching talks about helping to learn. In this book we consider that teaching is what happens in PE lessons, or when first helping a learner acquire a skill, and coaching is more to do with sport and improving competitive performance. In reality we tend to engage in both – coaches teach and teachers coach!

The style of instruction or teaching that we use is important. It is determined by a number of factors:

- the skill we are trying to improve
- the nature of the learning situation
- the nature of the learner.

We shall begin by looking at the different teaching styles that we may use.

Teaching styles

Teaching styles differ in two respects – the proportion of the decisions that are made by the learner and the proportion of the decisions made by the teacher. This can best be seen by looking at Figure 16.1.

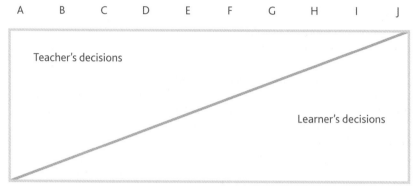

A   B   C   D   E   F   G   H   I   J

Teacher's decisions

Learner's decisions

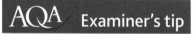 **Fig. 16.1** *The spectrum of teaching styles (adapted from Mosston and Ashworth)*

Mosston identified ten different styles on his spectrum.

Style A: Command

Style B: Practice

Style C: Reciprocal

Style D: Self-check

Style E: Inclusion

Style F: Guided Discovery

Style G: Divergent

Style H: Individual

Style I: Learner Initiated

Style J: Self Teaching

As you can see from Figure 16.1 as the teaching style moves from Style A Command Style to Style J Self Teaching the learner takes increasing responsibility for their learning – how it is conducted, how it is practised.

In the AQA specification we are concerned with just four teaching styles and these are adapted from the ones set out by Mosston – Command, Reciprocal, Discovery and the Problem-Solving approach.

Command style (Style A)

The **command style** of teaching occurs when the teacher makes all the decisions for the learner and may be described as an authoritarian style. All the learners are treated in the same way; there is no room for an individual to do anything their way. Learners take no responsibility for their own learning and are not encouraged to think why they should do something in a particular way. They are not required to think of alternative ways of achieving the objective.

AQA Examiner's tip

Exam questions will either ask you to identify which style will be used for a particular situation and why, or tell you which stye is being used and ask you to describe it, and suggest why it is being used.

Key terms

Command style: the teacher makes all the decisions, no input from the learner, no alternatives considered.

Activity

For one of the core skills in your selected physical activity plan how it could be taught using each of the teaching styles.

Reciprocal learning (Style C)

Reciprocal learning takes place when performers learn from each other. The teacher may demonstrate the skill or state what is to be learned and how it is to be done. The learners work in pairs. One learner is the performer and the other is an observer who comments on the performance, gives feedback and offers advice on how the performance may be improved. The learners then swap roles. This is a more cognitive approach (see Chapter 9 – Learning and performance, page 102) and leads to a more thorough understanding of the objective of the movement and how it may be achieved.

Discovery learning (Styles F/G)

In **discovery learning** the objective is set by the teacher, often in the form of a problem, and the learner has to work out the solution. For example in gymnastics the teacher may give the start position and the end position but ask the learner to work out how the transition may occur. The guided discovery method (Style F) requires the teacher to lead the learning by providing information, cues and asking questions to help the learner down the correct path. This process leads to a much deeper understanding of what is to be achieved and how it may be achieved but it is a longer process.

Problem-solving approach

The **problem-solving approach** is similar to the discovery learning style discussed above. The teacher sets an objective – how to get past an opponent – but the learner finds their own method of solving the problem. The solution will be determined by the learner's ability, physical attributes and current level of skill. This means that each learner can find their own solution, although some may be more effective than others. This allows for a greater understanding of the problem and how it may be solved and is a far more 'cognitive' approach.

Surely therefore giving the learner more control of the learning process is by far the best way of learning? This is not always the case however as you will see when we consider the advantages and disadvantages of each of the four styles and when we may use them.

When to use a particular style

As a coach or a teacher it is vital that the appropriate teaching style is used so that learning is optimised. When deciding which style to use four factors must be considered:

- the teacher – their knowledge and experience
- the activity – how complex or demanding is the task or skill and is there any risk involved?
- the learner or learners – their level of skill, fitness, prior knowledge, age, experience and level of motivation
- the learning situation – environment, size of group, equipment available, time available, etc.

Command style

If the teacher is more limited in experience and lacks confidence the command style allows them to retain full control of the session, using the limited knowledge they have. They may avoid having to answer awkward questions and retain confidence in themselves during the session.

If the activity is highly complex or has an element of risk the greater control of the teacher will help the learners grasp the basics and make progress in the early stages and will reduce the element of risk. For example when introducing trampolining the teacher may wish to adopt a command style at the beginning due to the risks involved.

If the learners have no prior experience of the activity or skill, or are young, then the command style allows the teachers to ensure they acquire the basic knowledge of what is to be done (the cognitive stage – see Chapter 9 – Learning and performance, page 102). Similarly if the learner lacks fitness or motivation then the level of teacher control may ensure that some progress is made.

A poor learning situation (large numbers, little equipment, limited time) may be more effective with the teacher regaining control. Similarly if the environment is difficult – bad weather, dangerous situation – then again the command style may be the most appropriate. The advantage of the command style is that it retains teacher control and therefore is most appropriate with poor learning situations, where there may be an element of risk or at the early stages of learning.

The disadvantage of the command style is that it does not allow for the development of understanding, will restrict development, prevent learners from taking responsibility for their own learning, and means they cannot come up with plan B or C if Plan A fails. They become restricted as performers.

Reciprocal learning

When the teacher is more confident or knowledgeable they feel able to let learners help each other. This may be limited help however, and the learner will still need the teacher's more expert support.

If the activity or skill is clear, has a clear progression and the essential elements are easily observed and commented upon, then reciprocal learning can be effective. It is often supported by prompt sheets given to the observer to help them see the key movements.

If the learners are not complete beginners and have some experience then this form of learning can be effective. If they are poorly motivated then it is unlikely they will give the observation or feedback role sufficient attention to be of much help to the learner. If the learners are immature they may find it difficult to give or receive criticism.

Reciprocal learning can often help when the learning situation is poor. If it is a large group with limited facilities the role of observer can support the teacher who may struggle to see all the learners perform due to time, and can keep half of the group actively involved even though there may be limited equipment. Reciprocal learning can develop a more in-depth understanding of what the learner is expected to achieve but it requires careful monitoring and frequent input by the teacher to ensure that correct learning is taking place. Learners can also gain confidence and improve their communication and listening skills by engaging in reciprocal learning.

Discovery learning

Discovery learning requires the teacher to have a good knowledge of the learner or the group and to have the confidence for them to be working without direct intervention or control.

Discovery learning works best when there are a range of possible outcomes or where the application of a skill or movement requires

 Activity

For your own sport devise observation and prompt sheets for each of the core skills and techniques.

decision making and judgement. It will also work well where the progression of the skill or sequence is clear and open to discovery. The use of a discovery learning style is less effective with a highly complex skill and may lead to the learner becoming confused or acquiring ineffective techniques which may then require relearning. If a task has an element of risk then a discovery learning approach, with its much lower level of teacher control, may not be advised.

Discovery learning requires engaged and motivated learners to work best. The use of a discovery style often motivates learners as they can gain great satisfaction by learning for themselves, with a high sense of achievement and personal fulfilment. With younger learners, with a shorter attention span, discovery learning can only be used for short periods of time, or needs to be constructed so that they experience frequent bursts of 'discovery' or learning to maintain their enthusiasm. More mature learners are able to stick with the problem and work at it until a solution is found.

Discovery learning can help overcome the disadvantage of a large group but it is a more time-consuming approach and is hard to use in limited time situations. It also frequently requires a reasonable level of equipment and fair weather conditions if the lesson is being conducted outside.

Problem-solving approach

The advantages and disadvantages of the problem-solving approach are very similar to those discussed under discovery learning. A method of teaching known as 'games for understanding' has been developed which has at its heart the need to develop understanding – why we do something before we worry about how we do it.

The diagram in Figure 16.2 shows how this approach might work.

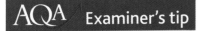

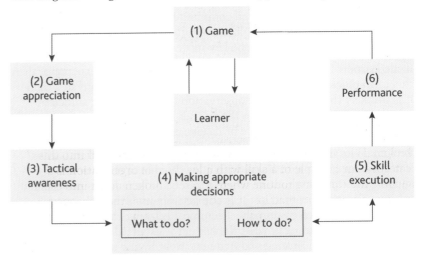

Fig. 16.2 *Games for understanding*

In games for understanding learners are asked to play either a simplified version of the game or a small element of the game.

Follow this process by referring to Figure 16.2.

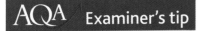

AQA Examiner's tip

If an exam question gives a learning situation and asks you to discuss which teaching style would be most appropriate bear in mind that a teacher could use more than one style in a lesson.

Stage 1 In badminton only give the performers two rules:

- The shuttlecock must cross the net.
- You win a point when the shuttle lands in your opponent's court, or the opponent hits the shuttlecock outside of your part of the court.

Stage 2 Ask them to play the game. After a few minutes of play learners can be asked questions – how do you score, how can you prevent opponents scoring?

Stage 3 'Tactical awareness'. The teacher asks 'how can you create space for the shuttle to land in your opponent's court?' Answer 'move my opponent to the back of the court'.

Stage 4 'Appropriate decision making' – if the opponents are at the front move them to the back. 'How?' Now there is a need to teach a skill such as the overhead clear and the reason why the learner should acquire this skill, which then leads to improved performance.

The games for understanding approach has at its heart the need to develop understanding of why the performer needs to develop a skill and when or how they may use it – it is a cognitive approach. It can equally be used within a full version of a sport or for the development of tactics. For example when playing an invasion game such as hockey or football a corner is won. Question – 'how can we score from here?' or 'how do we defend the corner?'

How to practise a skill

Skills vary greatly in terms of their complexity and their level of organisation. A complex skill requires a large amount of information processing, as a great deal of perceptual information has to be processed and there may be high levels of decision making to be made. When practising these kinds of skills they may be broken down into sub-routines. An example of a complex skill would be a basketball jump shot after a dribble. The player may well break the skill down into sub-routines or its component parts (the dribble, the stop, the jump and the arm action of the shot) as it may be easier to practise these component parts separately.

The level of organisation of a skill refers to how easy it is to break the skill down into component parts. A highly organised skill such as running or cycling must be practised as a whole because it cannot be broken down into sub-routines. Most continuous skills fall into this category. An example of a skill with a low level of organisation is a gymnastics tumbling routine where it can be broken down into the various elements for practice. It is the case however that whenever a skill is broken down into smaller components or sub-routines it must be practised as the complete skill as there is an inter-relation between the components which is also part of the successful performance of the skill. If it is not practised as a whole then the flow, timing and sequencing of the movements may be lost.

When deciding how to practise the skill the coach should consider a range of factors:

- How motivated is the performer?
- How experienced are they, their level of maturity?
- The type of skill to be practised – open/closed, serial or continuous, level of organisation and complexity?
- The environmental conditions, time available, etc.?

Activity

Develop lesson plans using a games for understanding approach for either improving one or more of the core skills in your pactical actvity, or using the skill in a competitive situation.

AQA Examiner's tip

Swimming is an example of a serial skill that can be broken into sub-routines.

Having considered all of these factors the coach must decide whether the skill may be practised as a whole or in its constituent parts.

The different methods of practice

There are four main methods of practising a skill – whole, part, progressive part and whole-part-whole. Which method to use is a key decision for the coach and for the performer.

The whole practice method

In the **whole practice** method the skill is practised as a whole, without any attempt to break it down into sub-routines. In reality all skills should at some stage be practised as a whole. It is only by doing this that the performer gets the correct 'feel' for the skill and receives the appropriate internal or kinaesthetic feedback. Skills that have a high level of complexity and are difficult to break down should be practised as a whole.

Progressive part method

The **progressive part** method of learning or acquiring a skill involves breaking down the skill into a series of parts and then 'chaining' them back together, one part at a time. A gymnastics routine might be learnt or practised in this way. Suppose a performer was attempting to learn a five-part routine. She would learn Part A, then Part B, then link Part A and B together, then learn Part C and then link them together.

$$A > A+B > A+B+C > A+B+C+D > A+B+C+D+E$$

The part and whole-part-whole method

In the part method a skill is broken down into constituent parts. You can do this with skills that are complex but low in organisation. For example a swimming stroke may be broken down into arm action, leg action, body position on the water and the breathing technique. This allows the performer and the coach to concentrate on each specific part and to improve them. It may be found that the breast stroke leg kick has a 'screw' action and by isolating that part of the skill by using a float the swimmer can focus their attention on getting the correct feel for the leg kick.

The **whole-part-whole method** is a development on the part method and where possible should be used in favour of the purely part method.

In the first instance the performer tries the skill as a whole. In terms of the learning stage this would be a performer moving from the cognitive to the associative stage (see Chapter 7 – Skills, page 78). This gives the performer a 'feel' for the movement in its entirety and develops their understanding of the skill. Then the skill may be broken down into parts, each part improved or perfected and then the skill is practised as a whole. It is very important to reintegrate the part being practised into the whole so that the performer does not forget the sequence of actions or the links between them. Therefore all the elements of the whole-part-whole method should be used within the same training session.

Using the letter sequence as before a skill may consist of five parts (ABCDE):

- Perform (ABCDE) as a whole
- Practise part B on its own
- Perform (ABCDE) as a whole.

AQA Examiner's tip

When discussing how to practise it is always creditworthy to point out that all learners should attempt the skill as a whole at some stage – even if a part-learning approach has been used, so that they understand the sequencing and the feel of the whole movement.

Activity

Analyse the core skills for your practical activity and decide which ones can be practised using the whole, progressive part or whole-part-whole practice method.

Link

The progressive part method is sometimes known as chaining and is most successfully used with serial skills. For more information, see Chapter 7 – Skills (page 78).

Key terms

Whole practice method: the complete skill is practised without any attempt to break it down into sub-routines.

Progressive part: a method of practice where a skill is broken down into parts, each part learnt and then linked in and practised as a sequence.

Whole-part-whole: skill is performed as a whole then broken into parts, a part is practised, then the skill is practised as a whole again.

In general it is better to use the whole-part-whole method as it retains the performer's feel for the whole skill and the connections and transition from one part to the other.

When to use the different methods of practice

A coach must think carefully about which method of practice to use. They must take into consideration:

- the nature of the skill
- the stage of learning of the learner
- the maturity and experience of the learner
- whether or not there are safety considerations.

In reality the coach or teacher will have to be flexible and is likely to use all three methods at some stage in a performer's development. For example you might (if possible) start with the whole method allowing the performer to feel the whole movement and to experience the flow and to gain a kinaesthetic sense of the movement. The coach and the performer can then analyse any weaknesses and break the skill down into its constituent parts and practise the weakest elements. After time spent working on these weak areas the performer is allowed to try the whole movement again. Both the whole and the part methods have their advantages and disadvantages and these are given in Table 16.1 below.

Table 16.1 *Advantages and disadvantages of the whole and part methods of teaching*

Whole method	Part method
Performer appreciates the flow, sequence and feel of the end product or movement	Allows complex serial tasks or routines to be learnt more easily
The performer is able to develop their own schema (see Chapter 7) for the movement	Can work on specific, identified weaknesses
Must be used for skills that are high in organisation, hard to break down or have to be performed quickly	Allows the performer to build experience and confidence in complex skills
Easier to transfer the skill from practice to the competitive situation	Can eliminate some areas of danger, say in gymnastics
Prevents boredom setting if the performer loses sight of the whole skill	Allows for staged success which can build motivation

Having decided which method of practice to use the next decision for the coach is to determine how to structure the practice time that is available to them.

Structuring practice time

There are two main ways in which the time you have available to you may be structured – distributed practice or massed practice. When deciding which way to structure the practice time the coach must take into consideration:

- the age and experience of the learner
- the physical demands of the skill or practice session
- the motivation level of the performer
- the performer's stage of learning
- the nature of the skill and the time available.

AQA Examiner's tip

Make sure that you know both the advantages and disadvantages for each method, and have a bank of examples of skills that are most appropriately taught by each method. Try and have examples from your chosen physical activity.

Distributed practice: when the time available is broken down into smaller time blocks, with rest periods.

Massed practice: when the performer practises for the whole of the time available, with no breaks.

Distributed practice

Distributed practice allows the performer breaks or rests between performances of the skill or movement. During those breaks the performer may rest or may engage in activity unrelated to the main skill. This allows for mental refreshment and prevents the performer becoming fatigued or bored. Note that the performer should not engage in activity which would cause negative transfer – for example you would not send a tennis player off to engage in badminton during their break – see Chapter 7 – Skills (page 78).

Massed practice

As you might imagine in a **massed practice** session the performer works continuously and gets very little or no break during the practice session. It is a continuous session.

The advantages of each method of structuring the time are given in Table 16.2 below.

Table 16.2 *Advantages and disadvantages of distributed and massed practice sessions*

Distributed practice	Massed practice
Is better for beginners being introduced to the skill	Useful for the older and more experienced performer
For performers who are less fit	Used when the skill or task is simple
For performers who are less motivated, as this form of practice can maintain motivation	Used when it is a discrete skill, or a skill performed quickly
If practice drills are varied then useful for developing schema	Used when working with a performer who is fitter, to avoid fatigue
Used with continuous skills, or gross motor skills	Used with highly motivated performers
Better with complex skills requiring a high level of concentration	Useful when time is limited
Breaks can be used for mental rehearsal or mental practice	
Useful when the skill or task is physically demanding	
Useful when the tasks may have an element of danger	

The rest periods or breaks that occur in the distributed practice model should be used constructively, to further the learning or skill level of the performer. During the break the coach could do some of the following:

- Give feedback to the performer (this would be terminal feedback) and could be either about the outcome of the movement (knowledge of results) or about how well the skill was performed (knowledge of performance). For more information on feedback see the section later in this chapter.
- Maintain motivation by giving encouragement or by doing an alternative activity to reduce boredom.
- Ask the learner to engage in mental practice.

Variable practice

The coach must also consider varying the actual practice of the skill to ensure that the performer is able to use the skill in a variety of situations. This is particularly important for open skills and for the development of schema – see Chapter 7 – Skills (page 78). Closed skills should be practised in as near 'real life' situations as possible. For open skills varying the practice means asking the performer to perform the skill in slightly different conditions – changing the target area for a badminton or tennis serve, changing the number of defenders, adding in some spectators, kicking into the wind, etc. These different situations and the way the skill is adapted will be stored in long-term memory and then used later.

Mental practice

Mental practice or mental rehearsal is the rehearsal of the skill without any physical movement. For beginners it allows them to build up a mental picture of the skill and is vital in going from the cognitive to the associative stage or phase of learning. For more advanced and experienced performers it is a vital part of the warm-up and allows them to become focused on the forthcoming tasks, as well as reminding themselves of strategies or tactics. Rugby players will mentally rehearse penalty moves or back line tactics, gymnasts will visualise the routine enabling them to recall the timing of each part of the sequence. It is also seen as a very valuable way to control arousal and anxiety. By visualising the situation, for example a penalty flick or kick in hockey or football, the performer becomes more mentally accustomed to the situation and they fear it less. This helps reduce anxiety and improves performance.

There is some evidence to indicate that during the visualisation of a skilled movement there is some stimulation of motor nerves (but below the level required to cause an actual muscular contraction). Therefore whilst mental practice is better than no practice at all it is most effectively used with physical practice. Coaches and teachers should therefore build in the opportunity for all performers to engage in mental practice. Research indicates that mental rehearsal combined with physical practice is highly effective.

Having determined how we should practise a skill, whether as a whole or in parts, and how we should structure the practice time, we can then begin our practice session. As the session progresses however it is clear that performers will need guidance, to help them perform the correct movement or to prevent incorrect movements from being repeated and learnt.

The next section looks at the various forms of guidance that may be used.

How to guide an improver

There are three forms of guidance that may be used to help the performer acquire or improve a skill or movement – visual guidance, verbal guidance and mechanical or manual guidance. Which of the three you use is determined by:

- the nature or characteristics of the skill including its complexity
- the stage or phase of learning of the performer
- the teaching, coaching or learning environment
- the level of cognitive or physical maturation of the learner.

Guidance is obviously given to beginners as they start their learning process but is equally valuable for performers in the associative and the autonomous stages of learning as they progress to ever more accurate and effective movements.

Visual guidance

Visual guidance occurs when a learner is shown a visual image of the skill or movement, allowing them to develop a mental picture of what the

Key terms

Mental practice: the mental or cognitive rehearsal of a movement or skill, with no actual physical movement taking place.

Activity

Close your eyes and picture yourself participating in your physical activity, performing some of the required skills or tactics.

Key terms

Visual guidance: the use of images or demonstrations to help a learner.

skill looks like and the flow of the movements. This visual image may be shown in various ways:

- demonstrations by a coach/teacher or another performer
- still images – pictures, posters, etc.
- moving images – video or animations, particularly the use of slow motion.

Fig. 16.3 *Coach demonstration – must be accurate and clear*

It is vital that the demonstration or other visual image is an accurate one. A coach or teacher who is not able to demonstrate accurately should consider using a more skilful or experienced performer to show the skill or use some form of video.

For the beginner the use of a demonstration or video can give far too much information at the early stage. It is vital therefore that the coach draws the attention of the learner to a few key points and reinforces them. This is known as 'cueing'.

It is also important that the learner is in the optimum position to observe the key point that is being shown. For example you may want to view a long jumper from the side, about 10 metres or so back so that you can see the effect of the leg and arm movements, or view a tennis serve from the side to see the ball toss and from the back to view the actual arm movement.

The key points for the successful use of visual guidance are:

- Ensure that demonstration is accurate.
- Draw the learner's attention to the key points – 'cueing', and consider the use of slow motion.
- Ensure the learner can see the essential parts of the skill or movement.
- Ensure that the demonstration seems attainable – to show an elite performer demonstrating a highly complex skill may demotivate the learner as they may consider that they could never perform such a movement.
- Visual guidance may be combined with verbal guidance for more advanced learners.
- Allow time for mental rehearsal.

Activity

Collect visual images (still or moving) of each of the core skills from your practical activity. Try and build your collection so that you have examples of the correct technique shown from different angles.

▨ Visual guidance is better for less complex skills where there is less information to be absorbed.

Verbal guidance

Verbal guidance is often used with visual guidance when the coach describes the action that is to be learnt or how it can be improved. It is used when giving verbal cues to the performer about the key elements of the skill or technique. As well as drawing the learner's attention to specific elements of the movement a verbal cue can also be used as a 'trigger' for the kind of movement that is required – for example a shot putter could be asked to 'drive' the hip as they rotate at the front of the circle. Verbal guidance can be used with more advanced performers during the movement as they have more attention 'bandwidth' to spare and can listen to what is said. They also have a broader movement vocabulary and are therefore able to interpret the coach's words more effectively.

The key points about the use of verbal guidance are:

▨ most often used in association with visual guidance, particularly for beginners

▨ is useful when drawing the learner's attention to important elements of the movement – known as cueing

▨ Keep it brief – too long-winded a description loses a performer's attention, particularly beginners.

▨ may be used during a movement with more advanced learners, particularly those at the autonomous stage

▨ The description must be clear and precise – with the use of key words.

▨ Consider the complexity of the skill – it may be best to only use a demonstration.

Mechanical or manual guidance

The two terms **mechanical** or **manual guidance** are inter-changeable and refer to much the same thing. Manual/mechanical guidance involves either physically moving the limb or body of the learner in the correct way for the technique or skill being learned, or by physically restricting their movement so that only the correct movement can be achieved.

Fig. 16.4 *Gymnastics – manual guidance*

▨ Activity

For each of the core skills of your chosen practical activity consider when the use of verbal guidance would be appropriate. Write down the key or cue words that you might use. Record onto tape how you might describe the skill to a learner, then play the tape back and see if it makes sense to you.

▨ Activity

For each of the core skills in your physical activity devise a way that the learning of each could be helped by the use of mechanical/manual guidance.

Physically moving the performer is also known as 'forced response' and a good example is when trying to correct a 'screw kick' in swimming. The teacher or perhaps another learner would be in the water behind the swimmer who is holding onto the pool side. The supporter would then push or guide the learner's legs through the correct action so that they can feel the movement.

Physically restricting the performer's movements either by support or some mechanical device is often used when the performer is learning something that carries an element of risk. In trampolining for example the learner can be in a twisting belt which restricts movement, or in gymnastics when the coach supports the learner when doing a handstand or a vault. Similarly in javelin the coach could hold the rear of the javelin whilst the performer starts to pull the arm through – this enables the kinaesthetic feel of the movement. It is important however that the learner undertakes and feels the movement without the mechanical guidance as soon as possible – this avoids them requiring it as a 'crutch' and in also learning the wrong movement – there are subtle differences between performing with mechanical support and without.

The key points for the use of manual/mechanical guidance are:

- It can give the kinaesthetic feel for the movement but should not be retained for too long as it is not exactly the same as doing it unaided.
- Useful for individuals but not often helpful in a group situation.
- Helpful at an early stage to allow the performer to try the whole movement in a difficult or dangerous environment, e.g. when swimmers start by using a float or arm bands.
- Useful when correcting an element of a movement, particularly if the learner can isolate the fault for themselves.
- Learners may get incorrect internal feedback from the movement so should dispense with manual support or guidance as soon as possible.
- Coaches and teachers must be aware of supporting appropriately, especially with children and members of the opposite sex.

On a number of occasions we have referred to feedback being used. Feedback is a vital part of skill learning and it is the next area to consider.

Feedback

Feedback means that the learner receives information about the movement and its outcome during or after the movement, and from internal and external sources.

There are a range of different types of feedback and it is important to use the correct type at the correct time and for it to be appropriate to the learner. Feedback is vital to learning and can be used to correct errors or mistakes, to reinforce correct movement and aid its retention and to motivate the learner.

Types of feedback

Many of the different forms of feedback are opposites of each other and can be paired:

- intrinsic – extrinsic
- concurrent – terminal
- positive – negative.

Activity

As a group observe another PE class in school or college and using the worksheet provided try and identify the different type of guidance, how the practice is structured, the type of practice used and the type of teaching style used.

Key terms

Feedback: any information received by the learner as a result of a movement.

Others forms of feedback are:

- delayed feedback
- kinaesthetic feedback
- knowledge of results (KR)
- knowledge of performance (KP).

Intrinsic feedback

Intrinsic feedback, also known as internal feedback, is information that is received by the sensory system within muscles, tendons and ligaments. These sense organs known as proprioceptors feed information to the brain about the changing state of tension or length of muscles, tendons and ligaments and we then acquire our sense of movement and the position of our limbs and the whole body. In addition we use our sense of hearing – say for example when a tennis player hears the sound of the racket connecting with the ball – the experienced player will have a clear sense of how well they have hit it from the sound.

 Activities

1. Close your eyes and put an arm in the air. Describe the position of your fingers, hand and arm to the rest of the group. Keep your eyes closed and allow another member of the group to move your wrist, elbow and finger joints so that your hand is in a different position. Once again describe the position of the fingers, hand and arm. Why were you able to do this?

2. Also try closing your eyes and then bringing your two index fingers together so that they touch first time – how close did you get? How can you do this?

You have been able to complete the two learning activities due to the intrinsic feedback, also known as **kinaesthetic feedback**. The more experienced and skilful you become the more you are able to use intrinsic and kinaesthetic feedback, and such performers will also refer to it as a 'sense of where you are'.

Extrinsic feedback

Extrinsic feedback, also known as external or augmented feedback, is the information about movement that the performer receives from outside of themselves. This information can come from a coach or teacher in the form of verbal comments about their performance or by showing them what they did right or wrong. Extrinsic feedback can also come from teammates or indeed spectators. Most often used with beginners – those in the cognitive-associative phase of learning.

Terminal feedback

Terminal feedback is feedback that is given to the performer after the movement has been completed. If the feedback is delayed to some time after the performance it is known as **delayed feedback**.

Concurrent feedback

Concurrent feedback is feedback that is given to the performer during the performance. It is sometimes referred to as continuous feedback and it can come in two forms – intrinsic or extrinsic. Intrinsic feedback or kinaesthetic feedback is occurring all the time, even though the performer may not have the attention bandwidth to attend to it or be conscious of it. Concurrent feedback that is being given by the coach (think about the times you have stood on the touchline and heard the coach yelling to the players) during a performance. Once again the performers need sufficient 'spare' attention to be able to attend to what is being said.

 Link

You will have met the concept of feedback in Chapter 8 – Information processing (page 87).

 Key terms

Intrinsic feedback: information about movement that comes from the proprioceptors within the body. Internal feedback.

AQA Examiner's tip

Exam questions frequently ask you about feedback. It is vital that you understand the different types and can accurately state when each form of feedback is most appropriately used.

Key terms

Kinaesthetic feedback: a term for information that is received from the sense organs within the muscles, tendons and ligaments that give the body information about body position and movement.

Terminal feedback: information about the performance received after the completion of the movement.

Delayed feedback: terminal feedback that is given some time after the event.

Concurrent feedback: information about performance that is received during the movement, can be intrinsic or extrinsic.

 Activity

Try doing a skill movement which has an accuracy outcome – a free shot in basketball, badminton serve, etc. with your eyes closed. How accurate were you? How is it that you can be as accurate as you were without looking at the target?

The next time you are on the sideline of a match listen and watch to how much external feedback the performer is receiving.

Ask yourself the question – how much are they receiving, are they able to pay attention to it, how much information are they being given and expected to take in?

Key terms

Positive feedback: praise and acknowledgement of a correct or successful action.

Negative feedback: external information about how a movement was incorrect or could have been better, critical comments.

Delayed feedback: feedback given some time after the event.

Knowledge of results (KR): feedback in the form of information about how successful the movement was in accomplishing the task.

Knowledge of performance (KP): information given as feedback as to how well the movement was performed, regardless of the end result.

Activity

When undertaking the previous activity listen also for the balance between negative and positive feedback – make a mark on a piece of paper for every time either form of feedback is used. Was it appropriate in terms of the experience of the performers?

Positive feedback

Positive feedback occurs when the movement or skill is correct and is given in the form of practise. It is designed to reinforce the correct action and motivate the learner to repeat the action in the future. Coaches will often encourage less experienced learners with positive feedback even if only a small improvement has been made. This must be balanced with not giving the learner a false impression of how successful they are being as this can be demotivating.

Negative feedback

Negative feedback is received when the movement or action was incorrect or unsuccessful. This is generally considered to be extrinsic and could be in the form of comments from the coach, the performer seeing that the shot missed or was out, advice from the coach as to what was wrong and what should have been done. The more experienced, confident or motivated the performer the more negative feedback may be used.

Delayed feedback

Delayed feedback is a form of terminal feedback. The coach waits for some time after the performance before giving the performer the feedback. This allows the performer to reflect upon their own performance, to calm down after a period of high emotion and to get over the joy of winning or the despair of losing. The feedback should not be delayed too long as it may be hard for the performer to recall what they did. The coach should keep notes to ensure that the feedback is accurate and comprehensive. Delayed feedback can be both intrinsic and extrinsic.

Two final forms of feedback are knowledge of results (KR) and knowledge of performance (KP).

Knowledge of results (KR)

Knowing how you have done in terms of the outcome of your movement – did you score, was the stroke accurate, did you jump the longest , is vital for future improvement and motivation. **Knowledge of results (KR)** is about whether or not you achieved the task, or how close you were. At times the performer can see this for themselves or they may receive KR from their coach or teacher in terms of 'that was out by 5 cm', etc.

The coach may then go on to give feedback in the form of knowledge of performance (KP).

Knowledge of performance (KP)

Knowledge of performance is information about how well the movement was executed, how close to the perfect model the performer came. This may follow KR when the coach may provide information after a shot was missed as to why the shot was missed, and how it may be corrected in the future. This is essential in enabling the performer to improve the movement in the future. In general as the performer moves from the cognitive to the autonomous stage of learning the more KP is used. In addition with the advent of slow motion video and video analysis software it is possible to give detailed KP feedback that can then become visual guidance. It is also possible for a performer to send the coach the digital video, the coach to analyse it and send feedback even though they may be in a different country.

Although most KP is extrinsic experienced performers can also use intrinsic feedback to judge how well they are performing in terms of the general feel of the movement, but even the most expert of performers require the detailed analysis that can be provided by a coach.

Whilst discussing the different forms of feedback it should have become apparent that the form of feedback to be used varies a great deal and it is vital that the performer receives the right kind of feedback.

Which feedback to use

The type of feedback to be used is dependent upon a number of factors:

- the stage of learning of the performer
- the characteristics of the skill, particularly its complexity and how rapidly it is performed
- the performance situation
- the purpose of the feedback.

Of those four variables the most important is the stage of learning of the performer. Figure 16.5 shows how the most appropriate feedback to be used varies with the experience and skill level of the performer.

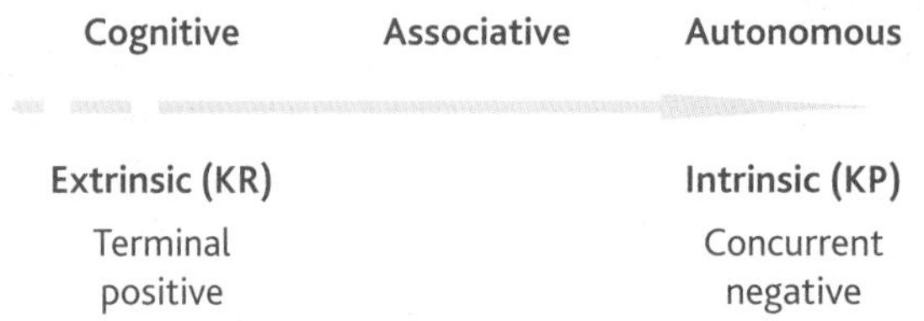

Cognitive	Associative	Autonomous
Extrinsic (KR)		Intrinsic (KP)
Terminal		Concurrent
positive		negative

Fig. 16.5 *How feedback varies in relation to the learner*

Feedback in relation to the performer's stage of learning

It can be seen from the diagram that as the learner moves from the cognitive to the autonomous stage of learning they are able to:

- Use more intrinsic feedback as they have greater feel for the skill and kinaesthetic awareness, they also know what the skill should feel like, and need the reassurance of the coach less.

- As they become more autonomous they need to give less attention to the mechanics of performing the skill and have spare attention capacity to listen to the coach, therefore they can move from terminal feedback to concurrent feedback.

- More experienced performers can be given more constructive criticism and advice without becoming demotivated. Therefore a coach can use more negative feedback as the performer becomes more experienced and skilful. Beginners need the reassurance of positive feedback (without giving a false sense of achievement).

- Performers in the early stages are very keen to know how successful they have been (KR) – almost to the exclusion as to how they achieved it. Experienced performers become more concerned with how well they have performed the skill (KP). It is important however that performers who succeed with an incorrect technique must have this corrected (even at the cost of temporary loss of success) if they are to progress to a higher level of performance.

- In addition beginners are likely to need more specific feedback – where to have stood rather than a comment that they are getting out of position.

Feedback in relation to the nature of the skill, purpose and learning situation

If a skill is highly complex, with a great deal of information processing it is likely that terminal feedback will be more effective due to the attention that the performer will be giving to the performance. In addition performers who are in the 'zone' will be blocking or filtering out any distracting stimuli.

If the purpose of the feedback is to build motivation, repair confidence and lower negative feelings then positive feedback after the event is likely to be best. Delayed feedback could then be used to go over the mistakes that were made after a period of reflection.

If the learning or performance situation is one where there is much crowd noise, or there were team celebrations or a sense of dejection at a loss or euphoria at a win then delayed terminal feedback is likely to be most effective. As many coaches have observed the time to build for the next World Cup or Olympic Games is as soon as the current one has finished.

Activities

 In classroom bounce a sponge ball on the edge of the hand or juggle it on the foot. Count the number of consecutive bounces gained in a minute. Coach your learner using different forms of feedback. Another member of the group should be observing and identifying on a worksheet the types of feedback being used.

 Read through the types of feedback and match them up to the learner, the situation and the nature of the skill. With a range of teaching/practice situations link the situation to feedback type.

The importance of feedback

Feedback is a vital part of learning. Little learning will take place without feedback. Performers cannot become critically self-aware unless they receive feedback, initially from external sources but increasingly through being taught to focus on their internal feedback. With feedback gained from a range of situations performers can develop schema that allow them to produce appropriate skilled reactions in changing circumstances – a vital component of high level performance. Micro improvements to skills and techniques are highly motivating to experienced performers and knowledge of the outcome equally so to the beginner. Every coach should spend time on learning which form of feedback to use and when.

✔ *You should now be able to:*

- construct a practice session and know how the performers should use the time available

- know which style of teaching to use for each learning situation and learner

- present the skill to the learner – as a whole or in parts

- help and guide the performer and know how that should vary in relation to the learner, the situation and the skill

- understand the importance of feedback, the type of feedback to be used in relation to the performer, the performance situation and the purpose of the feedback.

1   A teacher takes a class of young pupils for a badminton lesson and teaches them the overhead clear for the first time, then later on takes the 1st XV for a scrummaging practice.

How might the teaching styles differ between each of the learning situations described above? Justify your answer.   *(6 marks)*

2   For the learning situation in question 1 how might the form of feedback used by the teacher differ between the two learning situations. Justify your answer.   *(6 marks)*

3   Swimming may be taught using either the whole method or part method. What are the advantages of using:

(a)   the whole method?   *(3 marks)*

(b)   the part method?   *(3 marks)*

4   Learning enables performers to develop skilled use of their bodies.

(a)   Demonstrations are a form of visual guidance. Identify two other forms of guidance.   *(2 marks)*

(b)   What can a coach do to make demonstrations as effective as possible?   *(4 marks)*

Exam skills

AS Level Physical Education is assessed through examination and coursework. Unit 1 content is assessed through Section A of the examination paper. The theoretical aspects of the coursework, found in Unit 2, are examined as Section B of the exam.

The examination is worth 60% of the AS Level, and only available at the end of the course in May. Re-sits will be available in the following January if you wish to improve your marks. The examination consists of a two hour paper containing seven questions, each worth 12 marks, therefore having a total of 84 marks.

You will be asked to answer six structured questions from Section A and one from Section B, a total of seven questions. Section A will require candidates to answer two questions from each of the theoretical areas of applied physiology, skill acquisition and opportunities for participation, whilst Section B will examine the application of the theoretical knowledge concerning preparation for performance to a practical situation. There is no choice within the examination paper.

The quality of written communication for this paper will be specifically examined in question 7 in Section B.

Each question is structured. That means it is sub-divided into different areas. A single question could ask about two or three different topics from the specification. You have to answer every question; there is no question choice.

Preparing for the examination

You need to revise. You need to revise every topic area because there are no question choices in the examination. Revision is at best time consuming and difficult to motivate yourself for. But it is necessary.

It might help if we look at an analogy. Exams could be seen as being just like involvment in a physical activity. You are out to show just how good you are. In activities this demonstration is for the opposition; in an exam it's for the examiner.

Most of you will accept the idea that preparing for a physical activity is important; so is preparing for an exam. Most of you will practice for a physical activity. This is what you must do for the exam. In physical activities the best form of practice is realistic – remember schema theory. So for exams the best form of practice is past examination papers. Initially this will obviously be difficult – there are no past papers. But this specification is very similar to the previous specification and so exam papers from the previous specification are quite appropriate.

Many schools and colleges will run revision classes for you – make sure you attend. Several private companies will offer Easter revision courses or intensive revision days. If possible go to these as well. Learning in a different way and in a different environment is always beneficial.

Revision is time consuming and difficult, but so is training outdoors on a cold November evening. What your coach will do on such occasions is to make it fun and have regular changes in what is being done to maintain interest. You must do the same when revising. Your coach should not let you simply play a game as a practice. You must not simply read your notes for revision. Remember what you learned about memory – there are limits to what can be stored in short-term memory and storing things in long-term memory involves rehearsal, meaningfulness and over-learning. Try some of the following:

- Get organised – find a base where you can work and even leave all your 'stuff' in place where it won't get disturbed.
- Set a time limit for revision – many and often is better than few and long. If you want to revise for longer than an hour then set yourself two clear periods for revision, with a good break between the revision sessions.
- Work to a plan – maybe revise a topic each day – and stick to the plan. Allow time for leisure/non-revision sessions.
- Get a copy of the specification – highlight (in red!) those areas that you are not sure about – revise these first.
- Provide yourself with rewards – breaks/biscuits/coffee/TV programme after completing some revision.
- If you prefer it then revise with headphones and music.
- Have a break after about 20 minutes; then return to the revision.
- Review what you have revised – after that break test yourself.
- Try to produce images from your notes – diagrams/flowcharts/ mindmaps/tables – we remember pictures better than words.
- Reduce information down to key words and phrases – these are easier to remember.
- Produce revision cards – your own are better than any others.
- Don't leave it all to the last minute – there are three sections to revise and each one has many topics with those sections. Revision should begin soon after or even before Easter.
- There are some topics that tend to come up on nearly every examination – revise these the most and make sure you know the answers to likely questions.

On the day

- Get plenty of sleep – you perform best when you are refreshed.
- Don't revise the morning of the exam – you wouldn't train before a game – you'd get tired – so does your brain.
- It's a competition – arrive as you would for a match – with plenty of time to get ready and with the correct equipment – take spares if necessary.
- Don't talk to the opposition – your fellow pupils – get in the 'zone'.
- Stay calm – if you are too worked up you will be unable to perform at your best.
- Enter the examination room early and do all that you can before the start – write you name etc. on the answer booklet.
- When you are told to begin just simply read the questions – don't start writing straight away.
- If there are questions you are confident about then do these first, leaving those where you are uncertain until last.
- You haven't got to answer the questions in the order in which they have been set.
- Always remember that the examiner knows the question. Don't start your answer by stating the question.

▮ If you can't remember something leave a space for the answer, it might come to you later.

▮ Keep checking the time – it's a two hour exam – you have to answer seven questions – that's 17 minutes per question. Call it 15 to allow for reading through the paper at the beginning and allowing time for a final read through.

▮ If you appear to be running out of time start to use bullet points, but don't do that for question 7 – that needs sentences for the answer.

▮ Question 7 requires you to show good use of technical terms – use them!

▮ At the end, read through your completed paper – have you answered every question; could you add something to one of the first questions you attempted?

▮ Use highlighter to identify the important words used in each question.

▮ Interpreting questions

One of the hardest parts about doing PE exams is trying to understand what the examiner wants as an answer. To understand this better you need to look at exam questions in more detail.

There are usually three parts to a question:

1 A **command** word which tells you what the examiner wants you to do.
2 A **subject** word which tells you which area of the specification the question is about.
3 A **subject qualifier** which tells you in more detail what aspect of the subject you need to talk about.

For example, in the following question –

'Explain how the reaction time of a performer might be improved'

The command word is '**explain**'

The subject word is '**reaction time**'

The subject qualifier is '**improved**'

▮ In the following examples, the command word has been **circled**, the subject has a **rectangle** around it and the **subject qualifier** has been underlined.

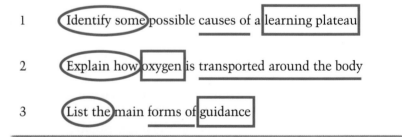

1 Identify some possible causes of a learning plateau

2 Explain how oxygen is transported around the body

3 List the main forms of guidance

▮ Command words

Examiners have a number of command words that they regularly use, and each has a different meaning – learn their meanings!

The more commonly used ones are listed below:

Account – Give reasons for.

Briefly – Be concise and straightforward, but not a list – use sentences.

Classify – Divide into groups or categories.

Comment on – Summarise the various points and give an opinion.

Compare – What is wanted is a point-by-point identification of the main similarities (when **contrast** is used as well look for differences). Use words like larger, quicker, more in your answer, or start sentences with words like however, as compared to, whereas.

Define – or **what do you understand by**, or **explain the meaning of** – Needs a short answer giving a precise meaning of the term.

Describe – Very commonly used – On its own it means what is the examined feature like. Can be linked to other words – ' describe the characteristics of' or 'describe the differences between' or 'describe the effects of' or 'describe and explain'. 'Describe and comment on' requires more than just a description – also needs some judgements about the description.

Discuss – Needs you to argue both sides of issue – produce a written debate with a conclusion.

Evaluate or **assess** – Weigh up the importance of the topic – similar to **discuss**.

Explain – Give reasons or causes – very popular. A description is not enough.

How – same as **describe**.

Identify – **State** or **name**. Point out and name – short answers.

Justify – Usually goes with questions where you have to make a decision about something and then justify you decision – explain why you arrived at your decision

Outline – Note the main features.

Suggest – Put forward an idea or reason.

Index

Page numbers in **bold** refer to **Key terms**